PRAISE FOR *HANGAR 4*

"*Hangar 4* takes readers on a candid journey that expertly captures the physical, mental, and emotional demands of two decades of service as a combat aviator. A must-read from one of the best assault support pilots of our generation."

—Chris Roy, Colonel, United States Marine Corps, USMC CH-53E Combat Veteran

"A warrior's tale of modern helicopter warfare: insightful, articulate, and raw. It tells the story for my generation in the way that *Chicken Hawk* and *Bonnie Sue* did for Vietnam-era combat aviators. Required reading for every military professional and military history buff."

—John Ruffini, President of PopASmoke, USMC Combat Helicopter and Tiltrotor Association, USMC CH-53E Combat Veteran

"*Hangar 4* is an intimate look into the life of a professional warrior striving to balance duty with family over two decades of war. Highly recommended for anyone interested in leadership, what it means to serve, and the nitty gritty of life in a Marine Corps helicopter squadron at war."

—Dan Sheehan, Author of *After Action* and *Continuing Actions*, USMC AH-1W Combat Veteran

"An extraordinary account of Marine Corps aviation during the Global War on Terror. Isaac Lee's memoir will impact those who served and those far removed from America's wars. His remarkable combat service lends particular credibility to the importance of family and successful transition."

—Joseph Costello, MSW, former Director of the San Marcos Vet Center

"Isaac Lee's memoir reads like fiction, but it's real life. *Hangar 4* ranks up there with the great war memoirs of our time. His honesty about the demons that rise from the combat aviator experience is brutal, but will hopefully help others who suffer in silence. A masterpiece!"

—Thomas M. Wing, award-winning author of *Against All Enemies*

"LtCol (Ret.) Isaac Lee pens a memoir which perfectly captures the emotional kaleidoscope of the military experience—the good, the bad, the very bad, and even the occasionally hilarious—in an authentic way that only a combat vet can."

—Benjamin Spada, award-winning author of *FNG* and *The Warmaker: Black Spear novels*

"Isaac Lee's book *Hangar 4* demands you read the next page and the next. It's a saga of a USMC aviator's career, triumphs, and personal life. Recommended reading."

—Garry G. Garretson, President of Veterans' Writing Group of San Diego County

HANGAR 4

A COMBAT AVIATOR'S MEMOIR

LIEUTENANT COLONEL, USMC (Ret.)

ISAAC G. LEE

FROM THE TINY ACORN...
GROWS THE MIGHTY OAK

This book is a memoir. It reflects the author's present recollections of experiences over time. Some names and characteristics have been changed, some events have been compressed, and some dialogue has been recreated.

Hangar 4
Copyright © 2023 Isaac G. Lee. All rights reserved.

Printed in the United States of America. For information, address Acorn Publishing, LLC
3943 Irvine Blvd. Ste. 218, Irvine, CA 92602

www.acornpublishingllc.com

Interior design by Kat Ross
Cover design by Damonza
Photo credit for the cover: Sergeant Juan Vara, USMC.
Al Asad, Iraq, 2005

ISBN-13: 979-8-88528-080-8 (hardcover)
ISBN-13: 979-8-88528-079-2 (paperback)
Library of Congress Control Number: 2023919281

For Kerry

Thank you for being my best friend throughout this journey. Especially when I didn't make that easy to do. You were the glue that kept our family together. You're a great Mom to our children. Your intelligence, sense of humor, genuine desire to help people, and your passion were always present. I am forever grateful. Love you!

For my children

You are both amazing young people. Thank you for your patience and support during our time as a Marine Corps family. You are both capable of achieving anything you want.
I am beyond proud to be your Dad.

For the Marines

From June 1997 to June 2017, I had the privilege of contributing to the greatest fighting force the world has ever known. The Marines I served with were a daily inspiration. They were willing. They were fearless. They were the best our nation had to offer. If Hollywood assembled a team of their best writers, they couldn't possibly dream up a cast of characters more remarkable and entertaining than the Marines who exist in every squadron and battalion in the Marine Corps. The blend of intellect, badassery, and jackassery in the Marines that comprise those units is truly awe-inspiring. Marines will say and do the funniest things you have ever heard or seen two seconds before and two seconds after a near-death experience. They have mastered the art of being unflappable. There is no more exemplary group of people on the planet. It remains my greatest honor to be one of you. I love each of you. Don't ever change. Just keep being you.

CONTENTS

FOREWORD

The names in this work are accurate for all those who granted the author written permission. Pseudonyms were utilized in three individual cases.

Throughout my Marine Corps career, music was always present. Certain songs always remind me of specific portions of this journey. There is a playlist in the back of this book that lists music I associate with each chapter. Every time I hear those songs, they take me back to that time or place.

This work has been reviewed and approved by the Department of Defense Office of Prepublication and Security Review (DOP-SR). The views expressed in this publication are those of the author and do not necessarily reflect the official policy or position of the Department of Defense or the U.S. government. The public release clearance of this publication by the Department of Defense does not imply Department of Defense endorsement or factual accuracy of the material. In addition, the appearance of U.S. Department of Defense (DoD) visual information does not imply or constitute DoD endorsement.

PROLOGUE

In June 1997, I arrived at Marine Corps Base Quantico, VA, for Officer Candidates School (OCS). My fellow officer candidates and I had no idea that four years and three months later, the events of 9/11 would trigger the longest war in our nation's history. That first summer, we were just hopeful officer candidates. Our collective goal was simple. Graduate from the ten-week course and earn commissions as second lieutenants in the United States Marine Corps. Roughly 65% of us would achieve that goal.

By December of 2000, I had completed OCS, The Basic School (TBS), Flight School, and had been promoted to first lieutenant. I checked into Marine Heavy Helicopter Squadron 465 (HMH-465) at Marine Corps Air Station (MCAS) Miramar, CA, with a ton of motivation and zero clue. My experience at Miramar, famous for the 1986 movie "Top Gun," would prove to be nothing like the highly entertaining film, which I may or may not have watched one hundred or more times in the months leading up to my departure for OCS.

Located in central San Diego, MCAS Miramar is one of the nicest military installations in the country. In 1993 the Base Realignment and Closure (BRAC) Commission recommended that the Marine Corps close air stations at Tustin and El Toro and relocate to Miramar. Navy Fighter Weapons School "Top Gun" was slated to move to Naval Air Station (NAS) Fallon, Nevada. The rest of the Navy's aviation assets from Miramar relocated to naval air stations in other parts of the country.

In 1999 the BRAC recommendations became a reality. A few months later, I checked into HMH-465 "Warhorse" at MCAS Miramar. The HMH-465 squadron spaces occupied the middle of Hangar 4 on the Miramar flight line. That home was still new to the squadron when I walked in the door. At the time, the CH-53E was also the newest aircraft in the Marine Corps aviation fleet.

HMH-465 shared Hangar 4 with two other CH-53E squadrons. Hangar 4 was home to HMH-462, HMH-465 and HMH-466. HMH-361, the fourth CH-53E squadron at Miramar, utilized squadron spaces next door in Hangar 5. About twelve years later, Hangar 4 would be expanded to include HMH-361.

I spent ten of my twenty years as a Marine flying and fighting as a member of one of those four squadrons. Through seven overseas deployments, the finish line was always Hangar 4 on the Miramar flight line. That was home. Making it back to Hangar 4 translated into surviving another deployment.

For the lucky ones, your significant other would be there to pick you up when you returned. Kerry ensured I was one of the lucky ones, seven out of seven times. Deployments are difficult and not at all conducive to family life or relationships in general, but deployment homecomings can be awesome. In the spectrum of human emotion, returning home from a combat deployment takes the cake.

Stepping off the aircraft and scanning the crowd with all of their signs and American flags is surreal. When you find your family in the crowd, that first eye contact is special. The ensuing family embrace is simply impossible to describe.

I thought a lot about writing this book before I finally sat down and did it. I kept an extensive journal of my career as a Marine aviator for numerous reasons. Writing nightly allowed me to decompress as I reflected on the events of the day. I knew I would never remember everything that happened, and I also figured my kids might want to skim through it someday to see what the old man had been up to during his frequent absences.

That journal provided the primary source material for this project. In 2008, I began to reflect on my first three combat deployments. I also decided to try and write version 1.0 of this book. It was too soon. The emotion flooded back, returning me to a combat stress level. I woke up in the middle of the night, expecting to hear indirect fire. I started to drink so that I could sleep again. Finally, I put down the journal and let myself move forward.

Fifteen years later, I am now a retired lieutenant colonel six years removed from wearing the uniform. My home office is filled with plaques, photos, and other mementos from my time in service. Two decades of memories fill the walls and shelves of a single room. I see the memorabilia every day, but most days I don't closely examine it. It represents things that remain anonymous in the background as I go about my day. But every now and then, I will stop and closely study one of the plaques or photos.

I catch myself reading the names on the plaques and studying the other faces in the photos. Those names and faces mean something to me. We shared an adventure more grandiose than any of us could have ever imagined before it began. We did everything together. We fought, flew, worked, ran, ate, slept, talked, laughed, cried, lived, and sometimes died. Together.

When one of us died, we all did our best to console the family. And each other. The combat experience brought out a level of greatness from many who might have never discovered that quality within themselves. We shared the purest form of love and admiration for one another. We often talked about the enemy and the mission, but that was not why we were doing it. Instead, we did everything for each other. I will always think of my fellow Marines as family.

At this point, most of us who survived the experience have moved on. We disappeared into cities and suburbs across the country to live seemingly ordinary lives. We work in new careers, raising families even as we individually work to reconcile all that we experienced. The common thread is that we all share a permanent bond. That bond is timeless, and it will live within all of us forever. We know who we are, who we were, and in most cases, why we volunteered to do it all in the first place.

Thinking of them is what finally compelled me to sit back down and share this story. I struggled with the idea of anything resembling a memoir. Who the hell am I to write a memoir? But, after much deliberation, I decided a memoir would be the only way to properly share the story. In doing so, I hope that, by extension, I will be telling the story of every other Marine who spent time in the Marine Corps CH-53 D/E squadrons throughout the Operation Enduring Freedom/Operation Iraqi Freedom (OEF/OIF) period. Especially those who served in the CH-53E squadrons of Marine Aircraft Group 16 (MAG-16).

My experience took me on an emotional journey that produced a lasting impact. I became someone I would never have imagined I would be capable of. On the darkest nights, in some of the most dangerous places on earth, I would repeatedly strap myself into a machine and do whatever was necessary to support the Marines on the ground in combat.

I also had to be the guy my wife, kids, extended family, friends, and fellow Marines all needed me to be. I mastered compartmentalization out of necessity. The cumulative effect of that lifestyle came with many strings attached. One of my primary motivations for retiring as a lieutenant colonel, rather than sticking around for another promotion, was knowing that I needed to unpack all of that sooner rather than later. My path could not be sustained. I had to walk away before it caught up to me.

I also needed to better understand who and what I had become in order to become the best version of myself going forward. I went to work with a Vet Center counselor one week after flying a CH-53E for the last time. That work through counseling will continue indefinitely. If my story helps just one fellow service member reconcile what they experienced, the writing of this memoir will have been worth it.

It was also important to me to tell this story in the language of the Marine Corps. I thought about sanitizing the language, but I would have felt like a total sellout. Marines curse like it is an art form. I chose to reflect that when and where appropriate. I also felt it was important to share my perspective when these events took place. Even when my perspective was flawed.

The majority of the ass chewings I received in the Marine Corps resulted from me speaking up and saying something to a senior officer that my peers were thinking, but that no one would say aloud. Describing these events as they transpired and felt at the time is the only way to paint an accurate picture of what I observed, thought, and felt when they took place. My goal is authenticity. Hence the language and perspective have not been massaged.

When I applied to Officer Candidates School (OCS), I didn't just want to become an officer; I wanted to become an aviator. When I received the opportunity, I set off to Marine Corps Base Quantico, Virginia, to make the most of the opportunity given to me. What unfolded over the next two decades exceeded my wildest expectations. If someone had told me beforehand that my career would play out in the manner it did, I would have laughed in disbelief. I had no business living this adventure and even less business surviving it.

My experiences covered the gamut of the emotional spectrum, often lingering on the extremes. The highs were really high, the lows far too low. The one constant? I was always in the company of more truly amazing people than one person ever deserves to know. This book is for all of them. Semper Fi, Marines.

AUTHOR'S NOTE

HMH Mission: Support the MAGTF Commander by providing assault support transport of heavy equipment, combat troops, and supplies, day or night under all weather conditions during expeditionary, joint, or combined operations.[1]

Assault Support: Those actions required for the airlift of personnel, supplies, and equipment into or within the battle area by helicopters or fixed-wing aircraft. Assault support includes fixed-wing transport, in-flight refueling, and helicopterborne operations; such operations may be tactical, administrative, or logistic in nature. The general categories of assault support are combat assault, air delivery, aerial refueling, air evacuation, tactical recovery of aircraft, equipment and personnel, air logistical support, and battlefield illumination.[2]

1

OPERATION MATADOR

On May 8, 2005, two CH-53E helicopters from Marine Heavy Helicopter Squadron 465 (HMH-465) inserted the Regimental Reserve Platoon "Beowulf" from Regimental Combat Team 2 (RCT-2), 2nd Marine Division, as part of OPERATION MATADOR, the largest coalition offensive staged against the Iraqi insurgency since the end of the second battle of Fallujah the previous December. I was the CH-53E Flight Leader for the mission.

"Seat Belt and Harness."

"Adjusted."

"VLEA Control Dial."

"Set."

"Seat Cushion, and Exposure Suit Blower Switches."

"Off to the right."

"Cockpit Window Emergency Release Handle."

"Shearwired."

My copilot and I glide through the prestart checklist in our CH-53E helicopter. It is a challenge and response cadence, but we are silent for this initial portion. We have done this so many times, it is as automatic as putting on our boots.

The small blue light that hangs around my neck guides us in

the dark silence. When we finish the prestart checklist, I reach across the console from the left seat and slap his left shoulder with my right hand to let him know I believe the prestart checklist is complete. Next, I shout, "Ready Four!" and hold up four fingers despite the fact that it is pitch dark and our crew chief positioned in front of the aircraft can't possibly see my hand.

My crew chief hears my call and replies by yelling, "Four's Coming Hot!"

Finally, I reach up and throw the lever forward that ignites the Auxiliary Power Plant (APP) in our CH-53E helicopter.

As the familiar high-pitched whine of hydraulic fluid turning over the APP start motor kicks in, my comfort level increases. Thus far, everything is as it should be. The aircraft looked good on preflight, felt right as I strapped into the left seat, and now it sounds right as well.

The cockpit smells of hydraulic fluid, dirt, and stale sweat. The smell of JP-5 exhaust fumes slowly overcomes those scents as our APP lights off and spools up. When I fly, I either chew gum or dip Copenhagen snuff. Tonight, I'm going with gum. I toss a stick in my mouth, and my fifth sense is satisfied. I am confident I will lead this mission to a successful outcome. We will execute like professionals, and most importantly, live to fight another day.

Although it is after midnight, it is still well over 100 degrees outside and even warmer in the cockpit, where I am wrapped tight in body armor, a survival vest, and my helmet. I can't bitch, though. During the day, it is closer to 120 degrees outside, so at the moment I am reasonably comfortable.

"One and three generators on."

"ICS check."

"Loud and clear on the left."

"Loud and clear on the right."

"Lima Charlie outside."

We resume our checklist without talking. Both my copilot and I are quickly and efficiently turning on all systems in the cockpit. Lights, radios, navigational aids, Global Positioning System (GPS), Aircraft Survivability Equipment (ASE), Forward Looking Infrared (FLIR), Radar Altimeter, and our Automatic Flight Control System (AFCS) are all quickly coming alive and warming up.

My body armor and survival vest tightly grip me. My helmet is heavy with Night Vision Goggles (NVGs) attached to the front and a battery pack attached to the back. My single monocle Heads Up Display (HUD) is attached to the right tube of my NVGs and plugs into the aircraft via a cord just above my left shoulder. All of my gear feels exactly as it should.

Some aviators complain about the amount of gear we must wear in a combat environment. I'm not one of them. Some guys skimp and at least remove the ten-pound "chicken plate" that attaches to the front of our body armor. I always wear it. I have no aspirations to be the dumbass who died when he took a round right where his chicken plate is supposed to be. Fuck that. I also always wear my gloves. Not only because I want the fire protection, but because I have always been what pilots refer to as a "button masher." I like being able to make finite control inputs to both the cyclic and collective, and I don't want to be fighting the trim. The gloves make button mashing more comfortable.

Over the radio dash two asks for a "Mickey." On our radios, we have multiple frequency options. Clear frequencies were standard radio frequencies. Secure frequencies were, in fact, "secure" because we were running them through an encryption device. The "Anti Jamming" (AJ) frequencies were HAVE QUICK and SINCGARS nets, which were secure because they "hopped" between multiple frequencies in a perfectly timed sequence. To enable that sequence, all players using those nets needed accurate time of day via their GPS.

On occasion, we couldn't acquire the time synchronization from the GPS in our own aircraft. Someone else in the flight would have to send it out over the air. That was called "sending a Mickey," the reference being the time on a Mickey Mouse watch. With the push of a button, I send the Mickey. Our radios are synched up ahead of radio checks.

I have already glanced around outside to determine just how dark this low light level night will prove to be. Low light level means there is little to no moonlight available for our night vision goggles to amplify. Less than .0022 lux, to be exact. On this night, it is straight zeroes. As dark as it gets.

Low light brings an increased degree of difficulty to any mission, particularly in the landing phase. When we are back in California, we spend countless hours executing training flights in the desert ranges around Yuma, Arizona, but no training range back home possesses the darkness and dust levels we encounter in Iraq. The landing we will need to execute on insert tonight will be of the highest degree of difficulty encountered by an assault support helicopter pilot.

The CH-53E is a beast of an aircraft. At 100 feet long and over 53,000 pounds without cargo, the "Super Stallion" creates a tremendous amount of downwash. In the landing phase, down-wash results in extreme brownout for the pilots in the seats and the enlisted aircrew in the back. It will take all of us being at our best to get the Marines of Regimental Reserve Platoon "Beowulf" safely inserted tonight.

Pilots fly two types of missions in combat. All requests for aviation support go through an Air Tasking Order (ATO) process, where they are prioritized and assigned to different aviation units to support. These Assault Support Requests (ASRs) cover the gamut. They can be anything from moving passengers and cargo between Forward Operating Bases (FOBs) to large-scale tactical operations with high levels of coordination. The former are referred to as general support missions. Marines in CH-53E squadrons typically refer to them as "hauling ass and trash."

The big tactical operations are typically referred to as "named operations" because they are always designated with some offi-cial-sounding name. Tonight we are part of "OPERATION

MATADOR." I still don't know what the connotation of dodging bulls had to do with anything. Some major at higher headquarters must have decided that it sounded cool.

We have yet to conduct a named operation on this deployment on a low light level night. Until now, higher headquarters pushed all named operations to high light level periods when the moon is up to increase our chances of success. But this is no ordinary mission. Tonight, a Task Force of the most elite of America's special operations forces will conduct a raid in the lawless border town of Husaybah, Iraq. The sand berm that defines the Syrian border runs north and south just outside the western edge of town.

Tonight's target is the High Value Target (HVT) in charge of Al Qaeda in Iraq, and as such, he tops our list as the most wanted man in the country. We have been chasing this asshole for a few weeks, but tonight is the night we will get him. At least, that's the plan.

The Task Force typically has air support available from the 160th Special Operations Aviation Regiment (SOAR). Commonly referred to as the "Night Stalkers," the 160th SOAR is the only military aviation unit that belongs to Special Operations Command (SOCOM), and they support the majority of the special operations missions in-country. We have been invited to play a supporting role tonight since the Night Stalkers MH-47 Chinooks are not present.

The Night Stalkers have established a Restricted Operating Zone (ROZ) around Husaybah. A ROZ is a bubble of airspace the rest of us aren't allowed to enter. It is a deconfliction measure that will enable them to operate freely in the objective area without interference from anyone else. Our mission tonight is to fly two CH-53Es up and around the east side of the ROZ to the northwest corner of the city, right on the Syrian border. There we will insert 48 "Beowulf" Marines into a landing zone on a small cliff that overlooks the town of Husaybah to the south. Their mission is to be the blocking force for any squirters who try to flee across the Syrian border.

The plan sounds simple, but like all things in our beloved Marine Corps, it has taken a full week of every field grade officer in the country trying to fuck it up for us to reach a plan that almost makes sense. Field grade officers are the rank of major through colonel. Company grade officers are captains and below. A significant divide exists between the ranks of captain and major, and promotion from captain to major is often referred to as "the lobotomy." As a result, all captains and lieutenants feel obligated to shit-talk majors.

At this point in my career, I believe that damn near everyone with the rank of major and above would probably send all of us on a one-way mission to hell while they sat in the rear, ate chow, and wrote each other up for medals for their stellar "leadership." This opinion is convenient for captains as we aren't there yet. If I remain in the Marine Corps and become a major, I will be obligated to hate myself.

There are, of course, exceptions to this rule. One of those exceptions is Major Doug "Bullwinkle" Glasgow. Bullwinkle is the Future Operations Officer (FOPSO) for Marine Aircraft Group 26, our higher headquarters. Bullwinkle is a CH-53 pilot, former Marine Aviation Weapons and Tactics Squadron One (MAWTS-1) Instructor and survived a mishap in Afghanistan during the initial invasion. Bullwinkle is a legit warfighter, and he has been my primary source of assistance from higher headquarters in developing the plan for tonight's mission. Bullwinkle is good shit, and even though he is not flying tonight's mission with us, he offered to come down and sit in our ready room on a Quick Reaction Force (QRF) standby.

From the beginning, all that the Task Force asked for from the Marine Corps was a one platoon force inserted into a blocking position by our squadron, HMH-465 "Warhorse." At one point, the Marine Corps allowed the planning to explode into a full-blown Battalion Insert. What initially started as a section requirement, which was two aircraft, ballooned to a division, which is three to four aircraft, and ultimately a flight, which is five or more aircraft. Typical Marine Corps shit. Total overkill. We can't let the Special Operations Task Force catch the HVT without having every Marine in this desert somehow involved in it! Thankfully, that plan was eventually scrapped, and we got back to one section of CH-53Es, inserting one platoon. I will take any shred of sanity I can get.

"Ready three."

"Three's coming."

I hit the start button on my #3 engine speed control lever. I instantly hear the high-pitched squeal of 4000 psi of hydraulic fluid turning over the starter in one of our three 4380 shaft horsepower engines.

"NG is spooling up."

"20 percent."

"Introducing fuel."

"Fuel flow is good."

"Light off outside."

"T5 inside."

We will repeat the process for all three engines, which we start in reverse order. Once the #1 engine is online, I make a quick assessment of the cockpit. Again, all five senses remain satisfied.

"Crossfeed going 3-3-1. Ready to release outside."

"Ready to release."

"Releasing on three… "

"One, two, and three... the head is released."

Upon the release of the rotor brake, our seven-blade rotor head - 79' in diameter - comes to life, as do the rest of the gauges inside.

"Quad Tach Triple Torque on the left."

"Same on the right."

"She's alive."

I constantly scan the clock on my GPS. It is 30 seconds to

radio checks, and they will start on time to the second. Exactly 30 seconds later, I key the button on my cyclic control grip to start radio checks. "Whiskey, flight check in ... two zero clear."

"Loud and clear, two zero clear."

"Go two one."

"Two."

"Flight check in ... two one clear."

"Loud and clear, two one clear."

"Go secure."

"Two."

"Flight check in ... two one secure."

"Loud and clear, two one secure."

"Go active."

"Two."

"Flight check in AJ1."

"Loud and clear AJ1."

"Go AJ3."

"Two."

"Flight check in AJ3."

"Loud and clear, AJ3."

"Push comm. Two."

"Two."

The process is repeated for the second radio.

Things are moving along right on schedule. We don't need to call for taxi for another 90 seconds. Now there is idle time to spare, and this is not a good thing. I think of Kerry back home. We are eleven hours ahead of Pacific Standard Time, so she is probably picking up our daughter from preschool right now. She has no idea that her husband is turning up his aircraft in the middle of the night to execute an insert of 48 Marines as part of a major coalition forces offensive.

In a little over an hour, CNN will report on the initial stages of OPERATION MATADOR via the two reporters embedded with the Marines in the back of my aircraft. Although it is primarily a Task Force mission, they will never be mentioned by name in any report I will see or hear in the coming weeks. I quickly dismiss thoughts of my wife and daughter heading home from my daughter's preschool. It is a dangerous distraction.

My thoughts turn to the three other pilots, six enlisted aircrew, two reporters, and 48 Marines we will insert tonight. I am responsible for all of them. I think of the hundreds of loved ones that are attached to the 60 of us. All of the wives, children, girlfriends, parents, siblings, grandparents, and other extended family members and friends back home, doing day-to-day things and wondering how we are.

How many people will be impacted if I fuck this up? Every one of us living to fight another day is contingent on my plan and our execution. It is a plan I had assistance in developing, but at the end of the day, I own it. I am the flight lead, and I gave the mission brief. Such is the burden of being the squadron Weapons and Tactics Instructor (WTI). I am more concerned about our ability to safely get our aircraft down in the Landing Zone (LZ) than I am about the enemy threat. Internal to my aircraft, the fate of the 30 of us will rest on my ability as an aviator to execute that landing. The responsibility is daunting, and it is mine.

I dismiss those thoughts and re-focus on the mission. We will take off from our base here on Al Asad and rendezvous in the air with our rotary-wing escorts. As an assault support aircraft, we have no forward-firing offensive weapons. My enlisted aircrew tonight is comprised of a crew chief and two aerial observers. They will man three .50 caliber machine guns located in the two windows on each side of the cabin and one on the ramp in the back. These weapons are defensive only. They exist to put rounds on any target firing at us, but only to buy us enough time to escape. For a mission like this one, we require an escort from offensive aircraft for protection.

Tonight that escort is coming from Marine Light Attack Helicopter Squadron 269 (HMLA-269) in the form of a mixed section of skids. The "Gunrunners" are providing one AH-1W Cobra and one UH-1N Huey to shepherd our safe passage in and out of enemy territory. The escort flight lead is Andy "Babs" Thomas.

"Babs" is a peer of mine, and we were in the same platoon at OCS back in the summer of 1997. He received the callsign "Babs" because he was a cheerleader at Clemson. We also went through the WTI Course at MAWTS-1 together about a year prior. As WTIs, we are supposed to be the resident experts in our squadrons on missions like the one we are executing tonight. Once the requirement went back to a section insert, the two of us put this plan together. I feel fortunate Babs is leading our escort section tonight.

"Base ... two three and two four outbound."

"Base copies, two three."

As we start to taxi out, the Operations Duty Officer (ODO) comes back across our base frequency and quietly sings, "America Fuck Yeah." It is a tiny snippet of a ridiculous song from an even more ridiculous movie called *Team America World Police*, which we have all watched in our shithole barracks way too many times.

In my mind, I complete the line, "Comin' again to save the motherfuckin' day, yeah."

In the darkness, I grin as I feel the tension ease a bit. As we taxi outbound, the burn pit shines brightly on the south side of the field. The trash from our base in the desert never stops burning. With my NVGs amplifying the light, the flames almost completely wash out everything as I look to the southwest. Looking underneath the goggles with the naked eye, the fire casts an ominous orange glow across the night sky.

With clearance from the tower, we taxi out onto Runway 27 Right. My copilot is on the controls, and I'm doing everything else. I quickly run through the panel takeoff checklist. "Instruments looking good. AFCS is on and working for you, turns are up, brakes are off. Harness... I'm locked. Check yourself, caution advisory is normal, ASE gear is on."

With that our crew chief chimes in, "Ramp up, skid down and locked. Two is on board... right side clear to come up."

My copilot gently pulls power, and all three 4,380 shaft horsepower engines respond appropriately. We smoothly break the deck, get a quick power check, and transition to forward flight. We are in the game.

Once airborne, we level off at 500 feet above ground level (AGL). I ask my crew chief, "How is dash two?"

He responds, "Looking good. Right side three rotors," which tells me their location and how much distance separates us.

Captain Dave "Apollo" Payne is my dash two pilot tonight. He and I have been in HMH-465 longer than any other officers currently in the squadron. We started together over four years ago as copilots. Tonight, we are flying one of the most high-profile missions our squadron has ever flown. We are roommates in the barracks and work together in our squadron's Operations Department. We are closer than most actual siblings. We both have field grade officers as copilots tonight, a fact much joked about amongst the squadron company grade in the last few days. Comments like "those fuckers just want to ride along so they can try to get some Air Medals with combat V's" ran rampant through the company grade ranks.

In reality, they are with us tonight because we stacked the deck with four of the most qualified pilots in the squadron. My copilot is our Operations Officer (OPSO), who also happens to be my boss. Our OPSO is known among the squadron company grade as "Daddy" due to his constant badgering of all captains and lieutenants. "Daddy" isn't his actual callsign, but once it started getting tossed around amongst the company grade, it stuck. Apollo's copilot is our Squadron Executive Officer (XO). Both are good guys, for field grade, of course, and both are solid landing in the dirt. We are going to need all the help we can get tonight. With this being as high profile as it is, we can't afford to fuck up.

Once away from the airfield lights, the extremity of the darkness settles in around us as we are outbound on our route. We can't see anything at all in the inky darkness. It feels as if we are flying into a black hole.

The Beowulf Platoon Commander comes up and sits on the jump seat between the OPSO and me. He is also equipped with NVGs, and I can tell right away that he is confused. He takes a quick look around outside and says, "Sir, I think my goggles are fucked up. I can't see anything."

I glance at him and see the faint green glow being reflected on his eyes, so I know his NVGs are working just fine. I respond, "Your goggles are working. That's what low light looks like. You've just never seen it from a cockpit."

He then asks, "How are you guys going to land?"

I calmly tell him, "That's the interesting part." I can tell in the tone of his response that the young lieutenant isn't enjoying this.

"Sir, you fuckers are crazy."

I simply respond with, "Yeah." And we keep pressing on to the objective area.

2

LEARNING TO FLY

Growing up in Lubbock, Texas, I wasn't a kid who had pictures of airplanes in my room. Reese Air Force Base was on the outskirts of town, but I wasn't interested in that. Instead, I was interested in sports. I was a reasonably good kid and made good grades. I was also a decent athlete in a town where competitive athletics was a huge deal.

High school football reigned supreme in West Texas, but I was a better baseball player. My Dad coached both at one of the local high schools, making him a celebrity of sorts. I spent my spare time hanging around practice and going to games. I was a ball boy, batboy, and did whatever other odd jobs I got tasked with. I loved being there, and I absorbed as much information as possible every day. My Mom was an elementary school teacher and very nurturing. While I focused on sports, my younger sister was more interested in the arts. There was balance in the house. It was a good environment.

Watching my father lead his teams provided my first example of effectively leading an organization. He also made time to personally coach me. He is a teacher at heart, and sports are his preferred medium. The lessons always centered around leadership, work ethic, competitiveness, physical toughness and, most importantly, mental toughness. He thought he was developing an athlete and future coach. As it turns out, he was developing a warfighter. The lessons learned on the dusty sports fields of West Texas provided the foundation for everything I went on to do as a Marine Corps officer and aviator.

Off the field, I had a natural draw to push limits. I knew where the lines were, and I tended to operate right on top of them. For the most part, it was standard teenage jackassery coupled with the occasional fistfight. It was all good training. For the most part, the fear of getting kicked off of a sports team, coupled with the potential wrath of my Dad, kept me in check. Dad was hard on me, but I needed that. When it came time for high school, Dad and I decided it would be best if I went across town to play baseball for a coach who was a living legend in Texas. His teams were always in the hunt for the Texas State Championship. I would have to earn my place to play for him. It would also allow both me and Dad to avoid the criticism that comes with being the Coach's son. It was a win for both of us.

My high school baseball coach was old school hard, and he'd been the baseball coach there since the school first fielded a team in 1960. By the time I got there, he was in his 30th season. He pushed us hard, and as was his tradition, we won district all three years that I was on the team. His philosophy was simple. He conditioned us better than every team we played, and our focus was mastery of the fundamentals. The cherry on top was that he pushed us to be ruthless competitors, who always played with mental and physical toughness. Off the field, he expected us to get good grades, stay out of trouble, and always represent the program with class. Despite being a three-year letterman and two-year starter, he didn't pay me a single compliment until I graduated. It was more great training for what was to come.

When I finished high school, I had opportunities to keep playing baseball, but I knew I didn't possess the physical tools necessary to make it to the big leagues. I didn't want to end up being one more guy hanging around my hometown and talking about how awesome it was when he played sports in high school. I knew a bunch of guys like that, and I refused to end up being one of them.

I enrolled in classes at Texas Tech. I honestly believed a college degree was a ticket to whatever was next. I just wasn't sure yet what next would be.

The best thing that was happening was that our family felt like it was in a good place. My parents had married young, and it hadn't always been easy. But things felt like they had really settled. They had a house on the outskirts of town that became a gathering place for a lot of people, including my buddies. We all enjoyed spending time out there. It also helped me realize they would be fine without me around. I went to class, I worked multiple jobs, and in the absence of being part of an athletic team, I spent the rest of my time drinking Lone Star Light with my buddies. Fun, but unfulfilling. Over time it made me more determined to find a meaningful life path. I also knew I wanted to be part of a team.

The summer before my senior year, I went home one night after working an internship shift, which I hated, and found my Dad sitting out in the driveway, drinking one of his signature screwdrivers. From my parents' driveway, we could see the T-37s in the landing pattern at Reese Air Force Base.

I grabbed a beer, pulled out a lawn chair, and joined him. I proceeded to tell my Dad that I hated my internship and was no longer interested in anything I was studying in school. I could tell right away he wasn't enjoying my perspective. I had one year left of college, and now I was telling him that I didn't want to pursue anything that had to do with the degree I was close to completing.

He looked at me. "Well, what are you going to do then?"

I looked over at those T-37s in the pattern at Reese and said, "I'm going to do that. I'm going to be a pilot in the military."

He looked at me like it was the dumbest thing I had ever

said. Given the situation and the randomness of my comment, I couldn't fault his reaction. He got up and walked into the house without saying a single word. I knew right then that's what I was going to do.

Over the next several months, I dove into learning about my potential options in military aviation. Just becoming an officer wasn't enough. I wanted to fly, and I was hell-bent on figuring out how to do that. The irony is that I had been a passenger on a commercial airplane just three times at that point in my life. For some reason, I had a gut feeling it would be a great fit for me.

With very few exceptions, everyone I told about my new plan looked at me like I was insane. Nobody thought I could pull it off. I must have heard the phrase, "You can't do that," at least a thousand times. The administration was leading a military drawdown. Military flight contracts were hard to come by for anyone who wasn't at a service academy or at least in a Reserve Officers' Training Corps (ROTC) program. The odds were not in my favor. The cumulative effect of that sentiment just made me even more determined to pull it off.

A year later, I graduated from college, and it was starting to look like all of those people might be right. Then, Uncle Louis Schumacher came to town for a visit. Louis was my uncle by marriage via my Dad's sister. He was also the only United States Marine I knew. I first met Louis when he showed up at my parents' house with my aunt when I was seven years old. A young enlisted Marine, who cursed like it was his job, he was funny as hell and drank beer like it was air. In a matter of minutes, he became one of my favorite people.

Now a Staff Non-Commissioned Officer (SNCO), Louis heard that I was interested in the military, so on this visit, he started in on me right away about becoming an aviator in the Marine Corps. I was ignorant about Marine Corps aviation, but the more Louis talked, the more interested I became. Before he left, Louis connected me with an Officer Selection Officer (OSO) out of

Albuquerque, New Mexico, who covered my region. After one phone conversation, the OSO sent a Marine Corps sergeant to meet me on campus after school one day to take a Marine Corps Physical Fitness Test (PFT), followed by a written flight aptitude test. Based on the results of those two tests, the OSO called me a couple of weeks later and told me that I was likely to go to OCS with an aviation contract. Finally, it was starting to look like I might pull this off!

The process wasn't fast. In the fall of 1997, I was a college graduate and had taken a job coaching baseball at a local high school while waiting to leave for OCS. My OSO called to tell me I'd been accepted but that my flight physical had not been processed in time to go with an aviation contract. I could go in December as a ground officer or wait until June to go with the aviation contract. I chose to wait. I wanted my shot at flight school.

For the rest of the year, I coached and worked out like crazy. I went out for long runs almost every night. I wasn't sure if I was running towards the future or from the past. It didn't matter. Either way, I was running fast.

On June 8, 1997, my parents took me to the Lubbock International Airport to board a flight to Albuquerque, New Mexico. From there, the other officer candidates in my district and I would fly to Washington, D.C. for OCS at Marine Corps Base (MCB), Quantico.

OCS was advertised as a grueling ten-week program designed to ensure that only the best earned the right to lead Marines. I knew going in that the attrition rate was typically more than 25%. My strategy was simple. Don't get hurt, keep a low profile, be observant, and figure out which candidates knew what was going on. So long as I did what the best candidates did, I could stay off the radar. The other candidates were all smart and athletic. As a group, they were impressive. I was never going to be the most intelligent, strongest, or the fastest candidate. To succeed, I would have to be one of the hardest working and among the most mentally and physically tough.

After landing at National Airport in Washington, D.C., buses picked us up and took us south on Interstate 95 to MCB Quantico. OCS is located on the southeast corner of MCB Quantico, right on the Potomac River. It was the greenest place I had ever seen. It was also hot and insanely humid. I hate humidity, and Quantico humidity felt like Houston to me. It was oppressive.

That summer, I would long for the dry heat of West Texas on more than a few occasions. After a couple of days of processing, we were divided up into platoons and handed off to our drill instructors. As a member of Charlie Company, 2nd Platoon, I immediately started to execute in accordance with my plan. We were assigned racks in the squad bay in alphabetical order. As fortune would have it, the two guys next to me were a Citadel graduate and a prior-enlisted Marine "Mustang." I couldn't have asked for two better guys to cue off of. I paid close attention to everything they did and followed their lead. That was enough to keep me off the radar early while I was learning and settling in.

Within a few days, they both emerged as leaders in our platoon, and all of us were getting tight. By design, the experience demands teamwork, and our platoon gelled quickly. My only downfall was that I found the drill instructors to be hilarious. I had watched *Full Metal Jacket* at least twenty times, but these guys were the real thing. Gunnery Sergeant Hartman didn't have anything on them. The things that came out of their mouths were equal parts awesome and hilarious. I got my ass chewed more than a few times for giggling. I couldn't help it. That shit was funny.

On August 6, 1997, our platoon completed "The Crucible," a new culminating event built to test our maximum capabilities. By that point in the course, our platoon had dwindled by more than thirty percent as candidates couldn't keep up with the mental and physical rigors of the program. The rest of us earned our Eagle, Globe, and Anchor (EGA). I was serving as the Candidate Platoon Sergeant on the day we completed The Crucible, so I had the honor of presenting EGAs to my fellow candidates. It was a heavy moment. I was physically and emotionally spent. It was by far my most significant accomplishment at that point in my life. But I was just getting started.

A few days later, my parents attended the graduation ceremony, during which my fellow candidates and I were commissioned as second lieutenants in the United States Marine Corps. The highlight was that Master Sergeant Louis Schumacher also made the trip, and he gave me my first salute. In line with tradition, I gave him a silver dollar in return.

There are few things less fucked up than a boot-ass second lieutenant or ensign in any military service. In other branches of the service, second lieutenants and ensigns are sent directly to training at their Military Occupational Specialty (MOS) School as soon as they are commissioned. However, the Marine Corps doesn't do that. Instead, the Marine Corps first sends all second lieutenants through a six-month training program called The Basic School (TBS) at MCB Quantico. As the name implies, at TBS second lieutenants learn the basics of being an infantry platoon commander and more about the Marine Air Ground Task Force (MAGTF). This training is in line with the "every Marine is a rifleman" mantra. It is also a perfect way to at least partially unfuck new second lieutenants in the woods of Quantico before releasing them to their MOS schools.

At TBS, I landed in Echo Company, Second Platoon (Section Alpha), led by an Infantry Captain named Randy Soriano. To this day, Captain Soriano remains the most quotable Marine I ever served with. "In a combined arms dilemma, the enemy doesn't know whether to shit or go blind!" Timeless. Captain Soriano also liked to joke that he had been "the hardest Marine in the Second Marine Division and quite possibly the entire Marine Corps."

Captain Soriano was a character, but he backed it up by consistently pushing us to our mental and physical limits. He was hell-bent on ensuring that we were the hardest platoon in the company. He was especially hard on those of us with aviation contracts. The general impression of the Air Wing is that the Marines who inhabit it tend to be relatively lax on Marine Corps standards of all types. Captain Soriano wanted to make sure that those of us with aviation contracts understood that not only were we there to support the infantry, but that we were still Marine Corps officers. As such, he pushed us to not only meet the standard but to exceed it by a wide margin. I completely bought into both his perspective and his methodology.

One night we were out on a ten-mile company hike, and during a short rest break, Captain Soriano pulled out a can of dip and threw in a healthy pinch. He then asked if any of us were hard enough to take one. I jumped all over that and threw a big dip into my mouth. For the rest of the hump, he kept looking back over his shoulder at me, grinning. "Lee, you aren't a pussy like most air guarantees. I like that." What he didn't know was that I dipped all the time. It was a carryover from my youth in Texas, where it is prevalent. My perspective was such that real dippers rarely even spit.

Regardless, it was a win with Captain Soriano. From there, I kept my head down, and worked my ass off through the rest of the program. He had a significant impact on the Marine I ultimately became. By the end of our time at TBS, I enjoyed it so much that I even contemplated giving up my aviation contract to pursue being an infantry officer. After some deliberation, I talked myself out of it. Flying was my original plan, and I wanted to take my shot at seeing it through. I was going to flight school.

Before I left home to go to OCS, I met a young couple from Northern Virginia. She was getting her doctorate at Texas Tech, and he ended up teaching at the high school where my Dad was now the Vice-Principal. They had become friends with my parents. When I left for OCS, they arranged for their parents to pick me up on weekends and take me to their homes to do laundry, call home, and eat something other than the OCS chow hall food. I appreciated that. On one of those visits, my now mother-in-law reminded me that she also had a daughter my age named Kerry. I politely played it off and went on about my business.

During one of the first weekends of TBS, I made the mistake of telling my roommates that I sort of knew a young woman our age. They were instantly all over me to call her so that we could meet up with her and her friends. I made the call. The next thing I knew, one of my roommates and I were heading north on I-95 to meet Kerry and her friends in downtown D.C. That first meeting was pretty great for the first few hours, but my roommate and I were fresh out of OCS, about 15 pounds lighter, and well out of drinking shape. At the end of the night, it caught up to us.

Kerry smartly dumped us in her car and took us to her parents' house to sleep it off. When we woke up in my now in-laws' basement the following day, it took me a minute to get my bearings. If she were anyone else, I would have likely never called her again out of embarrassment, but the family connection meant I needed to circle back and smooth this one over. After an awkward departure, I gave her a call later that afternoon. I asked her if I could take her to dinner the following weekend. For some reason, she agreed.

We went to dinner at a little place in "Q Town," a street on MCB Quantico that is home to a few small businesses. Marines could hit Q Town and drop cammies off at the cleaners, get a haircut, buy uniform items, an endless amount of Marine Corps swag, and grab a bite to eat. We sat there at a little restaurant full of Marine Corps paraphernalia and talked for a long time over some mediocre food. In retrospect, it was a cheesy place to take her, but it didn't matter in the end.

From that point forward, we spent every weekend together. We were from two different planets, but we enjoyed our time together and figuring one another out. She was highly intelligent and articulate. She had grown up going to marches in downtown D.C. with her Mom. She was strong, and she had opinions. Yet, underneath her tough exterior, I saw a genuine mix of caring and goodness. We had a shared sense of humor that wasn't always appropriate. Most importantly, she matched my level of intensity and passion. She was real. She was truthful. I trusted her instantly, and that had always been difficult for me. Everything about our relationship just felt right. We spent our weekends taking in the sights in downtown D.C. We went to museums during the day and bars at night. We took weekend trips to Philadelphia and New York City. We had a never-ending conversation about all things.

We were falling in love, but I did not see it working long-term. She had a life and a bright future there. She had just started a career in Washington, D.C. She was close to her family and busy pursuing her passions. There was absolutely no reason for her to give that up to follow me around to wherever the Marine Corps sent me. It was a relationship that started with an expiration date. In less than six months, I would head to Pensacola, Florida, for flight school, and we would both continue on with our respective lives. I felt certain our relationship would be short-lived, a memory I expected to look back on fondly.

While that was going on, my platoon mates and I spent our weekdays learning to lead, fight, and survive in the woods of Quantico during a Northern Virginia winter. Unfortunately, our culminating exercise, "The War," was cut short because a large portion of our company came down with hypothermia. Nevertheless, it was great training that pushed us hard and built on the confidence we had gained from OCS.

Most importantly, a small group of us in Second Platoon, who would be heading to flight school, had become really good friends. Chris Dalton, Dave Wright, Ian Dagley, Kurt Hendrix, and Mark Franko were all headed to Pensacola, Florida, as well. The six of us decided to pair off as roommates who would all live close to one another.

On March 6, 1997, we graduated from TBS and prepared to head south to Pensacola. Kerry and I said our goodbyes, and she was there when I pulled away in my Ford F-150, headed south for the next phase of the adventure. Kerry and I never even talked about what was next for us, but I assumed that I had just said goodbye to her for the final time. I was bummed about it, but I knew that staying in D.C. made the most sense for her. And I was a better man thanks to the time we'd spent together.

A couple of days later, my buddies and I pulled into Pensacola, Florida, and set up shop in an apartment complex. Dagley and I were roommates; Hendrix and Franko lived right above us. The shenanigans started immediately. Dalton and Wright lived in a different apartment complex not too far away, but the six of us hung out together most of the time. We checked into Marine Aviation Training Support Group 21 (MATSG-21). In what remains one of the greatest deals in military history, we would spend our first few months of flight school in what was referred to as "the pool." Meaning, we had absolutely nothing to do while waiting to start training. Our only requirements: stay in shape on our own time and show up once a week for an accountability formation. Glorious.

Our little crew from Echo Company, Second Platoon, was inseparable. We somehow managed to stay in shape despite spending most of our time hanging out at Pensacola Beach, drinking beer, and attempting to look cooler than all the other Marine Corps and Navy personnel doing the same thing. At night we hung out at the local watering holes like Flounders, Capt'n Funs, McGuire's, and Seville Quarter. It didn't suck.

We had endless conversations that covered all topics and learned everything there was to know about one another. More often than not, the conversation drifted back to what aircraft we wanted to fly and how badass it was going to be when we all got our wings and headed to our first fleet squadrons. Our bonds grew closer, as did our actual training date.

Dalton had impressed all of us since we started OCS. His

father was the Secretary of the Navy at the time, but he handled it like a pro. He was smart, tough, worked his ass off, and never once played the card. He just wanted to succeed on his own, and we all respected that. He was a total stud. Wright was from Northern Virginia, had attended Radford University, and had previously been enlisted in the Marine Corps Reserve. He was also a walking comedy show who promptly bought a boat he named "The Sea Chicken" when we arrived in Pensacola. We often loaded up cases of beer and fishing rods and went deep-sea fishing. The fact that we made it back to shore every time is a miracle.

Dagley was a Purdue alum and the unofficial ambassador for the state of Indiana. He was big, loud, and had a huge personality. You couldn't not love that guy. Franko was our token Naval Academy graduate. Wicked smart but still just a great guy. We tended to give all the Naval Academy grads a hard time on general principle, but Franko made the cut.

Hendrix was unique. After graduating from college, he enlisted in the Navy. After completing his enlistment, he had then worked as a paramedic back home before deciding to pursue a commission in the Marine Corps. He was a few years older than us and needed a waiver to head to flight school at the ripe old age of 29. Hendrix was like our big brother. He mostly told us we were idiots for doing whatever we happened to be doing at any given time, but he also took care of us and set the example. Despite being a few years older, he could outrun and outswim all of us. He was a fucking stud, and we all kind of looked up to him.

The days flew by as we waited to start training. We were all fairly certain that we were ten feet tall and bulletproof. Typical young lieutenants. At that point in the journey, the thought of someday flying in combat was nothing more than an intangible idea, absent the emotional burden that comes with it. We didn't know that we all stood on the cusp of executing multiple combat tours that would test our physical and emotional limits.

In early May, Kerry called and told me she wanted to come for a visit. Although surprised, I wanted to see her. She arrived on Saturday morning, and she stayed until Thursday. Five pretty great days. By the time I dropped her off at the airport, I wasn't sure where the two of us were headed, but I was happy to be on the ride.

A couple of weeks after Kerry left in early June, I officially started Flight School. Aviation Preflight Indoctrination (API) is composed of six weeks of academics and a ton of swimming. Dagley and I classed up together, which was great. We studied together, and he kept our training days entertaining. The program is a six-week weeding out program that is all firehose academics and trying not to drown. API included courses on aerodynamics, engines, navigation, and more swimming than any rational human would ever want to do. We spent our mornings in the classroom and our afternoons in the pool, dunkers, and Pensacola Bay. The culminating water survival event was a one-mile swim in full flight gear followed by a multi-hour survival float in Pensacola Bay. It was a rigorous program, but it went well.

The next step would be primary flight training in the T-34C. The T-34C is a fully aerobatic turboprop airplane set up for two pilots sitting front and back. Primary flight training was offered at Naval Air Station (NAS) Pensacola, Florida, and NAS Corpus Christi, Texas. Some of us would have to go to Corpus no matter what, so Dagley, Hendrix, Franko, and I all volunteered to go to Corpus. I figured it might be the only time the Marine Corps would send me to my home state of Texas. Worst case, I would get some Whataburger and Texas barbeque out of the deal.

We were close to finishing API when we got a long weekend over the 4th of July. Dagley had arranged for us to hang out in Panama City, Florida, with some girls he knew from back home. What ensued over the next few days was a bit of a blur, and I learned that the 4th of July weekend in Panama City is a close second to Spring Break. It was insane. I came away with one real takeaway. I was only interested in the girl who still lived in Virginia.

As soon as we returned to Pensacola, I called Kerry. A week later, I picked her up at the airport. She was supposed to stay for five days. Instead, she started calling in sick to work and stretched it to twelve days. She knew she was putting her job back in D.C. in jeopardy. I knew that I was about to move to Corpus Christi, Texas. On day eleven of the visit, I asked her if she wanted to move to Corpus. For reasons that I still don't quite understand, she said that she would meet me there. When that visit concluded, she flew back to D.C., quit her job, sold everything but her clothes, and prepared to meet me in Texas. Not too rational, but we were young, very much in love, and just wanted to be together.

Dagley and I rented an apartment in Corpus, aware that Kerry would become our third roommate. Kerry arrived about a week after Dagley. I had a lot going on at once. Kerry, plus it was game time. The real part of flight school was starting.

During flight training, every academic and flight event is graded. If you fail one, it is called a "down." If you fail two events, you go before a board that determines whether or not you continue in training or get reassigned to a ground MOS. Staring down the barrel of several exams and a few hundred flight events, I felt the pressure. Every single day would be game day for the next couple of years. I checked into Training Squadron Two Eight (VT-28) at NAS Corpus Christi. Time to dive in headfirst and leave it all on the field.

Upon check-in, I was assigned an "On-wing," which is an instructor with whom you fly the majority of your initial familiarization flights. My on-wing was a Marine captain CH-53E pilot. He was an okay guy, and a decent instructor, but the instructor I took to was a Marine Corps major named Will Hardy. "Wild Bill" was his callsign. He was an AH-1W Cobra helicopter pilot who'd flown in Desert Storm and had also done an exchange tour with the 160th Special Operations Aviation Regiment (SOAR).

As far as I was concerned, the major's resume made him the most badass instructor in Corpus by a wide margin. Major Hardy also looked like a real-life action figure. He stood about 6'3", was jacked, and had a shaved head and a square jaw. His wallet said Bad Motherfucker on it. All the Marine Corps students were in awe of him. He seemed like way too much of a legitimate badass to be hanging around as an instructor at primary flight training, but there he was. I got the opportunity to fly with him one day early in the syllabus, and the flight went well. Major Hardy kept a close eye on me and became a real mentor to me from that point forward.

On February 13, 1999, Kerry and I were married in a small ceremony in Corpus Christi, Texas. I couldn't take any actual leave since I was in training, so we settled on that date since it was during Presidents' Day weekend. A small group of family and friends made the trip to Corpus Christi, and several of my peers provided the customary sword arch for us to walk under when we stepped out of the church. From that day forward, we would be on the adventure together.

Several weeks later, Major Hardy and I went on a cross-country flight to Marine Corps Air Station (MCAS) Yuma, Arizona. MCAS Yuma is home to Marine Aviation Weapons and Tactics Squadron One (MAWTS-1). MAWTS-1 puts on a semi-annual Weapons and Tactics Instructor (WTI) course, and the graduates are considered the best of the best aviators in the Marine Corps. Simply stated, WTI is the "Top Gun" of the Marine Corps. Major Hardy was a WTI graduate and a huge proponent of the program. He was happy to go back and visit. At the time, I had no idea how big of a piece of my life that Yuma and MAWTS-1 would later become.

As we approached MCAS Yuma, Major Hardy radioed to request clearance into Range 2507 South, part of the Yuma range complex. MCAS Yuma is where it is because there are huge range complexes to the base's west, north, and east. That's where the Marine Corps plays war. Major Hardy and I blazed into Range 2507 South in our T-34C at low altitude, and he pointed out all the prominent landmarks in the range. We buzzed past LZ Bull, Mount Barrow, and Blue Mountain Airfield. At the time, I didn't fully grasp that I would end up spending countless hours flying and training in that range.

We wrapped up the range familiarization and headed into MCAS Yuma to land. Once the aircraft was buttoned up, Major Hardy headed to the BOQ (Bachelor Officer Quarters). As a bonus for me, Uncle Louis was stationed at MCAS Yuma at that time. So instead of heading to billeting, he picked me up at Base Ops. I spent the weekend at his place, drinking beer and talking about the adventure I was having thus far. It wouldn't be the last time he and I would spend a weekend like that.

Like most Marines, I thought I wanted to fly jets when I started flight school. As I neared the end of Primary Flight Training, my grades were strong enough to be very competitive for a jet slot if I wanted it. Upon completion of primary training, students "select" jets, helicopters, or heavies. Your graduating class gets ranked based on grades. You all fill out a wish list of your preferences, then receive your aircraft assignment based upon those preferences and your class rank. The first person gets their first choice. The last person gets whatever is left.

The options for jets were FA-18 Hornets, AV-8B Harriers, and EA-6B Prowlers. The options for helicopters were CH-46E Sea Knights, CH-53E Super Stallions, AH-1W Cobras, or UH-1N Hueys. The Cobras and Hueys were organized together into combined Light Attack squadrons, commonly referred to as "skid squadrons." The KC-130 Hercules transport aircraft was the final option. Despite initially leaning towards jets after flying with Major Hardy and some of the other Marine Corps instructors with rotary wing backgrounds, I began to lean towards flying helicopters.

A couple of days before making my final selection, I asked

Major Hardy for advice. I told him I was on the fence between jets and helicopters. He looked right at me and said, "Lee, here's the deal. Mach two is just a number on a dial at 20,000 feet. Now flying 50 feet off the deck at 150 knots, looking into the eyes of the man who's trying to kill you... that will make your balls crawl up into your stomach."

I was sold. Helicopters it would be. I had no idea how accurate his description would prove to be.

I finished up in Corpus in June of 1999, and Kerry and I packed up our apartment and headed back to Pensacola, where I would complete advanced helicopter training in the TH-57B/C helicopter. Dagley selected jets and headed to NAS Meridian, Mississippi, to chase his dream of becoming Blue Angel #2. Hendrix and Franko both selected helicopters and headed back to Pensacola a few weeks ahead of us. We all moved into the same apartment complex when we got back to Pensacola. Dalton and Wright also moved over there to join us.

For the next six months, we all studied, flew, worked out, and still spent too much time drinking beer at the beach. We were together all the time. Hendrix would always show up with a cooler full of food to make fancy appetizers. The rest of us were a lot more basic. Kerry was a part-time wife and a full-time mom, sister, and counselor to the rest of those guys. She was always right in the middle of it, trading barbs and laughing. She also kept all of us out of trouble.

By the time I reached advanced flight training, I had a good system in place for studying and preparation. I was naturally a decent stick, which helped. I credit the countless hours I spent as a kid playing football, baseball, and video games for that piece of it. Advanced helicopter training went well. As I hit the home stretch, I was in the running to finish at the top of my class. I spent a lot of time thinking about my choice of aircraft and potential location. In the end, I decided that I would be happy with either AH-1W Cobras or CH-53E Super Stallions on the west coast.

3rd Marine Aircraft Wing (3rd MAW) was based out of Marine Corps Air Station (MCAS) Miramar in San Diego, California. The CH-53s were on MCAS Miramar, and the AH-1Ws were on MCAS Camp Pendleton, CA. The idea of living in San Diego and flying out of those air stations sounded awesome. In March of 2000, I graduated at the top of my class and was selected to be a CH-53E helicopter pilot at Miramar.

Kerry and I were both super excited about the prospect of moving to San Diego and finally getting to a real fleet squadron. Hendrix and Wright both took CH-46s out of MCAS Miramar. Dalton got CH-53s out of MCAS Miramar. Franko selected CH-46s but on the east coast. He was the only one saying goodbye. The rest of us would head for Southern California.

Before going to San Diego, we had to take a detour at MCAS New River in Jacksonville, North Carolina. MCAS New River is home to the CH-53E Fleet Replacement Squadron (FRS), where newly winged CH-53E aviators learn the aircraft and fly a basic familiarization syllabus before heading to their fleet squadron. Kerry and I packed up and headed to North Carolina for that brief stint of training.

Jacksonville, North Carolina, is home to the 2nd Marine Aircraft Wing (2nd MAW) and II Marine Expeditionary Force (II MEF). Marines affectionately refer to the city of Jacksonville, North Carolina, as "J Vegas." Both Marine Corps Air Station (MCAS) New River and Camp Lejeune are located there on opposite sides of the New River. MCAS Cherry Point, North Carolina, is just up the road. Jacksonville is small-town North Carolina completely overrun with Marines. You can't go anywhere in that town without feeling like you are on base. Kerry and I rented a townhouse on the river, and I went to MCAS New River to check in to Marine Heavy Helicopter Training Squadron 302 (HMT-302) to knock out my training in the CH-53E.

The CH-53E is a marvel of 1970s and 80s engineering. At 99 feet and 0.5 inches in length, 17 feet and 2 inches in height (to the top of the main rotor head), and weighing in at 37,000 pounds without fuel, the CH-53E Super Stallion looks like a real-life Transformer waiting to come to life. My first close look at it was intimidating as hell. It almost didn't look real. Three General Electric T-64 416 engines each provide 4380 shaft horsepower through an extremely complex transmission system, to a 79' diameter main rotor that turns at 179 RPM and a 20' diameter tail rotor that turns at 699 RPM. The tail rotor is canted 20 degrees to the left, which provides an additional 2% lift. When you fuel her up with 15,483 pounds of JP-5 fuel (2,277 gallons), you can take her out for just over four hours of flight time.

The CH-53E "Echo" is also affectionately referred to as the "shitter" by the Marines who fly and maintain it due to the dark exhaust trail the engines leave in its wake. Others simply referred to it as "The Big Iron" due to its size and strength. It was the biggest, strongest, and fastest rotary wing aircraft in the United States arsenal. Just an absolute beast of a war machine. As I stood in the hangar staring it down for the first time, I hoped I could rapidly get myself to a point where I could get the most out of that machine.

I spent the summer and early fall of 2000 learning the aircraft systems and knocking out my initial familiarization flights. With the canted tail rotor, the CH-53E hovers with 5-8 degrees nose up and 2-3 degrees left wing down. That hover attitude tends to give young aviators fits for a few hundred hours until they get used to it. I dove into the syllabus and quickly adapted to my new aircraft.

Kerry and I made the most of our time in J-Vegas. We hit all the local haunts. Smithfield's Chicken 'N Bar-B-Que, Andy's Burgers, and Sywanyks Scarlet & Gold were all adequately sampled. We made the most of it but left there quite convinced that we had made the right choice by selecting San Diego. I finished up training just after the Thanksgiving holiday.

We packed up again and headed west for San Diego. I had only been to San Diego once before on a high school graduation trip with a couple of my buddies. Kerry had never been there at all. We rented an apartment sight unseen, and we were excited about becoming residents of Southern California. At that point, it was just one big adventure for both of us. We drove across the country with zero clue that the next few years would push us to the extreme of human emotion and test every ounce of our character.

3

WARHORSE

KERRY and I drove across the country with a purpose. I was in my F-150, pulling a U-Haul trailer, and Kerry was right behind me in her little red Honda Civic. We didn't own much except for some hand-me-down furniture and our clothes, so moving was easy back then.

On the home stretch, we blazed across the desert through Yuma, Arizona, passing right by the little mountain on the northwest corner of town referred to as "Pilot's Knob." I remembered it as the course rules entry point Major Hardy and I had used to return to Marine Corps Air Station (MCAS) Yuma on our T-34 excursion a few months earlier. We continued along I-8 through El Centro, California, then started the big climb up from the desert floor into the mountain ranges along the eastern border of San Diego County. As we drove down on the western side of the mountains, the city started to come into view in the distance. I would soon become accustomed to flying back from the Yuma range complex and descending towards MCAS Miramar over these same mountains.

Once in town, we turned north on I-15 right next to Qualcomm Stadium and soon passed MCAS Miramar on our left. Seeing the base for the first time was surreal. A few minutes later, we took the exit at Carmel Mountain Road and pulled into our new apartment complex. San Diego would quickly become home.

A few days later, we had unpacked, and I put on my Service Alphas and headed to Miramar to check in. With more than three years of training complete, I was checking into my first fleet squadron. Finally, after countless hours of studying and a few hundred training flights, I was getting to play with the varsity.

Approximately three hundred Marines populate a fleet CH-53E squadron. There are just over thirty officers in the squadron, almost all of whom are aviators. The exceptions are a couple of maintenance officers and the Navy flight surgeon who heads up the squadron medical department. The squadron's Commanding Officer (CO) is a lieutenant colonel, and the department heads are typically a group of four to five majors. The rest of the officers are first tour captains and lieutenants. The majority of the squadron Marines are enlisted personnel, who work in the various squadron departments.

The primary departments in any squadron are S-1 Administration, S-2 Intelligence, S-3 Operations, S-4 Logistics, S-5 Civil Affairs, S-6 Information Systems, Safety, Medical, and Maintenance. The Maintenance Department is the cornerstone of every fleet squadron, as well as home to most of the Marines in the squadron. Operations can have the greatest plan in the world, but it can only execute if the squadron maintenance department has provided up aircraft to fly.

There is typically a change of command following every deployment where a new CO takes over the unit for the next eighteen to twenty-four month cycle. The same applies to the rest of the Marines in the squadron. After each deployment, some of the Marines leave the unit to move on to their next assignment. Newly school-trained aviators, maintainers, and S-shop Marines check in to replace the Marines who depart. I always thought of it as being similar to school. After every deployment, the seniors graduate, and you get a new group of freshmen. At the time, the expectation was that new check-ins like myself would be in the unit for four years and complete two deployment cycles. That would soon change.

I was assigned to HMH-465 "Warhorse." HMH-465 was part of Marine Aircraft Group 16 (MAG-16), which fell under the command of 3rd Marine Aircraft Wing (3rd MAW). Higher headquarters was I Marine Expeditionary Force (I MEF), located at MCB Camp Pendleton.

HMH-465 was formed in 1981 when the Marine Corps transitioned from the CH-53D to the CH-53E. As a result of the early 1980s formation, it was one of the newer squadrons in the fleet. When I checked in, the CH-53E "Super Stallion" was also the newest aircraft in the fleet. The squadron's history was neither long nor particularly strong. The squadron was rumored to have performed in a less than stellar manner during OPERATION DESERT STORM, and it was sometimes referred to as the "Peace Ponies" by sister squadrons for generally sucking. I had heard that more than once via the lieutenant rumor mill before checking in. I gave zero fucks about that. I was in the fleet. Whatever happened in the past didn't matter. I was about to do everything I could to help make sure we were the best squadron on the flight line going forward.

I parked across the street from Hangar 4 and didn't take the time that I should have to stop and look at it. I was too busy being paranoid about making sure that my Service Alpha uniform looked perfect. First impressions mean everything, and I didn't want to screw this one up. I was minutes away from being the newest boot ass lieutenant aviator in a fleet squadron filled with salty Marines.

Some of the captains in the squadron had already completed Marine Expeditionary Unit (MEU) deployments and held advanced flight leadership and instructor designations. There were Staff Non-Commissioned Officers (SNCOs) wearing cammies that were older than my time in service. Sergeants and corporals in the squadron had earned their stripes. I understood very well that my job was to work my ass off and become a positive contributor as quickly as possible. I knew I was going to have to earn the trust of every Marine in the squadron. I couldn't wait to get started.

Upon walking into the hangar, the Marines directed me to the S-1 Administration Shop. The Marines in S-1 were talking me through the check-in process when a captain named Jay "Spooner" Holtermann walked in. Spooner was checking back in after graduating from the WTI Course at MAWTS-1 in Yuma, Arizona.

After my experience with Major Hardy in flight school, I knew that graduating from the course and earning the WTI designation was the pinnacle instructor designation for a Marine aviator. Becoming a WTI was my goal before I had even finished primary flight training. Spooner was shooting the shit with the Marines, and I quickly observed that he had an easy demeanor, coupled with a high level of confidence. In Marine parlance, you could just tell that he had his shit wired.

As the newest member of the squadron, I introduced myself. I congratulated him on earning the WTI stamp and told him that was my goal as well. He was cool about it, but he looked at me with eyes that said, "Calm down, Boot, you have a long way to go."

It wasn't the smartest comment for me to make, considering that I stood there in my Alphas holding a check-in sheet. If you are going to have a goal, at least have the audacity to say it out loud. Neither Spooner nor I knew then that he would soon set one hell of a pace for those of us coming behind him. I intended to do my best to keep up with him.

When I headed downstairs to check in to Maintenance Control, I was greeted by the squadron Maintenance Control Chief. He was a gunnery sergeant named Lee Marty. To call Gunnery Sergeant Marty salty doesn't do justice to the term or to the gunnery sergeant. He sauntered towards the counter, looking at me like I had already fucked something up.

"Jesus fucking Christ, another goddamn lieutenant." He gripped a cup of coffee like it was his assigned weapon and had a big messy dip in his mouth. He was pushing height weight standards and rocking a moto horseshoe flat top. His voice sounded like a gravel truck, and his general appearance and approach radiated that he gave zero fucks.

As he reached the counter, the phone rang. He looked me right in the eye as he picked it up and answered with, "Four hundred and sixty-fifth rotary bomber squadron. Gunnery Sergeant Marty speaking."

He quickly dismissed the poor bastard on the other end of the line, hung up, and turned his attention back to me. As he signed my check-in sheet, he looked right at me with a highly suspicious expression and led off with a sarcastic, "Sirrrrrrr" before going on to say, "Just don't break my goddamn aircraft, and you and I will get along just fine."

He was like a real-life cartoon character. I would later learn that he lived up in Sun City, CA, and stopped at the casinos to gamble on his way to and from work every day. He drank Bud Light all night and coffee all day. Nicotine was his constant. The guy always had a dip in his mouth. He personified old-school air wing SNCO, and he immediately became one of my favorite people.

I made my way back upstairs and looked at the deployment plaques lining the walls of the passageway. Every plaque was covered with names, colorful callsigns, dates, and other random factoids commemorating each deployment. I peeked into the ready room, where the pilots plan, brief, and debrief every flight. The Operations Duty Officer (ODO) sat behind the desk, tracking the execution of the flight schedule. I was excited to be there.

Later that day, I met the CO. He was a stoic man of very few words. I had a lot of COs over the years, but in retrospect, he was high on my list. He was a genuinely good officer who cared about his Marines. He welcomed me to the squadron, told me to do great things, then sent me to meet my new boss. I was assigned to be a schedule writer in the squadron Operations Department. Operations was led by a major who'd previously been a test pilot. As the Operations Officer (OPSO), he was a hard-ass but also an extremely competent officer and aviator. That first day, he didn't say much other than to tell me to check in with the squadron WTI, his right-hand man.

The squadron WTI was a captain who had been a quarterback at the Naval Academy. He was a big Captain America looking dude with a square jaw and an aviator haircut that pushed regs. When I checked in, he looked at me in a way that communicated he would consider me a dumbass until I proved otherwise. He informed me that I got lucky checking in after he had already written the duty schedule, or he would have given me duty on Christmas. He probably should have done it, anyway. I couldn't wait to get to work.

I snapped in quickly and worked my ass off to contribute to the squadron. I worked hard to learn my ground job in Ops, and I studied like crazy to prepare for every training flight. After a few days, I had a few minutes to spare and went downstairs to the Flightline shop to ask if any crew chiefs would be willing to do a walkaround on the aircraft with me.

I employed this same tactic at the Fleet Replacement Squadron in North Carolina, learning a ton from a super motivated young crew chief named Ron Strzalkowski. The best way to master the aircraft was to learn from those who worked on it every day. The Flightline Marines at HMH-465 surprised me. Instead of telling me I needed to bribe one of the crew chiefs in Flightline, they sent me down to Avionics to ask for Chief Warrant Officer (CWO) 2 Fifer. I assumed this was some kind of a joke on the new guy, but I dutifully walked down to Avionics to take whatever prank was waiting for me on the other end.

I walked into Avionics and asked for CWO 2 Fifer. One of the

Marines looked at me like a suspect then pointed me towards the back office. In that office, I found CWO 2 Jonathon Fifer sitting with his feet up on the desk and reading something on a computer screen. He was a big, tall bastard with a flat top and a big ass dip in his mouth. Fifer looked like he should be playing defensive end for somebody.

I would later learn that he was an enlisted avionics Marine who became a homegrown crew chief before being selected for warrant officer. As such, he had made his way back to a CH-53E squadron, where he still flew as a crew chief but also served as the Avionics Officer. Our Aviation Maintenance Officer (AMO), Major Brad "Browner" Brown, and Fifer went way back, and Browner made sure that he got Fifer to the Warhorse.

In that initial meeting, I flatly told Fifer I wanted to master the aircraft and the Flightline Marines told me that he knew it better than anybody. He gave me a semi-expressionless look, then said, "Okay, be here early tomorrow morning and check out ten rags from the tool room."

The next morning, I was there as instructed with ten rags. He took me out to the line, and we did a full daily inspection on an aircraft. He talked, I listened, and when able, I jotted down notes. It was the first of many walkarounds that he and I would do over the next year. It was also the beginning of a great friendship.

From that point forward, all I did was work my ass off, study, and fly. Dalton was next door, doing the same thing in HMH-462, but the squadrons didn't mix at that point. Like, at all. Hendrix and Wright were down the flight line in HMM-166. We all worked hard, trying to establish ourselves in the fleet. Kerry and I explored San Diego in our limited spare time, and we started working with a realtor to buy a small starter house. A lot was going on, but it was all new and exciting.

Our squadron was slated to deploy in July of 2001, just six months after I checked in. A CH-53E squadron is designed to be broken up into three separate pieces for operational deployments. Our squadron would provide two Marine Expeditionary Unit (MEU) detachments led by majors. Those detachments would consist of four aircraft and approximately 60 Marines to become part of a MEU Aviation Combat Element (ACE). The remainder of the squadron is referred to as the Main Body, led by the CO and designed to support eight aircraft with approximately 200 Marines. Our Main Body was slated to train and operate out of Marine Corps Air Station (MCAS) Futenma in Okinawa, Japan.

Six months before deploying, we had conducted a Change of Operational Control (CHOP) of our detachment to the 15th MEU ACE. Captain "Spooner" Holtermann would be the WTI on that det, led by one of our majors. Every MEU is composed of a Command Element, a Ground Combat Element (GCE), a Logistics Combat Element (LCE), and the Aviation Combat Element (ACE). The ACE was built around a Marine Medium Helicopter (HMM) squadron of CH-46Es. Their CO serves as the ACE CO. With a detachment of CH-53s, AH-1Ws, UH-1Ns and AV-8B Harriers, the ACE could adequately support the GCE. The 15th MEU, along with the 11th and 13th, participates in a never-ending rotation off the west coast that provides multiple capabilities to the Department of Defense.

A MEU is built to be a rapid response force that can bring combat power to any "clime and place" in a matter of hours. Our 15th MEU detachment would set sail from San Diego when the rest of the squadron was deploying to Okinawa, Japan. Upon arrival in Okinawa, we would CHOP another detachment to the 31st Marine Expeditionary Unit ACE located right there at MCAS Futenma. The "Thirty Worst," as we called it, did not require the same six-month workup period as the 15th MEU. The remaining fifty percent of the squadron would be the "Main Body" portion of the Unit Deployment Program (UDP). While deployed, we would fall under the command of 1st Marine Aircraft Wing (1st MAW) and III Marine Expeditionary Force (III MEF).

I was initially slated for the 31st MEU, which I was excited about. On a Friday just before deployment, we all went to the Officers' Club on Miramar, and the OPSO told me that I would remain part of the Main Body with him. I was a little crushed about not going to the 31st MEU, but I decided it would all work out. No matter what portion of the deployment I would be a part of, it all sounded like one gigantic adventure.

Shortly before deploying, Kerry and I closed escrow on a small three-bedroom starter house up in North County. It was tiny and in dire need of a remodel. We would get to that when I returned home. Until then, we talked about how hard this first deployment would be. She had taken a job working with wayward teenage girls, which was right up her alley. We were staring down the barrel of deployment number one. The thought of leaving for six months weighed heavily on both of us.

On July 6, 2001, she dropped me off at the Bob Hope Theater aboard Miramar. It was our first deployment goodbye, and it was a tough one. I was worried about leaving her at home for six months, but I was also excited about going on my first deployment. This was the big adventure I had signed up for, and I wanted to make the most of it. We were newlyweds in our mid-20s, and we had no clue what *hard* actually meant.

4

FAR EAST CHRONICLES

THE SHENANIGANS STARTED SHORTLY after takeoff on July 6, 2001. Just over two hundred members of HMH-465 were aboard an L-1011 the United States government had chartered to take us to Okinawa, Japan, by way of Anchorage, Alaska.

Somewhere over the Pacific Ocean, the Marines in the squadron had gotten pretty loud and rowdy. It wasn't due to any pent-up anxiety about the deployment. They were mostly just pissed off that the aircraft had run out of alcohol. We weren't supposed to drink on those flights, but shortly after our 1030 takeoff, our CO talked the flight crew into opening up the bar, which turned into a precursor of many things to come.

After twelve hours of flying, we reached Okinawa and landed at Kadena Air Force Base. From Kadena, we boarded buses that took us on the short drive down Highway 58 to MCAS Futenma. MCAS Futenma was going to be home base for the next six months. MCAS Futenma is a tiny base in the middle of Ginowan City, which is basically a runway with hangars on one side and a few buildings on the other. Those buildings include a headquarters building, a couple of clubs, the obligatory gym, a chow hall, and several barracks. All of the officers lived in a small cluster of barracks on the northwest side of the runway. Barracks 223 was referred to as "Menopause Manor." That's where the CO, the majors, and the captains on their second deployment lived.

Myself, the other copilots, Fifer, and our Maintenance Material Control Officer (MMCO), who was also a first lieutenant, all lived in Barracks 218, which we referred to as "The Halfway House." Right across the parking lot from us was the "Crack House," an old broken down barracks our second deployment captains lived in on their first deployments two years prior. They told us that no less than ten times every fucking day. "You boots have it so good; we had to live in the Crack House!"

There was also an HMLA squadron on MCAS Futenma that was also part of the Unit Deployment Program (UDP). They made their copilots live in the Crack House because that building was still home to the "Scar Bar." They were supposed to live there to protect the sanctity of the Scar Bar from other units. Mainly ours. We also had a CH-53 bar, but it was on the third floor of Menopause Manor, where our senior officers lived. Ours was called the "Echo Chamber" in reference to the CH-53E, a.k.a. "Echo."

The officers of HMH-462 originally built the Echo Chamber. They took the common area lounge on the CH-53 hallway in Menopause Manor and decked it out with a full bar, a fridge, and a TV. Over the years, deploying west coast CH-53 squadrons had adorned it with everything from a foosball table to a velvet Elvis painting. HMH-462 had the callsign "Heavy Haulers" but was unofficially known as the "Screw Crew," a reference dating back to the Vietnam era. HMH-462 Marines wore the "Screw Crew" moniker like a badge of honor. As a result, the sign on the Echo Chamber door had their patented Screw logo right in the middle of it. Despite being a Warhorse, I thought that was pretty badass.

As a squadron, we immediately kicked out our 31st MEU detachment and fell into a work hard, play hard routine. Our Advanced Party had already accepted the aircraft from the squadron we replaced, so we organized quickly and started training. My buddy Dave Payne and I were both copilots and schedule writers, working for our OPSO and squadron WTI. The two of them pushed us hard, but I loved it. When I was in the shop, I worked my ass off to write the perfect flight schedule. In reality, I only added minor details to the plan that our squadron WTI put together.

One afternoon I took the flight schedule to the OPSO for signature, and he ripped into me. I had written "Humvee" in the notes about some external lift training. The OPSO went off, "Goddamn, Leftenant, a Humvee is what Arnold Schwarzenegger drives! In the Marine Corps, we have Highly Mobile Multi Wheeled Vehicles (HMMWV)!"

I appreciated his delivery so much I started laughing while he was still yelling at me, which made him yell more. I also never forgot that, in the Marine Corps, it's an "HMMWV."

My goal for the deployment was to become a Helicopter Aircraft Commander (HAC) so that I could sign for the aircraft and start working on advanced qualifications and designations. To become an Aircraft Commander, I needed to fly a couple of hundred hours and complete all the specific flights in the syllabus laid out in our Training and Readiness (T&R) Manual. I studied my ass off to make sure I was always ready for my flights. I wanted to make extra certain I fully understood every system on the aircraft to the level that a crew chief would. Naturally, I enlisted the help of Jon Fifer on that quest.

The bible for every Naval aircraft is the Naval and Air Training and Operating Procedures Standardization (NATOPS) Manual. To this day, I am convinced Fifer knew significantly more than the 900 + page NATOPS. He had been turning wrenches on 53s since I was in high school, and he had his shit wired. Every time I could break away from Ops, I would go check out some rags, throw a cranial on my head, and do walka-rounds with Fifer. He knew every system on that aircraft cold.

In the early stages of those walkarounds, he would take me

through the systems and tell me all about them while I took notes. We would follow every line, every component, and every connection. He knew the "weenie numbers" associated with all of it. Weenie numbers were what we called all of the numerical limitations and readings associated with every system. With an aircraft that size, my weenie number "gouge" packet alone was a 27 page document I had created in 10 point font. "Gouge" was the Naval aviation term for informally produced study material.

Eventually, we graduated to me guiding Fifer through the systems. He would ask me questions as I went, making sure I understood what was happening in the aircraft when I saw caution lights or unusual readings on the cockpit gauges. The education I received from those walkarounds was priceless, and it set the foundation for the remainder of my career as a CH-53E pilot.

I was the only married copilot in the squadron, so the rest of those guys wanted to go out on the weekends. With a wife at home, I had little interest. Instead, I tagged along with Fifer and headed over to the "Echo Chamber" in Menopause Manor. The senior captains kept that place stocked with beer and kept track of how much everyone drank on a little whiteboard behind the bar.

Beers were only .50 cents each, so you could have a hell of a time for less than five bucks. I loved that fucking room. The beers constantly flowed, but that wasn't really what it was about. It was about camaraderie and education. The majors and the senior captains were all there. I listened to them talk at length about their experiences in the squadron and the aircraft. Every story was a free flight. A free lesson learned.

I loved talking to Browner and the OPSO about what it was like being a captain in the squadron back in the days of Tustin and El Toro before Base Realignment and Closure (BRAC) consolidated the CH-53s down to Miramar. I learned as much about being a CH-53E pilot in that room as I did in the seat of the aircraft itself. In addition to the education, we also had a great time. We drank beer like professionals. The OPSO could drink a Coors Light every 15 minutes for eternity. We all greatly admired his skill.

We listened to an obscene amount of Motley Crue, Def Leppard, AC/DC, and Metallica. Over time, I became the unofficial DJ and bartender of the Echo Chamber, which was arguably my crowning achievement as a copilot. Nights often ended at sunrise on Saturday and Sunday mornings, all of us singing along to Motley Crue's "Home Sweet Home." That's when we knew it was time to shut it down.

Okinawa is also sixteen hours ahead of Pacific Standard Time, so once college football season started in September, the early game came on at 0300 Sunday morning. I was still an avid college football fan, and so were several other guys in the squadron. For us, it was one more reason to stay up all night in the Echo Chamber. The Armed Forces Network (AFN) would pick up several college football broadcasts, starting at 0300 and culminating in the "night" game being broadcast late Sunday morning.

We would all go to bed early Sunday evening to sleep it off and reset for the following week. The routine was equal parts ridiculous and glorious. This little concrete room in a barracks in Okinawa, Japan, had genuine significance to all of us. We were like a bunch of siblings, constantly talking shit and antagonizing one another. By the end of the night, there was always a lot of hugging it out before everyone staggered back to their rooms to hit the rack. What happened in that room was indicative that it's always about the people, not the place. To this day, that room has a special place in my heart.

In August, we had a couple of second deployment captains finally finish their HAC check flights. They were the last of their peer group. My peers and I all saw them as the guys not to be. There was a reason they were last. Despite their shortcomings, Browner and the OPSO thought it would be good for them to take a few of us copilots and some of our enlisted Marines on a cross-country flight to Osan Air Base in South Korea over Labor Day weekend. We called it a training detachment, but it was really just a short liberty trip to give some of the Marines a good deal. Since I worked in Ops, I became responsible for putting together the cross-country request and all of the other paperwork that needed to be filed for an international flight. I knew the extra work would be worth it.

Osan Air Base was built by the United States Air Force Aviation Engineers during the Korean War. By the time we visited, the base was home to the 51st Fighter Wing and served as the hub for the "Patriot Express" flights, bringing American service members and their families to and from Korea.

Our actual flight to Osan was a total shit show. Neither of the two HACs was a section leader who could lead a flight of two aircraft, so we technically had to fly as two single aircraft but stayed close enough to see one another. Shortly after a quick fuel stop at Kanoya Air Base in mainland Japan, somehow both aircraft managed to go inadvertent instrument meteorological conditions (IIMC) somewhere out over the East China Sea. In layman's terms, they got lost in the clouds on a flight that was supposed to stay entirely below the clouds.

In my defense, I was a passenger in the back during that portion of the flight. Miraculously we all made it to Osan, and after taxiing into the transient ramp, we unloaded the aircraft and waited for a ride. My fellow copilots and I wasted zero time in starting to shit talk the two HACs. That was always a preferred form of entertainment, especially when it was deserved.

There was no billeting available on base, so our entire detachment took up residence in a little dive hotel called the "New Seoul" outside the gate. The area outside the gate was called Songtan Station, and it was right next to the Central Market in the city of Pyeongtaek. The hotel entrance was situated in an alley. We bunked as many as six Marines in some of the rooms, but we didn't care. Getting to stay off base was a gift, and we knew it.

The hotel was run by an awesome mamasan. The Air Force had established a midnight curfew in Osan, and all service members needed to be off the streets and in their lodgings by midnight.

We immediately told the mamasan that we required a fridge full of beer in the lobby so that we could still hang out together and drink beer after midnight. We handed her a wad of American cash to make it happen. She was all over it, and the lobby beer fridge appeared within a couple of hours.

Before we left Okinawa, the OPSO had told me to take plenty of cash for shopping. When I asked why, he just smiled and said, "You'll see." I had never been much of a shopper, but he was right. By the end of the first day, I had dropped $600 on everything from my first tailored suit to these awesome Korean blankets I immediately shipped to everyone back home. I caught a lot of shit over those blankets initially, but to this day, there is one in my living room that is used often.

Osan had something for everyone. In addition to the shopping, the streets bustled with everything from little kids trying to pick our pockets to endless food stands selling some of the scariest food I have ever seen. Street vendors sold various local delicacies, including snakes, insects, and some mystery grilled skewers that we called dog on a stick. We did like a little burger stand with a sign that read "Ms. Lee McDonalds." Ms. Lee could be found grilling up these little cheeseburgers and topping them with fried eggs at all hours. I have to say those were pretty great on the walk back to the hotel after a night of drinking OB Lager.

There were countless seedy bars with mamasans and girls in the doorway waving at us to try and get us to come inside. Osan had several of these "juice bars," which are pseudo strip clubs filled with dancing girls who will sit and talk with anyone who buys them "juice." About once every ten or fifteen minutes, the mamasan would come around and yell at any of the Marines sitting with one of the girls, "You buy juice!" At roughly ten bucks a pop, it was expensive company, but many of our Marines loved the game. More than a few of them were broke by the end of that det.

The other copilots and I found a place that was much more my style. The "Whisky a Go-Go" had ripped off the name from the famous location on the Sunset Strip in Hollywood, CA, but this one was a true shithole dive bar. They had a limitless supply of Budweiser, OB Lager, Tequila, and Soju. Soju is a colorless, odorless, unregulated liquor in Korea that bars tend to mix with Kool-Aid. At the Whisky, they sold Soju in lime, cherry, and grape flavors. The danger of Soju is that it is unregulated, so you don't know if what you are drinking is 15% alcohol, 50% alcohol, or something in between. It is common for Marines to start pounding Soju because it tastes like Kool-Aid, then promptly lose their fucking minds.

While that was going on, the Whisky played nothing but American heavy metal music while a big screen on the back wall showed a never-ending loop of motorcycle crash videos. The Whisky was perfect. We instantly decided to be there every night. I will forever associate Rage Against the Machine's "Killing in the Name" with that place.

It took less than 48 hours for our weekend "training detachment" to go sideways. A couple of days after our arrival, the two HACs walked over to the base to check our two aircraft and discovered that both were hard down. Neither HAC was a Functional Check Pilot (FCP), so not only did we need the squadron back in Okinawa to send parts, we needed them to send a qualified FCP who could test the aircraft after the completed maintenance. As a bonus wrinkle, the weather rolled in with a forecast of low ceilings for the next few days. Our quick weekend trip began to rapidly trend towards a one-week plus mini-vacation, and despite it being kind of a shit show, we were all for it.

I was supposed to be promoted to captain on September 1st, but there wasn't anyone present who could promote me, so I ended up walking around as a first lieutenant for a few extra days. As far as the Marine Corps was concerned, I was a captain on September 1st regardless. The promotion ceremony and oath would be a formality. I was totally fine with that. Until then, the games would continue.

We spent our days roaming the city and buying shit we didn't need. Guys bought suits, blankets, personalized bags, leather jackets, and $20 knock-off Coach purses for their wives and girlfriends back home. In the evening, the other copilots and I would go to dinner then head to a little Baskin Robbins on the main drag that had a balcony.

From that balcony, we watched all the juice girls come out and walk to work. Right behind them came little groups of our Marines. We called that "the parade." It was like clockwork every night just before sunset. As soon as the parade was over, we would start walking towards the Whisky. One night we decided to start playing a game that we had heard the majors talking about that we called "you ain't shit until you spend a million of something." At the time, one million Korean Won equaled about $750.00 US dollars.

We started taking turns making million won withdrawals from an ATM so that we could walk into the Whisky that night with a big gangster roll and throw it on the bar. That million won not only paid for our drinks for the night, but it gave us the right to determine who could come into the place. From that point forward, we could turn the Whisky into our little private party. It was glorious.

When it got close to curfew time, we would head back towards the hotel and sweep through the juice bars to grab all of our Marines, herding everyone back to the hotel. That usually pissed them off, but a few of them either had enough game or enough money to bring the juice girls back to our hotel. Mama San always had the beer fridge full in the lobby and made us huge trays of some great yaki mandu. We would then stay up until all hours drinking OB Lager and talking shit.

One night, we made it back to the hotel and realized that we had lost my friend and fellow schedule writer, Dave Payne, somewhere along the way. We knew he'd been with us at the last juice bar stop, but we realized we hadn't seen him since. We knew we had fucked up, and Dave was probably in deep shit with the strict midnight curfew. About an hour later, the Air Force MPs stopped by and asked us if First Lieutenant Payne was ours. We said yes, and they asked us to send a couple of guys with them. A few of our more sober copilots left with them to find Dave, who'd gotten separated from the group during our juice bar sweeps. When he realized he was on his own, he left the bar to return to the hotel. On the streets alone, he became an immediate target. Dave was out on the curb, trying to remember which alley to take back to our hotel, when a Russian guy came up the street and started a fight with him.

When our guys got to Dave at the police station, he already had a couple of stitches over one eye, and there was a badly beaten Russian lying on the floor behind him. Dave took a little damage, but the Korean cops and the Air Force MPs ensured that the Russian guy got the worst of it. The cops let our guys take Dave, but the Air Force told him he couldn't leave the hotel for the remainder of our time in Osan. Nevertheless, the story was worth it. A couple of months later, we would make "Apollo" Dave's official callsign, the joke being he was the first American knocked out by a Russian since Apollo Creed in "Rocky IV."

A couple of days later, the rescue squad arrived. Our Executive Officer (XO) and Fifer flew in to help us get the aircraft up and get the fuck out of there. Before that happened, we had some business to attend to. I still hadn't been promoted to captain. That evening we got the whole detachment down to the Whisky around dusk while still in our flight suits. Typically, that was a no-no out in town, but the XO let us do it for my promotion. We had the bartender cue up Metallica playing "So What" on the big screen, so that played in the background while the XO took me through the Oath of Office and promoted me. It was hands down the best promotion ceremony I've ever had. As soon as we were done, the XO ordered a round of Tequila shots, which he loved, and it was game on. Fifer and I may or may not have had to walk him back to his hotel a few hours later.

On September 9th, 2001, the aircraft were back up, and it was time to say goodbye to Osan. We had just had one hell of an adventure. We were all tired and had less money than we did a week prior. The back of each aircraft was loaded with Marines, several new bags filled with assorted purchases, Soju, and some memories that we would all cherish for a lifetime. It was exactly the type of adventure every young Marine hopes for on a deployment.

As we turned up to taxi out for our flight back to Okinawa, I felt on top of the world. I was a brand new captain in a fleet squadron out banging around the Pacific, having adventures with my fellow Marines. I couldn't have asked for a better start to my first deployment.

5

9/11

WHEN WE LANDED BACK at MCAS Futenma late in the afternoon of September 9th, the flight line was empty. There was a typhoon bearing down on the island, so the rest of the squadron had already folded and stuffed all the aircraft into the hangar in preparation for the storm. Once our aircraft were secured, we did what any good Marines would do and ran out and bought all the beer we could find.

The typhoon rule was that everyone was supposed to stay in their rooms and not drink. So, naturally, we decided to ride out the storm with a typhoon party in the barracks. We were on the second evening of that typhoon party when the first aircraft hit the towers. Okinawa is thirteen hours ahead of Eastern Standard Time, so it was getting relatively late in the evening there when we got the news.

Most of our officers were in the Echo Chamber that night. We did what Marine aviators do. We drank beer, shot dice, listened to music, and entertained ourselves by antagonizing one another in that special way that only Marines truly understand. Then, one of our officers ran into the room, turned off the music, and turned on the TV. After a few obligatory "What the fuck?" comments, we all realized what we were watching.

In that moment, our lives would be forever changed. Very little was said, but everyone in that room understood what was happening and what it meant for us. Like many before us, we knew that it was our turn to defend our country and everything it represents. I won't ever forget the weight of that realization. Our innocence would soon be lost.

Most of the aviators in that room would do multiple combat tours in Iraq and Afghanistan. Not all of us would survive those tours. The war would soon become very real for all of us.

6

PUT US IN, COACH

ONE WEEK AFTER SEPTEMBER 11TH, the Warhorse taxied a flight of four CH-53Es onto the runway at MCAS Futenma. We took off, heading for Guam. In a flight of any number of aircraft, the lead aircraft is referred to as "dash one," the second aircraft as "dash two," and so on. I was in dash three with Browner and Fifer for this flight. The OPSO was the Division Lead. Shortly after take-off, we executed a running rendezvous with a flight of KC-130s from Marine Aerial Refueler Transport Squadron (VMGR) 152.

VMGR-152 was callsign "Sumo," and they were permanently stationed out of MCAS Futenma. The KC-130 "Hercules" is an expeditionary cargo aircraft that can not only carry over 40,000 pounds of gear but can also aerial refuel other aircraft. The aviators and enlisted aircrew that fill Herc squadrons also happen to be some of the best aviators and most low stress guys in the Wing.

We were all headed to Guam as part of a Special Purpose Marine Air Ground Task Force (MAGTF). The days following 9-11 had been a complete clusterfuck. The squadron worked 24/7 to get ready to go somewhere. It seemed like the word on exactly where changed hourly. Someone up the chain finally landed on Guam as the destination, so we jumped through our asses to put the plan together and make it happen. The idea was to get a MAGTF established on Guam to receive follow-on tasking. None of us could quite put together how we might get to the Middle East from Guam, so the whole plan seemed suspect at best. We all thought this was just 1st Marine Aircraft Wing (1st MAW) trying to do something to get into the fight.

Flying from Okinawa to Guam in a CH-53E is mildly insane. In retrospect, it is probably one of the least intelligent things I ever did in a CH-53E. Day one was six hours over the open ocean to Iwo Jima. Yeah, that Iwo Jima. Day two was another six hours to Guam. In the event of an emergency, we would have had to ditch in the open ocean. In the planning stage, someone up the chain of command decided that putting a few Air Force Pararescue (PJ) specialists on the KC-130s would somehow miti-gate that risk. Because more people floating in the open ocean is better somehow? Regardless, I was flying in a division of fleet Marine Corps CH-53Es across the fucking Pacific Ocean, and I thought it was pretty badass.

Browner was a great instructor and a salty aviator. He had done his B billet as one of the pilots at Marine Helicopter Squadron One (HMX-1), the squadron that flies the President of the United States. They don't let just anybody into HMX-1. He was highly competent. He and Fifer had history back to their days as Captain Brown and Lance Corporal Fifer at HMH-462 when I was still a young college kid, and the two of them were tight. I loved flying with them. They knew what they were doing, and as a bonus, they were just great fucking dudes.

Somewhere in the annals of Marine Corps aviation history, some Avionics Marine figured out how to splice a standard audio jack to an Interphone Communication System (ICS) cord. This invention allowed aircrews to hook up any music player and push the sound into the ICS to listen to music while flying. I had a bunch of CDs I used to play in the Echo Chamber, and when we packed, Fifer told me to include them. When I asked why, he just said, "You'll see." The next thing I knew, we were flying across the Pacific Ocean listening to Fifer's own "Get ready for war" soundtrack. It was pretty great.

The KC-130s accompanied us to provide an aerial refueling capability. When topped off, a CH-53E carries just over 15,000 pounds of fuel, providing a little over four hours of flight time. One bag of gas wouldn't be enough for each leg. With nowhere to land en route to get fuel, it would need to come via aerial refueling. I had already completed my day and night aerial refueling training flights, but that was different. That was practice. If you couldn't get in the basket on a training flight, it didn't matter. You weren't going to have to ditch in the ocean.

When it came time for us to refuel for the first time, Browner had me try to get into the basket and take fuel first. I was in the right seat, which is the easiest seat to aerial refuel because the fuel probe is right in front of you when it extends from the bottom right side of the aircraft's nose. Aerial refueling is a lot harder in the left seat, where the pilot providing the instruction typically sits because you aren't looking right down the probe. A visual parallax exists between the two pilots since both pilots look at the refueling probe from completely different angles. I got into a good pre-contact position behind the basket, trailing the left wing of the KC-130, and started trying to plug. I missed my first couple of attempts and got frustrated. Finally, Browner took the controls and got into the basket right away. We got our fuel and disconnected. One plug down, two to go.

About halfway through Motley Crue's *Decade of Decadence* album, the OPSO called out that he had lost an engine over the radio. Granted, he had two more, but we were still 200 miles from Iwo Jima, and that wasn't a good situation to be in over the open ocean. That made the rest of the flight a tad more interesting than any of us wanted it to be. I was annoyed with myself for not getting in the basket. I let it get to me, and the same thing happened on plugs #2 and #3. I was frustrated with myself. Browner and Fifer told me to shake it off. I had to let it go. I would get another shot on the way back to Okinawa.

Over the course of the flight, we had finished two big bags of beef jerky, two cans of spicy peanuts, two bags of Jolly Ranchers, two cans of dip, and what seemed like ten gallons of water. We even had a contest to see who could go the longest without taking a leak. Browner won. That crazy bastard made it the whole way.

Iwo Jima is arguably the most famous battle in Marine Corps history, and we were now flying into the tiny strategic airstrip so many had died for. The airfield is right in the middle of the tiny island, and Mount Suribachi is on the southwest corner.

We approached from the west, Mount Suribachi our focal point. I temporarily forgot about my inability to get in the basket and appreciated the scene. I was looking at one of the most hallowed places in Marine Corps history. I thought about the iconic image of Marines raising the flag atop Mount Suribachi. As we set up on short final for the runway, I looked down into the water and spotted the remains of sunken landing crafts. I couldn't believe that stuff was still there. As a young Marine captain, it was a surreal moment.

After we taxied into the little airfield and shut down, we all piled out of the aircraft and went over to see if the OPSO and his crew were good. In what was typical fashion for him, he seemed completely unphased by flying for two hours minus an engine over the open ocean. He looked around and said, "So this is Iwo, huh? You know, it just looks like any other shithole in Japan to me." It was a good tension breaker after a long day.

The Japanese Self Defense Force (JSDF) personnel stationed on the island couldn't have been nicer. They put the KC-130 crews and us up in some nice clean barracks. Due to their austere location, their food was rationed, so they couldn't feed us, but we knew that going in. The KC-130 guys had grills and a bunch of meat that they brought with them for all of us. That was my introduction to how great it is to go on the road with the Herc guys. We had a nice cookout going when the OPSO tasked me to find some more beer.

I went to look for something resembling a store and ended up standing in front of a Japanese beer vending machine in a building that was definitely not a store. I had Yen bills but no coins. A group of Japanese officers in a conference room right next to the vending machine slowly emerged into the hallway and chuckled at my predicament. Despite the language barrier, they indicated that they would help me get the beer if I took photos with them. So I stood there and took a picture with about twenty of them, one at a time. In exchange, they grabbed a pillowcase from somewhere and filled it up with beer from the vending machine for me.

When I finally got back to the cookout, the OPSO gave me shit for taking so long. "Leftenant, what the fuck took so long?"

All I had was, "Sir, you don't even want to know." Somewhere out there are many photos of a young Captain Lee with a random assortment of JSDF officers. In the photos, I may or may not be holding a pillowcase full of beer.

We were ready to go the next morning, but the OPSO had to wait on the KC-130s to bring a new engine for his aircraft. I was now the senior Ops guy on the detachment heading for Guam. He called me over. "Hey, they don't know you're a boot captain, so as long as you sound like you know what the fuck you are talking about, you'll be fine."

I said, "Roger that, sir. I'm on it." Then I ran to my aircraft to strap in with Browner. It was classic "fake it until you make it" advice. It came in handy on that trip and many times since then.

The flight to Guam was uneventful but scenic. Flying low over the open ocean for that many hours, the vastness of the Pacific hit home. It was blue water for as far as we could see in every direction. Once we hit the Mariana Islands, we flew over the tiny island of Pagan, then buzzed Saipan and Tinian. Tinian was mostly overgrown, but the runways and bomb pits on the north field remain visible. It felt surreal to see yet another major historical landmark.

After landing on the long runway at Anderson Air Force Base

in Guam, we went to work. Billeting turned out to be some cots in old abandoned base housing, but it was better than a tent. The next day we wrote a schedule and started knocking out some training flights. What was initially billed as a Special Purpose MAGTF quickly devolved into a standard Ground Air Integrated Training (GAIT) exercise. After the big "we're going to war" spool up, it was beyond anticlimactic.

Meanwhile, we got word that our 15th MEU detachment was likely heading to Afghanistan to kick off the fighting in what would come to be known as Operation Enduring Freedom (OEF). We were excited that they would get into the fight and equally bummed we wouldn't receive the same opportunity.

We did get off base a couple of times to go out in town for a few beers. Naturally, most of our detachment ended up at a local strip club called "The Viking," where the star of the show was a performer known as "Violent Kay." Her whole schtick was to get dumbasses on stage and make them hold onto a giant ship's wheel while she pulled down their trousers and proceeded to crack a whip right on their bare asses. We had more than a few guys volunteer to participate in the show, which we all found hysterical.

One night one of our young Marines showed up with a girl he had met somewhere else. Before too long, she hopped up on stage and decided to become part of the show as well. A few minutes later, some Air Force guy in the crowd yelled out, "Hey, that's General so and so's daughter." She immediately gathered her things off the stage and bolted out the door. Our Marine who brought her got treated like a rock star for the remainder of our time in Guam.

We ended up staying in Guam for a little over three weeks. During our time there, we executed a fair number of training flights, but there was only so much you could do on an island that small. On October 7th, 2001, President George W. Bush announced that airstrikes targeting the Taliban and Al Qaeda had begun in Afghanistan. At Anderson Air Force Base in Guam, a steady stream of Air Force KC-10s and other transport aircraft stopped for fuel and sleep on their way to and from the bombing campaign. We walked over one night, and a couple of Air Force loadmasters let us look inside a C-17 that was loaded to the gills with bombs destined for Afghanistan. Most of the bombs had messages painted on them like "NYPD" and "God Bless America." Others were significantly less PC. Regardless, it was awesome to see that. For the time being, that was as close as we were going to get to the war on terror.

The flight back to Okinawa was good. As soon as we took off from Guam, Browner unstrapped and got out of the seat, and Fifer jumped in for him. Fifer plugged into the ICS, smiled, and said, "I sure hope you can plug on the way home because I definitely can't." It was a ballsy move on Browner's part, but it worked like a charm. I took care of our aerial refueling on the way back to Okinawa and never had another issue getting into the basket for the remainder of my career.

We got to Iwo Jima earlier in the day for the trip back, so our CO had arranged for the JSDF to give us a ride up to the top of Mount Suribachi before it got dark. It remains the coolest piece of dirt I've ever stood on. It was humbling to stand up there and look down at the black beach sand below and think about how many people had died over the control of this little airfield on this tiny little island in the middle of the Pacific Ocean.

Iwo Jima means "sulfur island," and the black volcanic sand still smelled strongly of sulfur in the ocean breeze. The whole scene was heavy. We then went down to the beach and watched the sunset over Suribachi. I put some beach sand in an empty Gatorade bottle I would take home with me. To this day, that sand is in a Sake bottle on a shelf in my office.

The remainder of our deployment proved to be uneventful. We were told to spool up to deploy to Afghanistan about once every other week, but it never happened. We celebrated the Marine Corps Birthday Ball in the Echo Chamber in November. A couple of weeks later, the officers had a potluck Thanksgiving

Dinner in the same room. That weekend we had a Kangaroo Court, and all the guys in my peer group received our first callsigns. Mine was "Socrates" pronounced "So" then "Crates," also known as the *Bill and Ted's Excellent Adventure* pronunciation. They tried to make fun of me for studying so much and producing a ridiculous amount of gouge. Everyone was always asking for copies of the gouge I had made for myself, which contained all of the Fifer knowledge on top of the standard NATOPS information. It would have made more sense if they had just called me "nerd," "notes," or even "gouge." It didn't matter though, that first callsign wouldn't stick for too long.

Sunday, November 25th, 2001, was the morning after our K-Court. While we shook off hangovers in Okinawa, Captain Jay "Spooner" Holtermann led a flight of six CH-53s in the longest amphibious airfield seizure in the United States Marine Corps history. By that afternoon, the 15th MEU would seize a desert airstrip in Southern Afghanistan called "Rhino." They were out there doing real shit, and we were stuck in Okinawa getting drunk and fucking around.

That week I completed my Helicopter Aircraft Commander (HAC) syllabus, so I was at least going back home as a more useful member of the squadron. There were still another dozen or so advanced designations and qualifications I wanted to earn, with the pinnacle of those goals to graduate from WTI. I wanted to do what Spooner was doing. This Mickey Mouse Unit Deployment Program (UDP) bullshit had been cool for a little while, but now that the war was on, that's where I, and every other Marine, wanted to be. I honestly thought we had missed our shot. This war was going to be over before it started. Or so we thought.

7

GROWING UP

WE RETURNED to Miramar from my first deployment in early January 2002. The "freedom bird" took us right to Miramar. It was my first time making it back to the finish line. As I stepped off the aircraft and saw all the families and friends waiting for us in Hangar 4, I paused to take in the scene. It felt like a huge weight off my shoulders. I had passed the test of my first overseas deployment. The thought of doing several more deployments seemed crazy to me at that point.

I made my way into the crowd and watched as my squadron mates started finding and reuniting with their loved ones. I eventually found Kerry and got to experience that first post-deployment embrace. She looked great. It felt so good to be home and even better to be back with her. We went straight back to our little house up in North County where we were inseparable for the next four days.

The Marine Corps refers to long weekends where you get extra days off by the number of hours. Three days off is a 72, and four days off is a 96. We were given a 96 upon return from deployment. On day five, I returned to the squadron, and we began to prepare for the next deployment cycle. The Marines who'd been in the squadron for at least two deployment cycles were receiving orders and preparing to leave. A group of brand new copilots and enlisted Marines right out of their Military Occupational Specialty (MOS) schools would replace them.

We would also be getting a new CO for the next deployment cycle. It felt good to no longer be one of the new boots yet to deploy, but I still had a lot of work to do. I was a Helicopter Aircraft Commander (HAC), but it was time to begin to work on my advanced designations. I needed to build hours, as well as to be recommended for each qualification and flight leadership syllabus. I volunteered for every opportunity possible to get those flight hours.

About a month after getting home, I took a little leave. Kerry and I planned to drive up Highway 1 to see the California Coast, San Francisco, and Napa Valley. Just prior to leaving, she found out she was pregnant. Like many military couples before us, we immediately conceived a post-deployment baby. We didn't know it, but we were enjoying some of our last moments of being blissfully ignorant about what this life would be like for us.

When I returned to the squadron, a lot was going on. Our new CO was a big personality, and Browner had moved up to be his Executive Officer (XO). We trusted Browner, but the jury was still out on the new CO. Regardless, I focused on making sure I took advantage of the available opportunities to grow into a real player in the squadron. I volunteered to ferry aircraft to and from North Carolina to facilitate the completion of some required aircraft inspections and heavy maintenance. Those cross-country flights would quickly give me the hours required for my next few qualifications.

After serving in the Operations Department throughout my first deployment cycle, I was finally assigned to be one of our maintenance officers. I was entrusted with the Flightline Division, home to all of the crew chiefs and the mechanics who work on engines and rotor systems. I loved every aspect of the job. I was finally getting to lead Marines! I knew I would have to earn their trust and respect. I was exactly where I wanted to be.

Shortly after that, our 15th MEU detachment returned from OEF and reintegrated with the squadron. They had real adventures in Afghanistan, and everyone treated them like heroes. They had been to combat. The rest of us still hoped to get our shot. I took Spooner out for his warmup flight after they got back. Cool for me. He was the guy I aspired to be.

It was a simple day flight around the airfield with a couple of instrument approaches and a few landings so that he could bust some rust and punch a current fly day. While we were flying, he talked about some upcoming national interviews he was scheduled to do about his experiences in Afghanistan. The country was still interested at that point, and in the CH-53E community and Marine Corps aviation as a whole, he was the man of the hour.

The real lesson I had learned from watching Spooner had nothing to do with interviews. He was the best of us, but he was also always the coolest motherfucker in the room. He knew how to handle being the guy. What he had just accomplished as a Captain WTI in a CH-53E squadron, and how he handled it, set the example for the rest of us to emulate for the next several years. He set the bar high, and my goal was to reach that level.

When I wasn't at the squadron, Kerry and I spent our free time and spare money remodeling our little house's interior. We did the vast majority of the work ourselves. We made that little house a home, complete with a nursery for the baby she was carrying. Life was really nice for a few months.

A few months later, I completed the Section Leader Syllabus, Terrain Flight Instructor (TERFI) Syllabus and was working through the Functional Check Pilot (FCP) syllabus. Being an FCP was the qualification I most wanted as a maintenance officer. It would allow me to test aircraft after the completion of maintenance procedures, and it would build in natural time to spend with my Marines on the aircraft. As I walked to the aircraft for an FCP evaluation flight on a July afternoon, I received a call on my first ever cell phone. Kerry had bought that little flip phone for me after finding out she was pregnant. I will never forget that call.

"Is this Captain Lee?"

"Yes, it is."

The caller said, "You need to pick up your wife at the Miramar Clinic and take her to Balboa Hospital right now. If you can't, we are putting her in an ambulance."

I dropped my gear right there on the hangar deck and told the guy I was flying with to let Browner know I would call when I knew what was going on.

Five minutes later, I walked into the Miramar Clinic. A nurse grabbed me and walked me to an examination room where Kerry was waiting. She looked like she was in rough shape and scared. She was in the midst of her 27-week appointment that day, and the visit had not gone well. Diagnosed with full-blown eclampsia, her life was in danger. The nurses talked fast and told me exactly what building and floor to take Kerry to when we arrived at Balboa.

We jumped into the car and headed south on Highway 163. As I drove, I said, "Kerry, this sounds serious, like you might have this baby today." I will never forget her response.

She said, "There's no way I'm having this baby today; if I do, it will only weigh two pounds."

We arrived at Balboa, and there was a team waiting for us. They immediately went to work on Kerry, and someone threw a set of scrubs at me. A few minutes later, a doctor walked in and pulled me outside the room. He bluntly told me that Kerry was extremely close to having a stroke that could kill her and handed me a stack of paperwork to sign authorizing an emergency C-section.

Kerry underwent an emergency C-section shortly after that, and our two pound six ounce daughter entered the world. It was touch and go for a few hours there, and I wasn't sure that either of them would survive. I spent a few hours contemplating what life would be like as a single father with a brand new baby. Or, what if Kerry lived and our daughter didn't? Both scenarios were tragic. At some point, a nurse appeared and asked me if I wanted to meet my daughter.

Our daughter was in the Neonatal Intensive Care Unit (NICU) under warming lights and had more tubes coming out of her than seemed possible. She was the tiniest little human I had ever seen, and she was covered in fuzz. I asked the nurse about the fuzz, and she informed me that it was called lanugo, which typically falls out while still in gestation a few weeks later. And so began my education into all things preemie. I still remember putting my pinky finger in her little hand. She tightly grasped it, her grip surprisingly strong. That tiny little girl came into the world fighting. We named her Tristen.

Kerry recovered slowly, and a few days later, I took her home. Tristen needed several weeks in the NICU. The entire situation proved to be an abrupt introduction to parenthood. We never felt sorry for ourselves. Other families in that NICU faced much more difficult futures.

The squadron provided us with incredible support. They immediately set up a volunteer effort to bring meals to our house so that we didn't have to worry about food preparation. Their generosity made an impression on Kerry and me, so much so that she would lead programs to deliver meals to all families with new babies in every unit we were a part of for the remainder of my career.

I returned to work and finished up my FCP syllabus. For several weeks the squadron only had me test aircraft as an FCP. That way, I always flew during the day. Kerry and I set up a rotation, during which she would head to the NICU while I would make my way to the squadron each morning. When I finished up for the day, I would transition to the NICU and send Kerry home. I sat there with Tristen until I started to fall asleep. Most nights, the nurses had me do "kangaroo care" with her after they pulled her out of the incubator and allowed me to hold her skin to skin on my chest. It was the best part of every day.

After nine weeks, we finally brought Tristen home. It was September, and about a month ahead of her actual due date. She was still tiny and on monitors, but she had gained strength and was over five pounds. That first day at home, Tristen and Kerry immediately fell asleep on the couch. I remember sitting there and just looking at them. The previous nine weeks had been a whirlwind of emotions, and I had managed to keep it together the entire time. But as I sat there looking at them, it all finally hit me. I walked outside, sat on the back porch, and cried for what seemed like an hour. Everyone was finally home safe.

We had heard rumors of follow-on war efforts at the squadron since returning from deployment, but a potential war in Iraq was starting to sound like a very real possibility. We were scheduled to go out to Marine Corps Air Ground Combat Center (MCAGCC) Twentynine Palms for a Combined Arms Exercise (CAX) a couple of weeks after we brought Tristen home. I went with the squadron. We were only about one week into the exercise when Kerry called me one day and broke down. She was sobbing and saying, "I can't do this; it's too hard."

Taking care of Tristen was a full-time job, and she was completely overwhelmed. I couldn't do anything to help her, other than apologize. We were both doing something extremely difficult, and we each had to do it alone. The hardest part was that we both knew this was likely just the beginning. I got off the phone and immediately got back into character. I was in the final stages of training for combat. I had to stay focused and keep my head in the game.

A couple of months later, I took leave for Christmas. We drove to my parents' house in El Paso, Texas. They had moved there from my hometown of Lubbock, Texas, a couple of years prior. It was a nice break for a few days. On the morning of January 3, 2003, Browner called me at my parent's house. He told me I needed to get back to Miramar as soon as possible. We were going to put the whole squadron on the USS *Boxer* and set sail for Iraq in a couple of weeks. Time was of the essence. It was happening. We were going to war.

A few hours later, the three of us were in Kerry's Ford Explorer and driving back to San Diego. Ohio State was playing Miami for the college football national championship, so I tried to distract myself by listening to the game on the radio. No satellite radio yet, so I ran through all the stations every few miles to find the broadcast again. I welcomed anything that kept us from having to talk about what we were about to face as a family. A few months prior, we were just a young married couple fixing up our little house in San Diego and excited about the future. The future had arrived, and it would be really fucking hard. No choice but to grow up.

THE MAGNIFICENT SEVEN

On January 17, 2003, Kerry drove me to the squadron. My bags were already on the USS *Boxer* (LHD-4) down on Naval Base San Diego. I was deploying to war on Kerry's 29th birthday. One hell of a present.

Saying goodbye to Kerry and Tristen at the squadron was hard. The reality of our situation weighed heavily on both of us. We didn't know if we would ever see each other again. Would Kerry remarry? Did I want her to? Tristen was so young, she would have no memory of me if I didn't make it back. I would just be some guy in old photos Kerry would show her. She might even end up calling some other guy Dad.

Moving on would be necessary for both of them. Acknowledging that reality contained the brutality of a shotgun blast. I decided that this would be the last time I ever asked Kerry to drop me off at the squadron for a deployment. It was simply too fucking hard.

After collecting myself and walking into the hangar, we got into formation, and our CO came out and gave a speech that mentioned how some of us might not come home. There is a time and a place for that speech, but that wasn't it. Some family members were still in the hangar, watching. Nobody wanted to hear that shit at that moment. I remember thinking that he was probably right, though.

We loaded up on buses and headed down to Naval Base San Diego to board the ship. While still on the bus, I thought again about the CO's words, and I started to wonder who might not make it. Nobody believes it will be them. But everyone else on that bus was probably thinking the same thing. The USS *Boxer* pulled out of port a few hours later and set sail for Iraq. Kerry drove over to Point Loma and took a photograph of the ship leaving. That photo is on the wall in my office to this day.

The USS *Boxer* (LHD-4) is a *Wasp* Class amphibious assault ship built to carry Marines, rotary wing aircraft, and AV-8B Harriers. LHDs are typically used to carry Marine Expeditionary Units (MEUs), but in this case, we had packed it to the gills with two entire squadrons and as many Marines from I Marine Expeditionary Force (I MEF) as she could carry. She was one of seven ships that made up Amphibious Task Force (ATF) West. The Navy more commonly referred to the group as "The Magnificent Seven."

In total, we had close to 3,000 Marines aboard those seven ships heading to the fight. There was a similar contingent inbound from the east coast. The majority of our Marines from HMH-465 were on the USS *Boxer*, as well as the majority of HMM-165, a CH-46E squadron. Both squadrons had a few aircraft and a small number of Marines on a couple of the smaller ships with us.

We represented just part of a massive deployment of combat power heading to the Middle East. Two west coast CH-53E squadrons were heading there. We were shipboard, and HMH-462 broke down their aircraft for C-5 transport directly into Ali Al Salem air base in Kuwait. There also an east coast squadron, HMH-464, sailing aboard a Navy ship. We would have a lot of heavy lift in this fight.

Before deploying, we had CHOP'd out another MEU detachment for the 15th MEU. Instead of getting our detachment back for deployment, they gave us a MEU detachment from HMH-466 that had just returned home from their deployment. We didn't have much time to integrate those guys into our squadron. We only had a boat ride to the Persian Gulf to ensure they gelled as part of our unit. We spent our days flying around the boat to increase our proficiency and conducting what felt like a never-ending series of planning exercises. Communications home were spotty, at best. We had email but emailing back home was often blocked for security reasons. Leadership wanted to ensure that none of us talked about the plan we were privy to.

We immediately started working a flight schedule to get our aircrews and the ship's crew as proficient as possible in conducting flight operations on the boat. Prior to deployment, I moved from being our Flightline Officer to being our Quality Assurance Officer (QAO). It was a more senior billet in the maintenance department, and as such, I was supposed to be our primary Functional Check Pilot (FCP). I loved testing aircraft and was typically on the schedule to do so every day that I wasn't flying a regular syllabus flight of some kind. I especially appreciated being able to test aircraft on the boat. It got me above deck and gave me a few extra practice landings on the spots.

With the exception of testing aircraft, it didn't take me long to determine that I hated being on the boat. Coexisting with the Navy is challenging, especially when you are literally in their house. There were blue and green hours in the gym. Blue hours were Navy only; Green were Marines only. We all joked about how crowded the gym was during green hours.

I hated the fact that enlisted sailors served us food in the wardroom. It was counter to the Marine Corps "leaders eat last" philosophy. Officer berthing was also right underneath the flight deck towards the front of the ship. I had a top bunk, so it felt like the skids and CH-46s were landing right on top of me on the nights that I wasn't flying. It was even worse when the blue shirts dragged the chains across the deck.

The planning and rehearsals were endless. We did everything from basic individual landings to practicing large-scale planning and launches to exercise the deck cycle. No matter how many times I landed on the spots, it still never felt comfortable. That was especially true at night. The Navy was doing their rehearsals for all scenarios as well. Now and then, the Navy would exercise the Close in Weapon System (CIWS) "Sea whiz" gun on the ship's stern. That thing sounded insane.

The company grade officers in our squadron took turns on different duties in the tower during flight operations, and as the Integrity Watch Officer (IWO), who made sure the flight deck was secure when flight operations weren't happening. Standing IWO at night was creepy as hell. Every hour you had to walk the entire flight deck with a flashlight and check the integrity of every chain on every aircraft. In the pitch-black, the roar of the ocean sounded deafening. When I reached the bow, I would always look out in front of the ship and watch as she pitched up and down, crashing through the water. I have never felt so small and insignificant.

While all of that was going on, our usual squadron shenanigans resumed. Drinking alcohol on the ship is entirely against the rules, but most of our guys had family members mail them secret stashes. Water bottles full of vodka, coke bottles full of whiskey, and other disguised packages arrived daily. Almost everyone had a secret stash. With an awareness that our life expectancies might be short, we weren't nearly as concerned about the rules as we should have been.

We finally pulled into the Persian Gulf on February 21st, and it looked like a scene out of a movie. There were Navy ships for as far as I could see in every direction. I remember going down to the Landing Force Operations Center (LFOC) in the ship, their radar screens displaying the entire Persian Gulf. Little blips showed the location of every ship. It looked like the entire Persian Gulf was covered up by the United States Navy.

On February 22nd, we started planning the offload of the

ground Marines with First Marine Division into a piece of the Kuwaiti desert named Tactical Assembly Area (TAA) Coyote. There were so many Marines, it would take four days of CH-53s and CH-46s flying ten aircraft per day for twelve hours a day. We began planning first thing in the morning, and at 2300 people we had never seen before still entered the ready room with new information. It was what we commonly referred to as a "goat rodeo," another way of describing completely disorganized chaos.

The planning ended up taking two days. Somewhere in there, we had email for a few hours one day, and I heard from my Dad back home. He reminded me that I had been conditioned for what was about to come on the dusty ball fields of West Texas. I appreciated the connotation, which helped a bit with the anxiety building inside me. I just wanted to rip off the band-aid and start the damn war.

On February 24th, I was dash three in a flight of five CH-53s that would start flying the offload. Most of the Marines were going into TAA Coyote, but we also took some to the air bases at Ali Al Salem, Al Jabber, and a small Kuwaiti Naval Base. Flying into Kuwait for the first time, I had three primary observations. There was so much oil there that it naturally bubbled up out of the desert, forming what resembled little black ponds. I also spotted a camel racing track that blew my mind. You could see the jockeys on those camels racing around the track. Fucking bizarre.

Lastly, the vast expanse of the desert was striking. It was just sand for as far as we could see. No terrain. Just a perfectly flat brown tabletop. We would soon discover that the top layer of sand was fine, like talcum powder. It would make for some extremely challenging landings for those of us flying the Big Iron.

When we landed in TAA Coyote for the first time, it looked like we were in the middle of nowhere. The Marines unloaded, and I looked out the window and saw them just standing there with packs on their backs holding their rifles. I wondered what they were thinking at that moment. It must have sucked for them to watch as we pulled power and flew away. I was done bitching about life on the boat.

Despite all the things I disliked about life on the ship, it was a hell of a lot better than what those grunts were about to do. I admired the hell out of them, though. We saw a contingent of white Land Rovers driving through the desert towards TAA Coyote as we pulled power. I didn't know who they were but thought it was a ballsy move to be driving toward those Marines, who were more than capable of lighting them up. On the second wave, we discovered they were reporters there to capture footage of us staging in the desert.

Day two of the offload was canceled due to our first encounter with a Middle East haboob. When the wind picks up, it takes that top layer of talcum powder sand with it, and the entire sky turns brownish-red. You can't see anything beyond a few feet. It was a definite no-go for helicopter operations. Some of us went up on the superstructure of the ship to see what it looked like from that vantage point. Nasty.

The following day we resumed the offload into TAA Coyote. Once we completed the off-load, the planning and rehearsals resumed. Some days we planned on the ship. On other days we flew into Kuwait to plan with other Marines. I completed my Division Leader check flight during one of those rehearsal flights. I was now legal to lead a flight of four. It was a nice distraction for me while we were all just marking time and waiting for the war to start. The one nice change was that with the infantry Marines offloaded, the green hours in the gym were significantly less crowded.

As individuals, we all tried to reconcile what combat flying would be like. The truth is none of us fucking knew. War remained an idea. A concept. Internally, I gave myself a series of never-ending pep talks. I tried to convince myself I was ready for whatever was to come.

An old football coach quote my Dad used with his players now seemed applicable. He called it "Rules of the secondary." "Deeper than the deepest, wider than the widest, when in doubt look about, and if you get beat deep don't stop running because you aren't playing anymore." I probably repeated that quote in my head one hundred times a day.

9

WELCOME TO THE SHOW

GROWING UP, I was an avid baseball player with dreams of someday playing Major League Baseball. The big leagues had long been referred to as "The Show." I didn't make it to that show, but I stole the term and applied it to combat. Everyone in the armed forces trains relentlessly for one thing. To be able to perform their jobs in combat. It's the ultimate show, and I was about to be right in the middle of it.

On March 8th, our squadron was tasked to provide four aircraft for the war's initial insert of troops into the Al Faw peninsula. This was going to be a massive insert with aircraft from multiple squadrons, and it would happen on a low light level night. Our CO took the most qualified pilots in the squadron except Browner. All of the other WTIs and Night Systems Instructors (NSIs) went. As the XO, Browner got left behind to keep the rest of us knocking out maintenance and testing up aircraft. He wasn't happy about it, and we all felt terrible for him. That said, we all wanted to go, too. Everyone wanted to get into the fight. Those who didn't make the cut for that first division of four started jokingly referring to ourselves as the B team.

Two days later, that changed when we got tasked to provide

an additional four aircraft for another insert that would follow the one that our first four aircraft would support. Shortly after finding out, I was in the back of a CH-46E "Phrog" with Browner, my buddy Aaron "Focker" Shelley, and a couple of our other pilots, heading to Tactical Assembly Area (TAA) Coyote in Kuwait for a planning session.

Focker and I had been buddies since flight school and checked into the squadron at roughly the same time. On our first deployment, he was part of the 31st MEU detachment, so it was nice to have him back. The next ten days were back and forth from the ship to TAA Coyote, where we planned, re-planned, briefed and planned some more. It seemed like every day, the word changed about when the bombing campaign would start and when we would cross the border to start the ground war. We were all sick of planning and ready for it to begin.

On March 16th, the Navy brought a bunch of doctors and nurses on board to ensure that the ship's medical department was ready to handle any surge in injured Marines once the war kicked off in a couple of days. They also tried to make dinner in the wardroom extra nice that night. They had steaks, crab legs, shrimp, and other stuff that should never be cooked in bulk. The whole thing felt like we were all being fed our last meal before marching off to die. It made for an uncomfortable vibe, and I didn't like it. At all.

On the morning of the 18th, we found out that our B Team mission was officially a go, but there was a twist. It wasn't the mission we had been planning for the last several days. It was a new mission with the Aviation Combat Element (ACE) from the 15th MEU. The CH-53E detachment on that MEU was from the HMH-361 "Flying Tigers." Back at Miramar, we referred to them as "Shitty Kitty" for a reason, so none of us were too jazzed about flying with them. At the same time, we were all excited about getting into the game.

The next few hours were a complete clusterfuck while we all got our gear together and got it up on the deck and into our aircraft. We had to take all of our Nuclear Biological Chemical (NBC) gear, and we all had two separate sets of that. We had the same set the grunts use on the ground and another set made for use in the aircraft. The two sets of NBC gear alone were almost a seabag full of shit that each one of us had to take. We also were told to take both our 9mm pistols and our M-16s with a full ammo can for both. Complete overkill.

If I'm in a situation where I need a full ammo can of 9mm rounds, I'm probably in a situation too bad to walk away from. The final piece was being issued our blood chits and told to sanitize our flight suits. When sanitizing, we removed all the patches so our rank and unit could not be identified if we were captured. We all had our last names and the last four digits of our social security numbers stenciled on the back of our flight suits to make things easier for the ship laundry. That information and our dog tags were the only things on our bodies that identified us. It was go time.

We finally got turned up and took off at 1500 with Browner and me in the lead aircraft. Immediately after takeoff, our aircraft got a Blade Inspection Method (BIM) caution light, indicating we had a problem with one of our main rotor blades. We pushed the rest of the flight on to Kuwait, and we turned back to the ship to roll to the backup aircraft. Rolling to the backup was a major pain in the ass with all of our gear, but we managed to quickly pull it off.

It was hot, and we were all sweating like we had just run a Physical Fitness Test (PFT) by the time we started turning up. Our number one engine flamed out on overspeed checks, but a few of our aircraft had been having that issue in the sandy environment, so we fired it back up and took the aircraft anyway.

We finally landed at TAA Coyote just after 1700 and headed to the primary tent to get the plan. The coalition's first objective was to secure the Al Faw Peninsula on the night of March 20th. Our A team would be part of that insert package, along with some CH-53Es from Dalton's squadron HMH-462 and a couple of Marine Corps CH-46E squadrons. They would all be inserting British Commandos. The 15th MEU was supposed to insert a backup force made up of a company of Marines and a Marine Reconnaissance Team. We were now part of that backup insert. If the British Commandos needed assistance with Al Faw, we would bring in our Marines to help reinforce them. If they ended up not being needed as reinforcements for Al Faw, we would insert them into the port city of Umm Qasr the following day.

The bad news was that the timeline seemed all screwed up. President Bush had given Saddam and his sons 48 hours to surrender, and that timeline was set to expire at 0430 the following day, March 19th. Then "A-Day," the aerial bombing campaign was supposed to run for 24 hours before "G-Day" when we kicked off the ground war. By that timeline, none of these inserts should be happening until the night of the 20th, but the 15th MEU Det from HMH-361 told us that we would be on standby for the insert on the night of the 19th. We finally decided that they were fucked up and walked back to our aircraft to bed down for the night. As we sat there, we saw a massive convoy of vehicles and tanks pushing out towards Highway 80, where they would head north to stage on the Iraqi border.

Since we were only 25 miles away from the Iraqi border in TAA Coyote, the Iraqis made it extra fun for us by constantly shooting missiles in our general direction. The assumption was that every one of them was a chemical weapon until proven otherwise. Each time one hit, everyone yelled, "Gas, gas, gas!" They also made the muscle-flexing gesture that indicates the same. We would all don our gas masks and wait until the all-clear was called. The system for this was that, once it was suspected to be all clear, the most junior Marine had to remove their mask while being observed for a reaction. Once it was obvious that the poor bastard wasn't going to keel over dead, the "all clear" was called for everyone else. Watching that happen made the seriousness of being in a combat environment feel very real, very fast.

The next morning, March 19th, we were back in the planning tent to receive an update on the timeline. The 15th MEU was still telling us that Al Faw would happen that night. President Bush's ultimatum had just expired a couple of hours prior, and A Day hadn't even started yet. None of it made sense. Right on cue, a massive sandstorm started up, and it felt like the whole planning tent was going to collapse. It was a shit show.

A couple of hours later, the Air Mission Commander (AMC) and Assault Flight Leader (AFL) from the 15th MEU CH-53E Det stood up and gave one of the worst AMC briefs I have ever witnessed. He said the brief was still in work, but he wanted everyone to understand the plan. We ended up sitting through what I would classify as a very rough rehearsal brief. We would never receive the "final" version.

That night we sat through an equally terrible AFL brief that was wholly focused on the CH-46s but included a guest appearance from one of the 15th MEU CH-53E Det pilots from HMH-361, who loosely talked about our portion of the flight. In the intel portion of the brief, their S-2 Officer told us that Iraqi Anti Aircraft Artillery (AAA) was right next to the Landing Zone (LZ) at Umm Qasr. There was no current plan to address that threat.

After the brief, Browner was pissed off and demanded some adjustments to the routes and talked to the Escort Flight Leader (EFL) from the skids about addressing the AAA near the LZ. That went on until about 2300 when someone finally came in and told us that Al Faw was off for the night. No shit, it was always going on the 20th. The war hadn't even started yet, but the fog of war was already present.

That night we sat on the ramp of our aircraft and shot the shit with a few dips of Copenhagen. Our crew chief for the flight was a MAWTS-1 instructor on loan to us for the deployment. MAWTS-1 had sent their instructors out to various aviation units to help plan and execute. He had a special canteen that he said was full of "Gunny Juice," which translated to Jim Beam. We all took a couple of pulls off of that between the "gas, gas, gas" calls when we were masked up. We kept waiting to hear the explosions from the bombs dropping for A Day, but we never heard anything at all. We had no clue what was going on.

The next morning, March 20th, we headed back to the planning tent and got another gas call right as we walked in. Everyone was masked up when one of the reporters provided some comic relief by completely losing his shit. He ripped his gas mask off and yelled, "I can't take this anymore!" All of the Marines predictably laughed at him before tackling him and putting his mask back on his face. A few minutes later, they brought in a young Private First Class (PFC) to do the unmasking drill, and the all-clear was called again.

Shortly after that, we were told that the war had started at 0530 that morning with strategic bombing aimed at Iraqi heads of state in Baghdad. That explained why we hadn't heard anything. Baghdad was over 300 miles away. We sat through another round of update briefs before finally being allowed to head back to our aircraft to go on standby as the backup for Al Faw that night. That night we all sat around one of our aircraft and one of our Marines had a shortwave radio, picking up the news from the British Broadcasting Corporation (BBC). They reported that the Iraqi Information Minister said we were all committing suicide in Kuwait because we were terrified of the Republican Guard. We all got a chuckle out of that. We then saw our A team guys fly over and land in their pickup zone a couple of miles away. The Al Faw mission was about to happen. A few minutes later, a Marine from the MEU pulled up on a four-wheeler and told us we were off for the backup that night and that the Al Faw insert was being pushed back to 0300. We would insert the Marines at Umm Qasr the next morning.

I had a hard time going to sleep that night. It was our third night sleeping in the back of the aircraft. A few miles away, our guys were about to fly an extremely difficult low light level insert, and we were going to get into the fight the next day. I was equal parts terrified and excited. After all that planning, briefing, and preparation, it was finally about to start. I repeatedly ran through the flight plan in my head. Imagining what it would look like. I thought about our escort aircraft giving us a "Winter" call as we approached the objective area to let us know the Landing Zone (LZ) was safe. If we received a "Devil" call instead, it would mean the LZ was hot and would be contested. Training was over. The enemy was now real. I eventually fell asleep around 0130.

At 0630 on March 21st, we were back in the briefing tent for our final intel brief. We learned that the Al Faw mission had been aborted when one of the CH-46s had crashed, killing the four Marine aircrew and eight British commandos on board. After the abort, the Brits said to hell with it and just drove across the border to start fighting. We also heard that one of our tanks positioned on the border had its turret pointed backward, and one of our AH-1W Cobras had shot it, thinking it was the enemy. Amazingly, nobody got hurt when that happened. When our brief was over, we walked back out to our aircraft. My mind raced, and my heart pounded at that point. After all that preparation, it was finally go-time.

By 0730, we put on all our gear, and the five of us in our crew stopped for a minute to take a picture. Someone up the chain had decided we needed to fly with our NBC bottoms over our flight suits, which not only looked ridiculous, but was uncomfortable in the desert heat. It also made zero sense. If someone thought we needed to wear NBC gear, it should have been the aviation NBC gear - all of it. At least our legs would be okay. That was comforting.

Fifteen minutes later, we were in the seat and awaiting word to turn up and depart. It turned into a long wait. At 1315 we finally learned that our L Hour in the LZ was set for 1400. We were carrying the recon Marines, a couple of their dirt bikes, and one of their Interim Fast Attack Vehicles (IFAV). Mercedes had designed the IFAVs to run quietly, and they had built them narrow enough to fit inside our aircraft.

Altogether, our cabin was full, and it was a heavy load. The four aircraft we provided from our squadron were four to make two. Meaning, we were flying two, and our other two were there as backups. Since HMH-361 managed to get all four of their aircraft out of the chocks, only two of our aircraft took off with the first wave, following the flight of four from HMH-361. Browner and I were in the lead, our dash two aircraft behind us. Dash three and four kept turning on deck in the Pickup Zone (PZ) at TAA Coyote, just in case they were needed.

When we finally took off, it was surreal. We were flying in a Terrain Flight (TERF) profile below 200 feet Above Ground Level (AGL) because, at the time, that was considered our best defense against Surface-to-Air Missiles (SAMs) and Man Portable Air Defense Systems (MANPADS). You could see the early evidence of the war on the ground at that low altitude. It was a short flight, and we were lining up for our final approach into the LZ at Umm Qasr before we knew it.

The LZ was a big parking lot between a couple of warehouses just north of the water in the port, and our final approach path was south to north, right over the water. We could see that the first couple of HMH-361 CH-53Es were shooting their approaches to the wrong spots. They were too far south in the LZ, so there wouldn't be room for all six aircraft. There was also a bunch of sand covering the parking lot, so there was significant and unanticipated brownout in the LZ. We expected asphalt!

The combination of those things made it difficult for the HMH-361 crews to get their aircraft on the deck, which hung us out to dry behind them. We ended up in the exact scenario considered taboo for any rotary-wing aviator. We were in a high, hot, and heavy hover scenario at 200 feet AGL with nowhere to go. I was on the controls, and Browner was busy running the radios and leading our flight. Browner didn't like being hung up and called for a wave off.

I started to pull power to take it around and immediately heard an audible popping sound. I then felt the aircraft begin to lose power and fall out of the sky. I initially assumed we were taking fire when Browner yelled, "We lost number one!"

A glance at our gauges confirmed that the popping sound I'd heard was a compressor stall in our #1 engine. Regardless, with one engine down and a full load, we were in a terrible situation. For about one second, I was super pissed off that I was going to die on my first combat flight.

I re-focused and brought my efforts back to getting us safely on the deck. Browner shouted, "Forward and down!" I attempted to get a little forward momentum going to clear the water and give us a chance. Just north of the water was a cinderblock wall. When it started to look like we were going to clear the water, I became concerned we would hit the wall, potentially breaking the aircraft in half. At 100 feet, we entered the dust cloud kicked up by the four CH-53Es that had landed in front of us. I was going to have to fly the remainder of this approach in the blind.

Later, our skid escorts would report that we had taken enemy fire right around that time. We never noticed it. We were too busy trying not to die.

I knew the ground would come back into view right around twenty feet above the deck. If I could have the aircraft attitude right and pull whatever power we had left, I might be able to arrest our rate of descent enough for us to survive the impact. Assuming, of course, I cleared both the water and the wall, neither of which I could see. I was thinking "forward and down" on repeat, and Browner was also saying it. Our descent lasted only a few seconds, but it felt like a lifetime.

As we blew through twenty feet above the deck, I saw the ground and pulled all the power we had left. It felt like a parachute popped, but with only a few feet remaining to arrest our rate of descent. We still hit the deck really hard. I immediately put my toes on the brakes and depressed them all the way. We were in a dust cloud, so I couldn't see out of the windscreen, but I could feel that we were still moving forward.

Browner yelled, "Brakes!"

I was already standing on them, but they weren't stopping us as we bounced across the ground. When the motion finally stopped, and the dust cleared, our rotor blades were only about five feet from the CH-53E at our two o'clock position. Our aircraft was sitting left wing down, and in addition to our #1 engine being offline, we now had a BIM light indicating an issue with one of our main rotor blades.

The recon team offloaded without incident and immediately jumped into a gunfight. While that happened, Browner got the #1 engine restarted. We all agreed we wouldn't stay there to shut down and troubleshoot. At that point, we considered our NATOPS procedures as advisory in nature only. I called the aircraft in front of us over the radio and told them we were ready to lift. We then pulled power and got the fuck out of Dodge.

As we flew back to Kuwait, we radioed our dash three to let them know we needed them to fill in for us on the second wave. We also heard one of the 361 aircraft call that they needed our dash four to fill in for them on the second run, so all four of our aircraft got into the fight. They were loading up when we landed back at the PZ at TAA Coyote to assess the damage to our aircraft.

We had blown our left main landing gear strut with enough force that the top of it blew a big hole in the top of the sponson and also took out a softball-sized chunk of one of our main rotor blades. We decided to cargo strap the landing gear strut to the aircraft's frame so it wouldn't fall off in flight, and we duct-taped the blade where the chunk was missing. With those expeditionary repairs complete, we turned her up and flew her back out to the boat.

Jet fuel comes in a couple of different varieties, and the Navy uses JP-5 aboard ship, which has a higher flashpoint and is thus less flammable. We had taken on some Air Force JP-8 out at the Forward Arming and Refueling Point (FARP), so the Air Boss put us in the Starboard Delta pattern until we dumped down to mins (minimums). Burning circles in the "D" while dumping fuel all over the Persian Gulf was somehow a fitting end to a fucked up day.

Once we got down to mins, the Air Boss brought us into Spot 9, where Browner gently sat her down before we finally shut her down. My first combat flight was in the books, complete with what would later be referred to as a "hard landing." That aircraft spent the next few weeks in the hangar bay of the USS *Boxer*, where our Airframes Marines put her back together.

It had been a hell of an introduction to combat flying and my first real brush with death. "Live to fight another day" was a common saying in Marine Corps aviation. If that was the objective, we had at least pulled that off. It had been equal parts terrifying and exciting. I had discovered the ultimate contest, and I was right in the middle of it. I wanted more.

After showering for the first time in four days, I grabbed some leftovers from the wardroom and then went to Browner's quarters to debrief. The other guys in the flight were there, and they all wanted to hear our story. We told it a couple of times, and the reaction was fascinating to watch. A few of the guys seemed bothered by it. I assumed they were struggling with the same thing that we all had after hearing about the CH-46E that went down with the Brits the night prior. Your first thought is, "Glad it wasn't me," and then the wave of guilt and reality kicks in.

We had come away okay, but our close call made it even more real for all of us. This was varsity, and we were all going to be a split-second decision away from not making it home for however long this war lasted.

After the debrief, Browner and I agreed not to tell the wives about our adventures at Umm Qasr until we returned home. There was no need to stress them out any more than they already were.

JALIBAH

PILOTS AND AIRCREW have to have a short memory. If you dwell on a single mistake or close call for any length of time, it can cloud your thought process and lead to a subsequent decision or moment of indecision that kills you. As an aviator, you constantly learn lessons, but you file them away immediately and keep moving forward. The same applies to positive moments and flights. Being great yesterday doesn't mean you won't fuck it away and get yourself killed today.

To this day, I spend very little time thinking about the past, either good or bad. Focus on what you can control - what is happening right now and everything that hasn't happened yet.

I knew the best way to move past the close call at Umm Qasr was to get back out there. I immediately asked to get back on the flight schedule as soon as possible. I didn't sleep much the night we got back to the ship as I replayed the events of the day over and over in my head. The next morning, I turned on the Armed Forces Network (AFN) in my room. The reality of almost buying it the previous day had set in, and I felt lucky to be sitting there. I was strangely upbeat. I felt like I had legitimately cheated death. I had written everything that I could remember about the flight in my journal the night prior, but I opened it back up and added some detail to what I had written before falling asleep. I wanted to make sure I captured everything I could remember about that flight.

Umm Qasr was all over the news. It was surreal to sit in my room on the ship, watching AFN and seeing the footage of what had transpired there the day prior. It was the first time in my life that I watched the national news and personally had something to do with the story. Thankfully, none of the American News Networks had footage of our hard landing. They talked about the firefights the Marines we had inserted got into while securing the port. It was a minor miracle we got out of there unscathed.

As a country, we had secured our first two strategic objectives with Umm Qasr and the Al Faw peninsula. The Army could now unload their ships in Umm Qasr, and the Iraqis couldn't get anything in or out of that port. It was wild to think I had almost died helping that happen. The news also reported that Saddam had been captured, which turned out to be total bullshit.

That night our CO, Browner, and a couple of the other majors flew a low light level deep insert of a Surveillance and Target Acquisition (STA) team. Browner stopped by before they left and said the plan was insane. He wasn't happy about it. I couldn't sleep that night. I finally heard them land around 0100. Once I knew they were safe on deck, I slept for a little bit. They made it back with stories about a wild flight deep into bad guy country. I couldn't wait to get to the point where I would get to be on flights like that.

The following day, I was back on the flight schedule and assigned as the copilot to one of my peers. A little behind me in the syllabus, he was a junior Helicopter Aircraft Commander (HAC). Our mission for the day was to pick up some "Marines" at Camp Commando in Kuwait and take them up north to set up an Enemy Prisoner of War (EPW) Camp. When we got to the Pickup Zone (PZ) at Camp Commando, a couple of CH-53Es were in the zone from the east coast squadron HMH-464. One of the Marines with them was a gunnery sergeant who had been in our squadron before executing orders to the east coast a few months earlier. He had always been a crazy bastard, and that hadn't changed. He launched right into a story about how he got into it with his new maintenance chief at the Marine Corps Birthday Ball. While he yammered on about his altercations with fellow Marines on the east coast, the "Marines" we were supposed to be inserting came out to load up. They wore Marine Corps cammies, but they didn't look at all like Marines. We soon realized they were interpreters who would help translate prisoner interrogations at the EPW camp.

We geared back up to take off. Our aircraft had one auxiliary fuel gauge that was dead, so it read zero. As a result, our crew chief visually checked the tank before takeoff to make sure it contained the fuel we thought it did. We had enough fuel to make the run and get back to the Forward Arming and Refueling Point (FARP) in Kuwait with 6,000 pounds of fuel remaining, so we had plenty of fuel. After turning back up, we took off and headed north for the Iraqi border. As we approached the border, we ran through our penetration checklist, ensuring that all of our systems were in the proper configuration for flying into enemy territory. With our penetration checks complete, we dropped down into a Terrain Flight (TERF) profile below 200 feet Above Ground Level (AGL) and checked in with the Direct Air Support Center (DASC) to confirm our clearance and routing.

For security purposes, higher headquarters was changing up everyone's flight callsigns on the Air Tasking Order (ATO) every day, so it was confusing as hell trying to keep all of the players straight, especially if you weren't working with them directly. You would hear a "Mudbug" flight check in with DASC, and we wouldn't know if that was an FA-18, some skids, or even some CH-46s. We carried full printouts of the ATO, so if you wanted to figure out who belonged to a callsign on the radio, you needed to rifle through several pages to quickly find the callsign. Beyond maddening.

We were down at 100 feet AGL and cruising at 130 knots when we crossed the border south of the Rumaila Oil Field. The Iraqis had set some of the wells on fire in the Rumaila Oil Field, and the flames were close to 100 feet tall. We dropped down even lower to mask ourselves, weaving through those giant flames at 50 feet AGL as we made our way north toward our destination. We started to transfer some fuel into our main tanks from the auxiliary tanks, but the auxiliary tank we had visually checked prior to takeoff wasn't transferring.

I started to run our fuel numbers on my kneeboard to ensure we could still complete the mission without being able to transfer any fuel from that auxiliary fuel tank. That tank essentially carried 4,000 pounds of fuel we couldn't use. According to the math, we could complete the mission without it, but it would be close. Weaving through the flames, vice flying in a straight line, wasn't helping.

By the time we reached the soon-to-be EPW camp to offload our passengers, it had turned into a shit show. The interpreters didn't want to get off the aircraft because they weren't sure what they were supposed to do next. That wasn't our problem, but getting them off the aircraft was. Marines would have been offloaded with all their gear in less than a minute. It took us about 30 minutes to get the interpreters off the aircraft and clear of our rotor arc so that we could take off. Meanwhile, we were burning fuel that was becoming more precious by the second.

We finally got back in the air, and I had to take over the flight. The other pilot I was flying with had mentally checked out. The stress of the situation was too much for him, and he shut down. It wouldn't be the last time I would see that happen to someone in combat, but this was my first time. I realized it was on me to get us home. A definite reality check. We were tucked in as dash two, and over the radio, I told dash one to take us straight to FARP "Texaco" in Kuwait.

I flew left-handed so that I could run and re-run the numbers on my kneeboard with my right hand. In that moment, I coined the phrase, "If you get excited, you get dead." It came out of nowhere, but I found myself silently repeating it.

Emotions cloud your thought process and, in extreme cases, can shut it down entirely. That had already happened to the guy sitting next to me. I needed to stay calm and think clearly. The calculations I was running on my kneeboard needed to be perfect to get us out of the situation. I had our crew chief on the jump seat, managing the Speed Control Levers to ensure our fuel burn stayed right on maximum range. Maximum range is the most efficient power setting to fly as far as possible on the fuel you have available.

It ended up being a close call, but we made it back to FARP "Texaco" just across the Kuwaiti border. Barely. We had one engine flameout before we even hooked up to fuel due to fuel starvation. We were as close as you could get to running out of gas without running out of gas. Soon after that, we discovered that during our visual check of the fuel tank prior to takeoff, the cap didn't re-seal securely, so the tank couldn't pressurize. The whole escapade was the result of a fuel cap.

Stay calm and think through it. That was the lesson for the day. I felt good about how our crew chief and I had done. I also knew it would take the other pilot in the cockpit a long time to reconcile that he had been unable to do the same. When we got back out to the ship later that afternoon, I told Browner about the flight. He was cool about it. We had gone below our NATOPS minimums for fuel, but it had been a unique situation. We ultimately saved ourselves and a thirty-million dollar aircraft.

After a couple of lost days due to another haboob, I flew a big insert to push Marines closer to An Nasiriyah for what would ultimately become one of the bloodiest fights of the war. The mission went off without a hitch. The Army (V Corps) and Marine Corps (I MEF) forces advanced toward Baghdad on two different routes. At our level, the impression was that the Marine Corps was quickly advancing on Baghdad, and the Army was struggling to keep up.

I wasn't originally on the flight schedule the next day, but at 0500, our schedule writer woke me up and told me I was leading a section for a popup mission not originally on the ATO. There had been rumors for a few days that we were going to move forward, and now it was happening. We had captured a small airstrip called Jalibah about 40 miles into Iraq. The mission was straightforward. Head down to Ali Al Salem to pick up some heavy lift external loads and drop them off at Jalibah. The flight was uneventful until we dropped our first external load at Jalibah. Our #2 Engine Oil Pressure light came on, and we needed to shut down to check it out. It didn't take long to determine that the issue was something we couldn't fix in the field. Our ongoing engine problems were quickly becoming more and more routine.

Thankfully, the Marine Corps had already begun to set up a small Operations Center at Jalibah, and the Battle Captain was a CH-53E lieutenant colonel from the east coast. I told him what was going on and that I needed to get in touch with my CO back on the USS *Boxer*. I needed permission to fly back to the ship with only two engines.

Technically, I wasn't supposed to do that, but I was comfortable with it and felt like we didn't have much choice. The Operations Center was already plugged into the Secret Internet Protocol Router (SIPR) chat, so I was able to get in touch with the Operations guys back on the boat using that. On the other end was my old flight school buddy, Dave Wright, who immediately tried to talk me out of flying back on two engines. He was giving me the book answer, but I told him not to worry about it and asked him to get my CO anyway. After a brief exchange, the CO was good with it, so I thanked the Battle Captain and started to walk to my aircraft.

Right then, some other colonel in the tent caught wind of what I was doing and lost his fucking mind. He started telling me that if I took off, he would make sure that I lost my wings for violating NATOPS. Thankfully, the Battle Captain stepped in, and cooler heads prevailed. It wasn't the colonel's call, and I was executing an order from my CO. I was also totally good with doing it. I got the hell out of there as fast as I could, turned up, and got airborne. We made it back to the USS *Boxer* without incident. At that point, I had flown four combat flights and had managed to have a hard landing, almost run out of gas, and then lost an engine and had to fly back to the ship on two. Not a great start, but I found it to be equal parts stressful and exhilarating.

A couple of days later, a UH-1N Huey crashed out at Jalibah. The pilot was a guy I had gone to flight school with. It was the first time someone I knew personally had been killed flying in combat. I immediately reminded myself of something I'd learned as a kid on the ballfields of West Texas. You can't win if you are worried about losing. I knew I had to immediately shake it off and stay focused.

One week in, things felt a little bit like playing Cowboys and Indians. The ATO seemed to be in a never-ending revision, so our flight schedule constantly changed. We rarely knew what to expect on a day-to-day basis. Guys would take off and immediately start getting re-tasked by the DASC. What had been planned and briefed was often immediately scrapped for a new plan that had to be executed on the fly.

On a couple of occasions, we had crews that ended up running out of crew day and had to shut down at some random Forward Operating Base (FOB) for the night, only to pick up follow on tasking as soon as they turned back up the next morning. Sections would take off and sometimes not show back up for a couple of days. It was damn near impossible to keep track of it all. I felt thankful to be working in Maintenance and not Operations at the time. We had to keep the aircraft up in maintenance, which was easier said than done, but at least it was straightforward and not changing every five minutes.

On April 1st, I flew in a day section, then we hot seated our aircraft into a night division that was going out as part of the Jessica Lynch rescue mission. Our squadron had received that tasking the night prior, and I was initially slated to be on that flight. I was still a little pissed that I got switched to the day section, but the squadron ended up stacking the deck with more senior pilots that were all Night Systems Instructors (NSIs). It made sense, but I was still annoyed. I wasn't quite on the A team yet.

The Lynch mission went well, and our crews had some good stories to tell when they got back. The mission was a huge news story, but the media coverage never mentioned the aircraft, only the Special Operations personnel they carried. It was evident that flying Assault Support helicopters would never be glamorous or even a news story. Unless you fuck it up.

We were supposed to start moving forward to Jalibah the following day, but that got pushed back one day to April 3rd. We had been flying supplies to Jalibah to set up for a week at that point, so I already had the route memorized. Depart the ship to Awhah, then through the following checkpoints: ACP 4, ACP4A, ACP 4B, ACP 5, Budweiser (right on the border of Kuwait and Iraq), Pabst, bypass Abita due to the unknown Anti Aircraft Artillery (AAA) threat that had been there for a week and then on to Jalibah, which had been named "Riverfront." All of the FOBs had been named after stadiums back home.

Jalibah was simply three parallel runways in the middle of nowhere. We used the southern runway as the CH-53 flight line, the northern runway as the skid flight line for the AH-1W Cobras and UH-1N Hueys. All of the aircraft took off and landed from the middle runway. To the North of the runways, the camp where we lived was nothing more than a tent city on the sand. The living conditions were miserable.

The first night we slept there, all of the officers in our squadron were in one tent, and our Captain WTI "Krusty" Ridgway lightened the mood. Krusty had come to our squadron after a year at resident Professional Military Education (PME) for captains back at MCB Quantico. Before that he had been in HMH-466 "Wolfpack" with our CO. When he returned to the fleet, he checked into our squadron, and we worked him up for WTI, which he attended and summarily crushed. Krusty was the kind of guy everyone in the squadron loves. He was a great officer, great aviator, and he had a huge personality. Said another way, he was funny as hell. That first night at Jalibah, the mood was slightly off in the officer tent. Krusty fixed that.

He had a headlamp on and fully buried himself in his sleeping bag. He started to loudly talk about how he was having himself and how incredible this imaginary chick was. We were all cracking up. A couple of the majors got offended and started yelling at him to cut it out, which made us laugh even harder. It was a great tension breaker.

The camp had piss trenches and little plywood shitters with steel drums full of kerosene under them. When the drums got full, some poor bastard had to pull them out and burn them. There was no privacy of any kind. In the mornings, we were all out there, brushing our teeth with water bottles and taking a leak in the piss trench. Female Marines would walk by, staring at us.

Krusty would yell to them, "Morning, ladies." Then he would grin and wave. It was fucking ridiculous, but we all got a laugh out of it. A few days later, the Seabees arrived and set up some field showers so that we could at least sort of rinse off every couple of days. Krusty made our group trips to the showers a lot more entertaining than they should have been. You need guys like him in that environment for the sake of levity.

They had also set up a little tent as a makeshift chow hall that was serving Tray Rations that we called T-Rats. They were basically nothing more than family style Meals Ready to Eat (MREs). Up to that point, we had just been living off the infamous MREs, which I didn't mind. The MREs had gotten much better since I was an officer candidate having to eat "Frankfurters, Beef," a.k.a. "four fingers of death," and "Omelet with Ham," a.k.a. "the vomelet," at OCS. Most of the remaining MREs were much better, and there were a lot of new ones. My favorites were "Chili and Macaroni" and "Beef Ravioli with Meat Sauce," which were tough to beat.

The best thing about the MREs, though, was what we called MRE postcards. With limited access to email, snail mail was still a big part of communication with family back home. I always cut the face off the box of the main course in my MRE and turned it into a postcard. You could write your note on the back and "free mail" where the stamp would have been, and it would get to whomever you were sending it to back home. I sent a lot of those to Kerry, Tristen, and other family members. It was also just a nice way to spend our limited downtime.

On April 7th, I was on night standby when we got tasked with an emergency resupply of MREs and water for Regimental Combat Team 5 (RCT-5) on the east side of Baghdad. I MEF had advanced to the city's outskirts, and RCT-5 was engaged in heavy combat. I was the copilot to the major we picked up from the HMH-466 MEU Det. A great pilot and a highly competent officer, his glass was always half empty. He seemed at least mildly pissed off at all times. He was one of those truly intelligent guys that found everything annoying. Regardless, it had the potential to be a crazy flight, and I would need to be on my A-game.

We looked at the threat board in the operations tent, and there was AAA everywhere between Jalibah and Baghdad. As far as we knew, no CH-53Es had flown that far north yet, so we faced a shitload of unknowns. There were also a lot of power lines in the area, and the Iraqis had painted them tan to make them even harder for us to see. At our typical TERF altitudes below 200 feet AGL, those power lines were as much of a threat to us as the AAA. It was also a low light level night, so that added layer would make the flight extra varsity.

Although I was an up-and-coming brand new Division Leader cruising past 800 hours of flight time, this was going to be a challenging flight for me. I was glad to be paired up with a more senior pilot who was also a Night Systems Instructor (NSI).

We came up with a route that would take us just to the southeast of An Nasiriyah, where the fight had been particularly nasty just a week prior. We pressed out to a point 45 miles east of Baghdad, then turned west. There appeared to be a corridor a few miles wide running east to west into Baghdad that was clear of AAA. Looking at it on a map, it looked like we were going to fly right down an alley that was flanked on both sides by AAA as we headed into Baghdad.

Our Forward Looking Infrared (FLIR) system wasn't working when we turned up. The FLIR was a thermal imaging camera displayed on a screen in the cockpit. It was particularly helpful for obstacle avoidance on low light level nights since it could display an image based on temperature differences when our Night Vision Goggles (NVGs) had no light to amplify. Without our FLIR, it would be completely impossible to see the power lines. As a result, we decided to trade one threat for the other and fly at 300 feet AGL vice 200 feet AGL. We wouldn't hit power lines, but we would be slightly more vulnerable to the AAA and even more vulnerable to Surface-to-Air Missiles (SAMs) and Man Portable Air Defense Systems (MANPADS). Given the circumstances, the choice to fly at 300 feet AGL made the most sense.

We pressed out on the route. In addition to the inky blackness of the low light night, it was also really hazy, which made overall visibility even worse and the ability to see anything resembling a horizon impossible. I was flying in the right seat and kept experiencing brief periods of vertigo that we called "the leans." When that happens, you feel like you are in a turn even when you aren't. I just kept scanning the gauges underneath my NVGs and pushed the "I believe" button in my head to stay straight and level until the leans passed.

Our crew chiefs were even complaining about vertigo in the back, which was a big red flag about the bad visibility. Looking out the windows in the back, our crew chiefs could always see the horizon better than we could in the cockpit, so it was really bad if they were struggling. Once we hit the checkpoint east of Baghdad and turned back west towards the city, the fight that was going on there made it look like one giant strobe light in the distance. Our NVGs were amplifying every little blast and explosion. It felt unnatural to be deliberately flying towards that series of explosions.

As we came upon the objective area, we could see what looked like a semi-circle on the ground pointing away from us. There were a lot of rounds going downrange from that semi-circle, so we knew the Marines we were dropping this re-supply for were engaged in a firefight. We were going to try and land just behind them to drop off their supplies. I flew the initial approach, and as we came through 100 feet, I noticed a couple of Army helicopters parked in the LZ below us. I wasn't expecting that at all, and I had to slide over to my left to try and avoid them.

Once I got down to 25 feet, I was also totally browned out and couldn't see anything. Everything felt off, so I called for a wave off and started to pull power. Our crew chief immediately yelled, "No higher!" A highly unusual call.

Our dash two was already waving off and wound up right above us. We almost ran into them! Our crew chief saved our asses.

At that point, I was squeezing the cyclic and collective way too tight. The major I was flying with took the controls, brought us back around, and got us on the deck. That attempted landing had exceeded my current skill level. Once on deck, a couple of Marines ran over and told us they were heavily engaged in a firefight. No shit. We quickly taxi-dropped their supplies. To taxi drop, you lower the ramp and pull a little power to slowly roll forward while your crew chiefs push your cargo off the ramp behind you. Then we got the fuck out of there. When we lifted, I had the controls back and started pressing back on our route to the east.

We were going to have to fly through that corridor between

the AAA one more time on the way out. We made it through the corridor unscathed, hit our checkpoint to the east, and turned back toward the south. We were all still fighting vertigo when we crossed the Tigris River. Our crew chief called out that we were taking fire from our three o'clock. The rounds passed right behind our section. Since we were all blacked out with no lights on, they couldn't see us. They were shooting at the sound, which was always behind the aircraft.

We headed to a FARP at a FOB called "Three Rivers" to get more fuel and prep for the next run of the resupply. It was so dark and visibility so poor, we struggled to locate the FOB when we heard an Unmanned Aerial Vehicle (UAV) call for "rocket launch." A couple of seconds later, that UAV was coming right at us and went straight over the top of us. At least it showed us where the FOB was. We landed without incident and learned that it would be about an hour before the Marines at Three Rivers could fuel us. By the time we got our gas, the DASC let us know that the follow-on runs wouldn't be needed. After taking some fuel, we headed back to Jalibah without incident.

The next day the CO joked with me about having more flight time and more adventures than anyone else in the squadron. It had just randomly worked out that way, but I knew that meant I was about to be on the bench for a while. For the next few days, I tested aircraft, stood duty, and gave what seemed like 100 haircuts. We didn't have a barber or a barbershop, so the Marines who were decent at giving haircuts got hit up to do so all the time. I had always been pretty good with a set of clippers, so I ended up being the default barber for most of the other officers in the squadron. I didn't mind. It gave me a way to kill some time. I also got good enough at it that I could even cut my own hair if I had a couple of mirrors to use to see the back of my head.

A few days into that routine, we got hit with another one of those crazy haboob sandstorms. We woke up in the middle of the night because our tent collapsed on us. Getting that tent put back up in the pitch dark in the middle of that storm was no fun. We were all covered with sand, and it was everywhere inside the tent, including inside our sleeping bags. It took a couple of days of shaking the sand out of everything to get sleeping back to something that was semi-tolerable.

Right around that time our CO lost his mind when one of our captains decided not to take off one day due to poor visibility. Our east coast sister squadron HMH-464 launched a flight as he was canceling, so it was a bad look for him. Nobody ever said it, but the "don't be a pussy" rule was ever-present. The CO was all over it, and his message to the squadron was that all of us captains were soft, so the field grade were going to lead flights for a while. I honestly didn't give a damn at that point. Let the majors lead the flights. That meant they would have to actually plan and brief the flights, instead of just showing up to the brief and poking holes at whatever captain planned and briefed it.

About a week later, Browner woke me up at 0400 to tell me that he needed to send me back to the boat to test up some aircraft there. The thing driving the decision was that some of the aircraft at Jalibah would need to be swapped out for fresh aircraft soon. We had left a few aircraft and a maintenance detachment on the ship for that exact reason. A couple of hours later I flew to the USS *Boxer*. At that point I was happy to get back to the boat. Just doing my laundry and taking a shower was a win.

My actual boss was our Aviation Maintenance Officer (AMO), Major Jeff "Cooter" Chestney, a great officer and a great pilot. I verified with him that he was okay with me going so that he didn't feel like Browner was too deep into his department. I was one of our most proficient Functional Check Pilots (FCPs), and as the Quality Assurance Officer (QAO), testing aircraft was what I should be doing if I wasn't on the flight schedule for something else. We needed to finish testing those aircraft up to swap them out with a few aircraft at Jalibah. So Cooter was all about me going back to the boat to help with that.

On day six of testing aircraft on the ship, our OPSO Eric "Dobie" Gillis sent me a message via SIPR chat that he needed me back in the fight the next day. Dobie had been the senior captain in the squadron when I had checked in a couple of years prior. He had also deployed as part of the 15th MEU with Spooner to Afghanistan. He had come right back to the fleet as a junior major and served as our OPSO.

I packed up my gear that night and flew back out to Jalibah the next morning. I had been told I would do my Night Systems Instructor (NSI) check ride when we got home from deployment and then attend the Weapons and Tactics Instructor (WTI) course in the fall. As a result, Dobie wanted to ensure I got as much action as I could in Iraq, especially at night. I had been gone for six days when I returned to Jalibah on April 19th.

Nothing had changed other than the chow hall was now serving breakfast. The food was still MREs and T-Rats, though, so nobody cared. The food remained at varying degrees of terrible.

It didn't take me long to notice that our tasking load had dropped way off while I was gone. With the battle of Baghdad now complete for more than a week, there simply wasn't a lot left to do. On April 27th, I finally got back out there for a flight as Krusty's dash two. Our mission was to make a couple of runs with passengers between Three Rivers and Division Main, located at Ad Diwaniyah. The flight was uneventful until we headed back to Jalibah and ran into a haboob that popped up out of nowhere. For the last 15 miles, we had to fly down at 100 feet AGL and 60 knots, just picking our way through it. We could barely see the ground at that altitude, and our forward visibility was close to zero. When we got back to the field, we just landed on the taxiway because it was the only thing we could see. By the time we landed, I was officially ready to get the hell out of Iraq.

On April 30th, I was in the ready room planning when we got word that Krusty's aircraft had gone down. He was dash two in a section with one of our other crews to move the 1st Marine Division Commanding General (CG) from Al Hillah to An Najaf. We kicked all non-pilots out of our ready room tent and calmly started working the mishap plan. We soon got word that Krusty and his crew were okay, but the aircraft was destroyed. Thankfully, the passengers were also on the other aircraft.

When they got back to Jalibah a few hours later, Krusty told the story. Their #2 engine caught fire while en route. While fighting the fire, they set up for an emergency landing in the desert, but it was too little too late. The fire burned through the flight control rods on short final for landing, and the aircraft yawed hard to its right. The result was that they hit the ground facing sideways and immediately rolled over. It was a miracle that they were all still conscious and able to get out after the violent motion stopped.

Once they were clear of the aircraft, the rounds from the .50 caliber machine guns in the windows started cooking off. The 1st Marine Division CG had personally run out of the other aircraft to get them. They ran with him back to the other aircraft in the flight and got the hell out of there while their aircraft was still burning.

Krusty was one of our captain WTIs and undoubtedly the most revered captain in the squadron. He was shaken, and seeing something like that happen to him was a sobering reminder to the rest of us that nobody was immune. That environment could get any of us at any time. The list of things that could get you was quite long.

We flew basic missions for the next few days while getting ready to retrograde back to the ship. I did run into a couple of my old flight school buds, though. I saw my former roommate Ian Dagley at Jalibah one day. I had heard from Dave Wright that he had crashed a Huey about a week prior, but Dagley said it wasn't that big of a deal. He just spread the skids a bit on a hard landing. Regardless, it was good to see him.

I also caught up with Dalton on a run down to Ali Al Salem,

where his squadron HMH-462 was living. Those assholes had a nice chow hall with real food and even had cold Cokes. After swapping stories with Dalton for a few minutes, I grabbed a few Cokes on the way out the door to give to my crew back on the aircraft. We all agreed they were the best thing we had tasted in weeks.

Cinco de Mayo was my last night at Jalibah. On May 6th, I flew back to the boat. Before crossing the Kuwaiti border, I noted that the last checkpoint on the Iraqi border was called "Budweiser." I looked down and thought to myself that I didn't believe this was the last time I was ever going to fly in the unfriendly skies over Iraq. Somehow, I just knew I was going to be back here again. Probably sooner rather than later. It just didn't feel like it was over to me.

We retrograded the whole squadron back to the ship and then kept flying assorted cleanup missions into Iraq for another few weeks. On May 18th, the 3rd Marine Aircraft Wing (3rd MAW) CG came on board to talk to us. He congratulated us for destroying 8 1/2 Iraqi Divisions in 25 days. None of us were sure about his math, but it didn't matter. It was over, and we had won. Two days later, on May 20th, I flew a milk run up to Division Main, and we took fire en route and had kids throw rocks and sticks at us on short final into the zone. Those people wanted us to get the fuck out of their country. I couldn't blame them. We were ready to go, too.

May 26, 2003, was Memorial Day. The ship had a "beer day" to celebrate our supposed victory. It was held in conjunction with a steel beach picnic, so everyone on board was up on the flight deck, and all the aircraft were stuffed into the slash. We had a big group from our squadron sitting right on Spot 7 in lawn chairs. Marines were assigned to distribute the beers, and the system in place was to highlight your name when you grabbed one. They just kept highlighting everyone's name over and over. Somewhere in there, everyone started going down to berthing and breaking into their secret stash of liquor to make cocktails as well. A few hours into it, I was headed down to berthing to hit the head, and one of my roommates asked me to grab his stash. I did it without really thinking about it. Everyone was doing it but what I was about to do was a lot bolder. It didn't dawn on me that was the case.

After heading back up to the flight deck and handing him his container, the Master at Arms grabbed both of us and told us to come with him. At first, I didn't think there was any way this would turn into a big deal. I couldn't have been more wrong. Two days later, I was standing at attention in front of my CO while he told me what my fate would be. My primary punishment was that I would not be attending the WTI course when we got home. Secondary to that, I would be standing a lot of duty during our ride home. They could have given me a Fitness Report (FITREP) that would have ended my career for all practical purposes, but they didn't. I was thankful for that, and I knew that Browner had a lot to do with it working out that way.

Although I knew it could have been a lot worse, I still took it pretty hard. I had always been an envelope pusher and a bit reckless, but it had caught up to me this time. I let the team and myself down in the process. It was a great lesson to learn at that point in my career, though. You never want to do anything that puts the fate of your future in the hands of someone else. That applied both in and out of the aircraft.

Regardless, it made a fifty-five day ride home feel like an eternity. For me, it was purgatory. My boss, Cooter, was great throughout the whole thing. He must have given me a pep talk of some kind at least once a week the entire way home. He kept reminding me that I needed to shake it off, because the squadron would need me to be the best version of myself for the next deployment cycle.

Our first two port stops on the way home were in Sydney, Australia, and Townsville, Australia. The CO and Browner let me off the boat one night at each place with the caveat that I had to hang out with them. One night they even utilized me to extract the MAG CO from a compromising situation. That helped put me back on the right side of the law. It was probably best that I wasn't out running wild with the rest of the guys. They came back with some epic stories. Those adventures might have gone too far if I had been in the middle of them instigating.

Metallica had come out with a new album, *St. Anger*, just before we reached Sydney, and Fifer grabbed me a copy on his first night out in town. It's my least favorite of all the Metallica albums, but the thrashing rage fit my mood at the time. I listened to it on repeat the rest of the way home. The last stop on the way home was in Honolulu, Hawaii. At that time, Uncle Louis was stationed there at Marine Corps Air Station Kaneohe Bay, and they let me off the boat for the entirety of the stop. I crashed at his place, and we went out and met up with the rest of the squadron every night. We spent most of our evenings at a little bar called the Irish Rose, watching a cover band that specialized in Van Halen songs. It was at least mildly cathartic for me.

I was in the infancy of processing my experience in Iraq, coupled with the fact that I had fucked up and lost my shot at WTI. It felt like a lot. And I still had to get home and try to reintegrate with Kerry and Tristen after being gone for several months. Kerry wasn't pleased about me getting into trouble on the boat, and Tristen would have no idea who I was. All in all, it wasn't a great place to be coming home from my first combat deployment. It had been one hell of an experience, but I had managed to end it on a sour note. It left me with a restless feeling that I had unfinished business as a combat aviator.

HOME

My HOMECOMING from OIF was bittersweet. We had a huge fly off on July 25th that brought all of our aircraft and most of the squadron off the ship and back to the flight line in front of Hangar 4. The final piece of my punishment was that the CO wouldn't let me participate in the fly off as a pilot. As a result, I just rode as a passenger on Browner's jump seat. It was great to see Kerry and Tristen, but the strain that both Kerry and I had been under was evident right away. Our reunion had a very different feel than my homecoming from my first deployment.

Tristen had just turned a year old, and Kerry had her first birthday party planned for a couple of days later so I could be there. As a result, we had some family in town for both events. Having them there on top of everything else was too much for us all. Those first few days passed in a blur. I was home, but every-thing felt off. I felt out of place. I still had that nagging feeling the war wasn't over. I wanted to redeem myself at the squadron, and I also needed to re-connect at home. Competing interests.

After our obligatory post-deployment 96, I was happy to return to the squadron and get back to work. We immediately had a Change of Command ceremony, and we welcomed our new CO, who had previously been in the squadron with us and had also served as the Detachment Officer in Charge (OIC) for Spooner's 15th MEU Det a couple of years prior.

He and our outgoing CO were very different, and they didn't seem to care much for one another, which worked out in my favor. As our new CO took command, Cooter moved up and took over the XO spot for Browner, who was also departing. I would miss Browner; he had been a great mentor to me. I was happy Cooter would stick around to take his place as the XO. Cooter was also one of those rare majors I trusted and respected. Having him with us for another deployment cycle was a big win for the squadron.

Right after the new CO took over, he and Cooter summoned me into the office and told me to forget what had happened on the way home from Iraq. They gave me a clean slate and told me they needed the best version of me for this next deployment cycle. It would be a quick turn, so we didn't have much time to get our shit together as a squadron. They expected me to remain the Quality Assurance Officer (QAO) to help keep maintenance strong, but more importantly, they wanted me back in the syllabus for advanced flight leadership designations and instructor qualifications.

Specifically, they wanted me to prepare to be a Night Systems Instructor (NSI) and a Weapons and Tactics Instructor (WTI). I would miss my original WTI opportunity, but I might get another shot if I met their expectations. It was the best news I had heard in a long time, and I felt fortunate to be given the chance to get back on track.

With the war supposedly over, our squadron was slated to resume the previously existing deployment rotation. We would immediately CHOP a detachment to the 11th MEU. Krusty and Focker would be part of that detachment. The rest of us would deploy to Okinawa, Japan, for the Unit Deployment Program (UDP) in December. Upon arrival in Okinawa, we would also provide a detachment to the 31st MEU.

That timeline would give us just five months between deployments rather than the standard eighteen months. We would also send some of our most qualified Marines to that 11th MEU detachment, which meant we would have a lot of training to complete for the rest of the squadron. With numerous new Marines checking in, we needed to get them trained and ready to deploy in a hurry.

The limited time to train prompted me to push our new copilots hard when I flew with them. I knew how important every hour of flight time was, so I did everything I could to teach them to take advantage of it. I was naturally a "button masher" pilot, one who tended to keep the trim buttons depressed to make myself really feel and fly the aircraft. I wouldn't use the altitude hold functions in our Automatic Flight Control System (AFCS) unless the rules for the mission profile dictated it in situations like flying the pattern on the boat. I wanted to literally fly the aircraft every second I could, and I taught them to do the same. There were no wasted reps. The margin between living and dying was too thin. I had seen it. I wasn't going to let myself or anyone else get lazy. Even though we were just going back to Okinawa, I still expected to get back into the fight soon. We needed to be ready for that.

One of my favorite things about being a west coast Marine was that we had ready access to great desert training areas near Marine Corps Air Station Yuma, Arizona, and the Marine Corps Air Ground Combat Center (MCAGCC) at Twentynine Palms, California. Believing that we would end up back in Iraq, I put myself and everyone who flew with me through the paces of desert landings every chance I got.

Landing a CH-53E in a dusty environment is both art and science. Only science is working against you. At a gross weight of over 50,000 pounds, when filled with fuel, the aircraft creates a violent downwash. In a dusty environment, that downwash puts all that dust airborne into a cloud the pilots must fight through to land.

The aircraft was designed and built with actual landing gear with tires. I always assumed the original designers only saw this heavy lift helicopter landing on hard surface runways, landing pads, or the decks of naval ships. But the Marine Corps fights in any "clime and place." I always imagined that somewhere, the engineers who designed the CH-53E were laughing. You crazy assholes are going to land those things in the open desert? Good luck! The art of landing them was literally in the hands of the pilots and enlisted aircrew. There was no system on board the aircraft to help with reduced visibility landings.

It took a lot of practice to master those landings, so we trained constantly. In training, we would fly a 300 feet AGL landing pattern, which allowed us to practice flying the final approach profile that we executed for almost every mission. If we did it right, we would roll out on our final approach at 150 feet AGL and 50 knots. From there, it was a straight descending, decelerating glideslope to our landing spot. The dust would initially kick up behind the aircraft, but as we continued to descend and decelerate, it would slowly catch up and envelop the aircraft between 50 and 25 feet AGL as we slowed to 10 knots.

Our crew chiefs in the back would lean out the windows and look straight down for a visual reference to the ground. In the cockpit, the pilots flew the remainder of the descent based on their calls, seat of the pants, and what our gauges were telling us. In the end, it always came down to a pilot leaning over and looking straight down over their shoulder, hoping to see a plant, a rock, anything that could tell them how high they were off the deck and if they were drifting. The pilot would then call "reference right/left" as appropriate, and the crew chiefs would give a final clearance to land. It was borderline insane. It was also pretty damn fun.

I also appreciated that the marine layer tends to roll in over San Diego on most evenings. So on night flights out in the desert, a recovery back to Miramar often required an instrument approach. There was no better way to maintain proficiency flying real instrument approaches than to do it. A long night of tactics and bouncing in the desert, followed by a precision instrument approach back into Miramar, was great training. We needed every bit of it to ensure that our crews would be prepared for the upcoming deployment.

I volunteered to deploy early as part of our advanced party and leave in November. The CO and Cooter said thanks and then informed me that they intended for me to do that whether I wanted to or not. Conveniently, I wanted to. For every deployment during which one squadron replaced another, the aircraft would stay in place. Each squadron would send an advanced party to execute an aircraft turnover. That turnover was fairly involved and required that each aircraft be taken through a Functional Check Flight (FCF) with pilots from both squadrons.

One of our junior majors would technically be in charge, but Fifer and I would be responsible for turning over and accepting the aircraft from our sister squadron HMH-361, the "Flying Tigers." I loved testing aircraft with Fifer, so the idea of the two of us getting to accept and test a full complement of eight main body aircraft and being on our own program for a month appealed to me.

Knowing that I would only be home for four months put Kerry and me in a situation where we never really adjusted out of deployment mode. We were still close, but we were both very aware that we would soon be separated and on our own again. She had done a great job of becoming integrated with the squadron. She volunteered for everything she could and spent time with the other wives and families. Those other wives became her local support system with our own families living so far away. They would soon fill that role for each other once again.

We tried to make the most of the time that we had. We didn't talk about it often, but the unspoken communication was always there. We held each other close while we slept. Every embrace counted. I tried to be as present as possible with Tristen. I always helped with feeding, diapers, and bath time. I spent as much time as I could playing with her on the floor. If I watched TV, I would sit her in my lap. It was important to me to be close to her. But I was always aware that she was still so little, she wouldn't remember me if I didn't make it back. That feeling settled heavily in my gut. I didn't always feel like a guy who was home with his wife and baby girl. I sometimes felt like a transient outsider in my own house. It wasn't anything that they were doing. It was me. I didn't want them to know I felt that way, but I knew Kerry sensed it.

After being home for a few weeks, I realized how much I was feeling the weight of all of it. I also knew that it wasn't just the combat experience. It was that I would soon be asked to do it again. The combat stress I felt wasn't so much from what had happened but knowing what could have happened. Was I lucky? Was I good? Was it some form of divine intervention? Was that real? I couldn't answer my own questions. I saw how dangerous a war zone could be, as well as the randomness and unpredictability of things like indirect fire. I had been a half-second fast enough to stay alive a couple of times. What were the odds I could keep that streak alive?

A heightened awareness coupled with the early stages of something else I couldn't quite understand or reconcile. Part of me liked it. Really liked it. Combat flying was like a drug, and I had gotten a taste of it. I knew it might destroy me, but I wanted more. When I acknowledged that to myself, I thought I was crazy.

During the week, I stayed busy at the squadron and spent most of my free time studying for my next qualifications. When I did have downtime, it was almost impossible to sit still or relax. My mind raced with an array of thoughts, and I felt restless. I started to drink more on the weekends. I needed to turn off my brain and get some sleep. Drinking helped. At least, that's what I told myself.

My drinking simply added to an already tense dynamic at home. Kerry was just trying to survive without me, and even when I was home, we both knew I wasn't always present mentally. At the same time, I felt like she was oblivious to what I was working through. That wasn't true. We both had expectations for one another that we couldn't possibly fulfill. We just didn't have the bandwidth to really help each other. Resentment started to build. We never verbalized it, but we thought we would try to figure it out after this next deployment. For the time being, we focused on just getting through it.

I left for my third deployment on November 12, 2003. There were only about twenty of us in the advanced party, so we flew commercial. We had to be at San Diego's Lindbergh International Airport by 0430 to get in line for customs, so it was a perfect excuse to catch a ride instead of having Kerry drop me off. I'd already decided after my last deployment never to have Kerry drop me off for deployment again. It was too hard. Fifer picked me up at 0330, and we were off for the next adventure.

We flew to Okinawa by way of Tokyo. Then, we took a bus from one airport to another in Tokyo. The trip lasted for just shy of 24 hours, and when we finally got to MCAS Futenma on Okinawa, we were all smoked.

We immediately started testing aircraft with HMH-361 to accept them for turnover. I loved testing with Fifer, and we were highly proficient at it when we were together. We could dial in the engines and the rest of the systems tight. The HMH-361 crews we tested with kept asking, "Why are you adjusting that? It's within limits."

Fifer or I would say, "It's not good enough." Then, we kept making it better. We got those aircraft quickly dialed into our standard.

Fifer and I had moved back into Barracks 218, "The Halfway House." As neighbors, we spent all our downtime together. We took turns cooking dinner in the evenings and played "NCAA Football" and "Grand Theft Auto Vice City" on my PlayStation 2. We ate and drank like every day was our last one on earth. All of that was just a backdrop for the two of us to have a never-ending conversation about the aircraft and the squadron.

On December 1, 2003, the CO called from Miramar to tell us that our main body was going to take the eight aircraft from Okinawa and return to Iraq. Our 31st MEU detachment would remain in Okinawa. He would have more information when the rest of the squadron arrived to meet us in a couple of weeks, but he wanted us to know.

It was happening. Even though I had been expecting that news, the reality of it weighed heavily. We were going right back to the show. Part of me felt excited. Another part immediately started questioning myself. Can I do this again? Can I be the guy that the rest of the squadron needs me to be? I didn't have a choice. It had to be the latter.

Fifer and I drank way too much that night while talking about how unprepared we were as a squadron. We were only a point five, and we had a bunch of green pilots and aircrew at every level. That was exacerbated by having to leave some of our stronger pilots, aircrew, and maintainers in Okinawa on the 31st MEU. As much as we both personally wanted to go back, we had concerns about the squadron. I ended up calling Kerry late that night to break the news. It was a terrible way to tell her, and that call did not go well. I regret that.

The rest of the squadron arrived in Okinawa on December 13th, and we had a big party in the Echo Chamber that night. The copilots looked like someone had just dropped them off on the surface of Mars. It was their first deployment, and they knew they were on a short pitstop in Okinawa on their way to Iraq. Meanwhile, they were in this room that everyone seemed to think was great while all the senior captains and majors were getting hammered. It was a bit of a scene, and the CO was right in the middle of it. He was a genuine liberty risk. Honestly, I loved that about him. It was one of the things he and I had in common.

Two days later, on December 15th, I took off from Okinawa with Chris "Suit" Roy, heading for Pusan, Korea. The Marine Corps had a deal in place with Korean Airlines (KAL) to perform what was referred to as Depot Level Maintenance on CH-53Es. I was taking an aircraft to drop off and testing an aircraft KAL had just completed to bring back.

Suit had been the best copilot in the squadron on our previous deployment to Iraq, and I had flown with him off the ship and into Iraq several times. He was always prepared and had a calm demeanor. His callsign ended up being Suit because he was all business. We spent a few days at Pusan and had some quality adventures. We had a Marine Corps gunnery sergeant as a liaison with KAL, but there was also a Korean civilian liaison, who was technically in charge of the Korean maintenance personnel doing the actual work on the aircraft. His name was Mr. Kim, and he was hilarious.

He had learned English through some immersion training with a family in Texas that had taught him every combination of curse words possible. First thing in the morning, he would greet us with something like, "Good morning, you piece of shit cocksucka, muthafuckas!" I loved that guy. At night, he would take us out to dinner and bars, and he paid for everything. His job was to give us a good aircraft and keep us happy. He delivered on both.

Even though it was freezing outside, we had a great week in Korea. On December 22nd, we took the aircraft we had just tested and flew back to Okinawa to rejoin the squadron. I was hoping to break down our aircraft, stuff them into Air Force C-5s, and quickly re-deploy to Iraq. But I wasn't that lucky. Someone had decided we needed to do more training in Okinawa first.

First Marine Aircraft Wing had put together a Ground Air Integrated Training (GAIT) exercise that we were going to have to participate in for "pre-deployment training." We were already deployed! The whole thing amounted to a total waste of time. I was beyond frustrated at how things were playing out. Christmas was a non-event. We all just cooked a bunch of food and drank too much. We were in purgatory, just dying to get on with it.

On January 21, 2004, we were still stuck on Okinawa and had to go to the base theater over on Kadena Air Force Base, to listen to the 1st Marine Aircraft Wing (1st MAW) Commanding General (CG) speak. The gist of his message was that 3rd MAW had done everything wrong during OIF I, and that 1st MAW was doing everything right in preparing for the real fight with North Korea.

As a young captain, he pissed me off. He wasn't in Iraq with us! How the hell did he know what we did wrong or right? And everything that 1st MAW was doing in Okinawa seemed like a complete waste of time to me. It was maddening.

On February 4th, we finally started flying our aircraft to Kadena to break them down to stuff them into C-5s for transport to Iraq. I had been away from home for three months, and it felt like we had wasted all that time. On February 11th, we had one aircraft remaining, but it had a bad engine that needed to be changed. The 1st MAW CG would be making a speech about us deploying to Iraq from Kadena the next day, and the brass wanted us to get that last aircraft over there. There was going to be a lot of media coverage, which seemed to be all that higher headquarters gave any fucks about.

The CO asked me to fly the aircraft that needed the engine change over to Kadena on two engines. I was always up for flying a semi-broken aircraft, but I thought this one was a bad decision. As the QAO, I felt strongly that we should just change the engine right there in Okinawa, where it was easy, instead of taking it to Iraq, knowing we would have to change the engine in a more austere environment. Regardless, I did what I was asked to do.

I flew it over on two engines with Fifer, dropping it off without incident. Fifer and I decided that, when we reached Iraq, we would make it our aircraft. He wanted to name it "Violent Kay," after the stripper we had encountered at "The Viking" in Guam on my first deployment. With Kay delivered to Kadena, we were finally ready to go back to war.

12

GOING BACK

THE MOVEMENT from Okinawa back to Iraq was painful. We took eight CH-53Es with us, so we were broken down into four sticks (groups) that would fly on Air Force C-5s. Each of those C-5s also carried two of our CH-53Es. I was on stick 2, and we were initially slated to depart on the afternoon of February 16, 2004. That original timeline slid and ultimately resulted in us living out of our backpacks and Camelbaks for three days.

The rest of our gear was already packed, palletized, and ready to go, so there was no getting it back. In Okinawa, we could have some additional creature comforts in our rooms, but that wasn't an option in Iraq, so I had already mailed that stuff home to Kerry.

Those three days were just a never-ending series of timeline changes and cancellations. We checked out of our rooms three times only to check back in. Each time, I called Kerry one last time. I grew tired of repeatedly saying goodbye. Keyed up about leaving, I couldn't sleep. It was maddening. On the morning of February 19th, we were up at 0100 and arrived at Kadena Air Force Base for our flight at 0430. We boarded our C-5 at 0840 and took off at 0900. We were finally on our way.

The idea of going back felt different than I expected. I had last flown across the border from Iraq into Kuwait nine months prior. As I crossed Checkpoint Budweiser on that day, I had a gut feeling that this return trip was inevitable. Now, it was here. Part of me dreaded it, but I also acknowledged that another part of me felt excited. I had gotten a taste of the combat drug, and I liked it. I liked it a lot. I was looking forward to feeling it again. I also looked forward to the lack of downtime. I learned on my previous deployment to Iraq that there isn't anything to do besides work, fly and maybe work out in a combat zone. There was a simplicity to the existence. I looked forward to that, too.

Our first fuel stop was at Travis Air Force Base in Vacaville, California. It was a seven-hour layover, so we walked to the gym and grabbed a shower. We also hit the base exchange to load up on stateside Copenhagen while we still could. Then we had something resembling a last meal at the exchange. Popeyes chicken and Taco Bell. Pre-combat meal of champions. About an hour after getting airborne again, one of our Marines got sick, so we diverted to Wright Patterson Air Force Base outside of Dayton, Ohio, for medical attention.

That unplanned stop resulted in a night in a hotel outside the gate. Our clocks were all messed up after starting in Okinawa, but we still ended up in some little sports bar downstairs around lunchtime. Once the owner found out we were on our way to Iraq, beers were on the house, and the Marines had a big time with that. I didn't last long and ended up heading back to my room to crash around 1500. I got back up at midnight and went back down to the bar. Most of the Marines were still in there and going hard. I asked the owner if they were about to shut down, and she said, "Hell no, we aren't closing until you guys leave. This is the most excitement we've had around here in months." And so it was.

A couple of hours later, we were on our way back to the base to load up. Fittingly, just before takeoff, the flaps on the C-5 got stuck down, so the crew decided to jump over to Dover Air

Force Base in Dover, Delaware, for repairs. Just what we needed. Yet another unplanned stop.

We offloaded into the passenger terminal at Dover just as a "Hero Flight" taxied in and started to offload Marines and Soldiers who had been killed in Iraq. It was a sobering reminder about where we were headed and what we were about to do. It appeared to have a significant impact on our first-time deployers. The awareness of death is ever present in a combat zone. Seeing those caskets made it real for those who hadn't previously seen them.

The flap issue turned into another night in a hotel, complete with beer and pizza. It was a rinse-and-repeat of our night in Ohio. Thankfully, nobody got into trouble. A few Marines had families not far away who came to see them. Kerry was about six hours away in Virginia, staying with her family, and we briefly discussed her coming to visit for a few hours. We ultimately decided it would just be too hard. We were both already in deployment mode. A few hours together might do more harm than good for both of us. I just needed to focus on what I was going to do and get my ass back home in one piece again.

We were airborne again at 1530 local time on February 22nd. Our last stop was at Morón Air Base, located just south of Seville, Spain. After a quick refueling evolution, we were airborne for Iraq. We landed at our final destination, Al Asad Air Base, Iraq, at 1930 local on February 23rd. We had been traveling for five days at that point. I was surprised at how cold it was as we loaded up on small buses to head to the makeshift Joint Reception Center to scan our IDs and get logged in as new residents. We had missed the cold season the previous year, but we were catching the tail end of it this time. I didn't complain. I knew how hot it would get very soon.

Al Asad Air Base was further northwest than we had been when we were fighting in Iraq the year prior. Al Asad was in the desert of the Anbar Province, just a few miles east of the green Euphrates River Valley. The population centers were concentrated along the Euphrates. The cities of Fallujah, Ramadi, Hit, Haditha, Rawah, Al Qaim, and Husaybah would soon become familiar. The base had been built in the 1980s by Yugoslavian companies under contract with the Iraqi government. The airfield had 13,000-foot parallel runways numbered 09/27 oriented perfectly east and west. The airfield also included hardened shelters initially built to protect Iraqi fighters and bombers.

Before the invasion the year prior, the base had been home to Iraqi Air Force MiG-25s and MiG-21s. On April 16, 2003, the base was secured by the Australian Special Air Service Regiment. The following month, it became home to the Army's 3rd Armored Cavalry Regiment. We were part of the I Marine Expeditionary Force (I MEF) that was now moving in to take over. It would serve as the primary base for the Marine Corps and a major logistics hub for all US forces for the remainder of the war. From Al Asad, Marine Corps Aviation could easily cover the entirety of Anbar Province. Not only the population centers along the Euphrates River Valley, but the sprawling expanse of desert to the west and southwest, as well.

As one of the first groups of Marines to move in, there would be a lot of work to do. We took over a few small buildings on the flight line and set them up as our squadron spaces. No running water, but we had electricity for lights, and that was good enough. Like American bases, the part of the base where the living quarters, chow hall and other amenities were located was separated by some distance from the flight line. Also, like back home, we called that side of the base "mainside."

We moved into some broken-down old Iraqi barracks on mainside. Those barracks reminded me of abandoned buildings from some post-apocalyptic movie. They had running water for showers, and toilets that couldn't take any paper products. The barracks were filthy, smelled terrible, and had several creepy murals painted on the walls in the hallways. But it was better than living in tents.

Our government brought in a shitload of cheap bunk beds, so

we set those up and started grouping everyone into rooms. In the officer barracks, I ended up rooming with Fifer, Suit, and another of our younger pilots from Suit's peer group. Suit had a calm and quiet demeanor complemented by a great sense of humor. He liked the Boston Red Sox, Dave Matthews and ate Tabasco Chipotle on pretty much everything. He fit right in with us.

It was a little over a mile from our barracks to the flight line, and transportation back and forth was an issue. That made for a long walk. They allowed a few local merchants onto the base, and the Army referred to them as "Hajis." Not at all PC, but the term stuck. Some of them had set up shop underneath the stands at the old soccer field in the middle of the base. Mostly they sold junky tchotchkes, weird souvenirs, and bootleg DVDs. One of the merchants sold cheap mountain bikes, so several of us bought those to use as our primary transportation around the base. Fifer and I bought a matching set. His was black; mine was red. We joked about how ridiculous we all looked riding back and forth to the squadron spaces on those dumb bikes.

Our Marines had gone to work putting our aircraft back together. As the Assistant Aviation Maintenance Officer (AAMO) and Quality Assurance Officer (QAO), I was very plugged into how that process unfolded. Getting a CH-53 on a C5 requires significant preparation, including removing the auxiliary fuel tanks, tail rotor, and main rotor. Reinstalling the main rotor system was a really big job. I was bouncing back and forth between overseeing that process on the flight line and sitting through in-briefs. The Army pilots supporting the 3rd Armored Cavalry Regiment gave us our in-briefs related to flying. On February 26, we had a full day of briefs with them. They had been operating out of Al Asad for almost a year, and they had lost a few aircraft and crews during that time.

They had just lost another OH-58 and its crew the day prior. The effects of that were evident in their demeanor, but they were total professionals about helping us get snapped in. A couple of weeks before leaving Okinawa, I saw a quote from a Marine General in "Stars and Stripes" that essentially said the Marines wouldn't lose as many aircraft as the Army because we were going to "do it different." In our opening brief, an Army Warrant Officer read that quote and followed with, "Good luck." I never felt like a bigger asshole for being a Marine.

The next day I was in the back of an Army Blackhawk with one of our other pilots, getting an Area Familiarization (FAM) from a couple of their pilots. They showed us all the primary places they had been going to and how they approached them. My primary takeaway was that they spent too much time lingering over and around the population centers in broad daylight. I kept thinking how pissed I was going to be if I died as a fucking passenger in the back of a Blackhawk on a FAM flight. They were likely just doing that to try and let us see everything, but we would be much more tactical around those population centers.

For the entirety of our last deployment, our tactics dictated that we fly Terrain Flight (TERF) altitudes at 200 feet AGL and below. The TERF hard deck was 50 feet AGL. Flying at those altitudes for extended periods was taxing for multiple reasons, but it was necessary to counter the threat of the infrared Man Portable Air Defense Systems (MANPADS) prevalent with the enemy. The proximity to the ground made it more difficult for them to lock on and chase our heat signature.

During turnover, the Army had told us they had tried flying at 300 to 500 feet AGL for a while, because they thought the threat of hitting wires or simply Controlled Flight Into Terrain (CFIT) was higher. After getting a couple of aircraft shot down by MANPADS at those altitudes, they dropped back down below 200 feet AGL. There was no "good" answer. Our Commanding General (CG) then told us we would go with 300 to 500 feet AGL. I didn't like it. I would rather bet on myself not hitting any wires or flying into the ground than take my chances with a MANPADS shot at a higher altitude. But it wasn't up to me. The decision was made.

As the QAO, I was also our primary Functional Check Pilot (FCP), so as soon as our Marines had an aircraft put back together, myself and our other FCPs were out there testing them up. We needed to get the mission going. We also assigned "combat crews" to each aircraft. Those groups of pilots and aircrew had some specific responsibilities to the maintenance department and got to pick the door art and paint their names on the aircraft. It was more symbolic than anything else. Fifer and I were both assigned to Kay, but we flew whatever aircraft maintenance needed us to fly. And although we were combat crew and would fly together quite a bit, we wouldn't fly together 100% of the time.

Once we started getting aircraft up, the most challenging part was that nobody seemed to really know what the mission was. When we had been in-country for OIF I, the mission was clearly defined. We were fighting a conventional force in the Iraqi Army and Republican Guard. Those forces had been eliminated, and there was a "friendly" Iraqi Security Force standing up in conjunction with the new Iraqi Government. There was an organizational void that fostered the formation of an insurgency. The new enemy was fragmented and difficult to locate or identify. Their goal was to win a war of attrition. If they could inflict enough casualties and damage upon us, our government might lose its will and send us all home. It was true asymmetric warfare, and it didn't feel at all like we were prepared for it.

We started receiving tasking that was primarily helping the Marine Corps get set up all over the Area of Operations (AO). One of our primary stops was a smaller airfield at Al Taqqadum, a.k.a. "TQ," where a Marine Corps CH-46 squadron and a skid squadron were setting up shop. We were just moving people and things around. Standard Assault Support Requests (ASRs) that had us "hauling ass and trash." There were no named operations or anything else exciting going on.

So far as we could tell, there wasn't any actual fighting happening anywhere, either. At our level in the squadron, the unrest was growing. There was a lot of grumbling along the lines of "Why are we even here? We aren't doing shit!" I didn't allow myself to get sucked into that way of thinking. Our job was to deploy, fight, and fly anywhere the Marine Corps told us to. We all needed to focus on that. Sitting around asking philosophical fucking questions about whether or not we should even be there would only hurt our focus. I was also confident we would figure out how to transition to a counterinsurgency fight once we settled in. As a country, that wasn't new for us. It had just been a while.

I had a few random aircraft emergencies out of the gate that weren't a big deal, but the CO commented that I needed to "watch it." Apparently, it was somehow my fault that I had a tire blow on a taxiway or a serious hydraulic leak. I was annoyed by his comment but shook it off. I hadn't done my Night Systems Instructor (NSI) check flight yet, but I was still one of the more proficient pilots who could fly nights, so I was doing a lot of those night flights right out of the gate. I had almost forgotten how damn dark it was on low light level night in Iraq. I was concerned about the degree of difficulty for our pilots. We were thin, and this was varsity flying. As a point five, we only had nineteen total pilots, and only eight of us were even Helicopter Aircraft Commanders (HACs). Two of those HACs were majors on their first combat deployment. Less than optimal.

We had a formation one day, and the CO mentioned that we should all probably be having our loved ones mail us liquor. Alcohol wasn't allowed in-country, but Marines always had a secret stash. We all just couldn't believe he mentioned it like that. It's one of those things you just don't talk about. Especially not in his position. Regardless, I had already learned my lesson the hard way on the way home from OIF. I wasn't inclined to roll the dice again.

Fifer and I were brainstorming at chow one night about

things we could do to mitigate the risk. In OIF I, we toyed around with the idea of putting a red lens on our right-position light. As a squadron, we had discussed trying it during OIF I, but we never actually did it. The standard configuration for any aircraft is a red position light on the left and a green position light on the right. This helps aviators identify which side of another aircraft they are looking at when it is dark. In Iraq, we always flew around with our overt position lights and anti-collision lights turned off to avoid being seen by anyone. Night Vision Goggles (NVGs) amplify all available light; red light is part of the spectrum that NVGs amplify best.

As a result, when we were on the ground and had our overt position lights on, the pilot in the left seat could see the ground outside really well. The pilot in the right seat could not. The green light just didn't amplify the same way. Putting a red lens on the right side would give both pilots the benefit of being able to see the ground much better. The idea was that in the landing phase, we could flip the overt position lights on to increase our chances of making a safe landing in a dusty environment. At that point, anyone in the vicinity would know we were there anyway. It wasn't like turning those overt lights on for a few seconds would give us up. Fifer and I decided that we needed to convince the CO to let us put red lenses on the right side of our aircraft. It wasn't like the Federal Aviation Administration (FAA) was in Iraq to give us a flight violation for it. We briefed the CO, and he was all about it. So we did it.

On March 18th, Al Asad was hit with the first of many mortar attacks during our stay. A few shells landed around the base theater and hospital, resulting in a few casualties. Most of us were back in the barracks when it happened, and a few minutes later, we got word that everyone was supposed to put on their flak jackets and Kevlar helmets and sit in the hallway. It reminded me of the bizarre tornado drills we used to do in elementary school while growing up in West Texas. A lot of our copilots appeared rattled, so I started making smartass jokes to try and ease the tension. I said, "This place is really about to fucking suck now." "I can't wait to see all the bullshit knee-jerk reactions that come down from this shit." It worked. After a few laughs, the lieutenants ran around the rest of the night quoting me.

The next morning the bullshit knee-jerk reactions started right on cue. We now had to wear our flak jackets and Kevlar helmets any time we were outside. We also started making sandbags to fortify all of the buildings. It all seemed a little ridiculous to me at the time. If a mortar was going to randomly land next to me, I wasn't so sure my flak jacket and Kevlar helmet would save my ass. Riding our bikes around with that stuff on seemed extra ridiculous, but it was what it was. Next came glow belts. We had to have them on any time we were outside as well. Countless jokes would be made about sergeants major losing their fucking minds over Marines who weren't wearing glow belts. We were all going to have to live with it.

A couple of days later, I was in a section that was tasked with taking some intel Marines out to photograph a few Bedouins who were out in the open desert a few miles away from the base. We took some small arms fire from them and headed back to Al Asad. The next night the Quick Reaction Force (QRF) standby launched and grabbed them. Apparently, they were the Al Qaeda operatives behind the mortar attack on the base. Welcome to fighting an insurgency.

On the evening of March 29th, I was watching a movie in my room when one of our majors came to get me. He was our Aviation Maintenance Officer (AMO) and my boss. He told me that the Operations Department was struggling and that it was coming to a head. We had an inexperienced major in there as the OPSO and the captain WTI, who had gone to the class in my place after I got in trouble for the boat incident at the end of our last deployment. They needed some help.

The Command's solution was to move me out of my billet in maintenance and back into operations to help "fix it." I didn't like their solution for obvious reasons. I had been in maintenance since returning from my first deployment to Okinawa, and I loved it. I loved working closely with our Marines, and I loved testing aircraft when I wasn't flying a regular flight. I also didn't like the idea of having to help "fix" a department being run by two officers senior to me. At the same time, I knew we needed to do something because our Operations Department was struggling, and I could help to improve it.

The next morning, I was in the squadron spaces early to complete all of the Fitness Reports (FITREPS) I now owed my former maintenance Marines. I was diligently knocking those out when another mortar attack hit. I heard the first one that hit, and it was close. I looked out the window and saw a black smoke cloud just beyond our aircraft on the flight line. It was just over 100 yards away. There were six rounds total, and one hit near a barracks building occupied by another unit, blowing the windows out of it. Once the commotion stopped, I put on my flak jacket and Kevlar helmet and sat back down at the computer to keep working on my FITREPS. A few of the maintenance Marines laughed about how only I would be that calm. At the time, I just laughed and didn't think anything of it. When it stopped, we went out to check the aircraft. Thankfully, none had taken any damage. I conceded I would just have to get used to wearing my flak and Kevlar. A lot.

A few days later, I got a care package in the mail from my parents. It contained a bunch of Texas magazines like *Texas Monthly* and *Texas Highways*. I sat on my rack and leafed through the magazines. I came across an article about the Panhandle South Plains Fair. Growing up in Lubbock, Texas, I attended that fair every year as a kid. I even went a couple of times when I was in college.

As I scanned the article and looked at the photographs, I quickly became aware that I was feeling zero emotion. It didn't bother me, but I was aware of it. That article would make me feel at least a bit nostalgic if I'd had normal emotions. Something.

Anything. But I felt nothing. That made me think about "home" and what the word meant to me at that point. Home was wherever Kerry and Tristen were. I missed being around the two of them, but I didn't feel a lot of emotion about that either. I felt a little guilty for being an absentee husband and father. But that was it. I remained very aware that I might not ever see them again. But I couldn't feel any real emotion about that, either.

It made me realize how compartmentalized I had become. In a combat zone, my total focus had to be on the mission. The job. I was taking everything else and stuffing it down so deep, I couldn't feel it anymore. Even coming to that realization didn't incite an emotional response. It just was. It was who I was becoming in my evolution as a warfighter.

I took over as the Pilot Training Officer (PTO) in operations, which primarily made me responsible for putting together appropriate aircrews to support our daily flight schedule. It was a detail-oriented billet typically filled by the Squadron WTI. Even though I hadn't gone to WTI yet, I learned how to be a PTO when I worked in operations as a schedule writer on my first deployment. It was a big job, but I was up for it because I felt confident I could execute it in a way that would be best for the squadron.

I immediately re-wrote our existing weekly plan and started to hash out the following week. I put together trackers to spread the flight time around appropriately within the different peer groups. I also wanted to be certain everyone would keep progressing toward additional qualifications. I had to have the crews arranged in a way that balanced all that while also ensuring the mission for each flight could be safely executed. We had two copilot schedule writers who initially interpreted my re-working of the plan as criticism. I had to show them it wasn't at all. It wasn't their fault. They didn't know what they didn't know. They quickly got on board with the new methodology I was employing.

As we headed into April, we settled into our routine. Our

sister squadron, HMH-466 "Wolfpack," had also arrived in-country and settled in just down the flight line. They were a full 1.0 squadron, and all the company grade officers in the two squadrons got along well. But our COs didn't like each other, so our CO started pushing us to one up the Wolfpack in every way possible. The CO set a flight hour goal for us at 300 hours for April and spent time at higher headquarters campaigning for every big tactical mission in-country. Some of the captains in the squadron started referring to him as "helium hand," because he volunteered us for everything.

A 300 hour month was an aggressive target for a point five, but it wasn't like we had a choice. Our XO Cooter had been doing a great job of keeping the CO in the box, but we all knew that nobody would be able to talk him out of this one. When the CO directed us to go hard, Cooter looked at us and said, "Get 'er done." Just like Larry the Cable Guy, which was his humorous way of saying what we already knew. We were doing it.

I was supposed to be preparing for my NSI check flight, my final prerequisite for attending the fall WTI class upon return from deployment. There were rumors I might be able to do that flight in Iraq before we went home. The NSI check flight had to be administered by a MAWTS-1 instructor, so I was doubtful they would send one out just for that. Despite that, I spent a fair amount of my downtime studying. I had always made my own "gouge" packets to study in preparation for advanced designations and qualifications. NSI would be no different. I had made my NSI gouge packet on the USS *Boxer* during our last deployment. As per usual, it was very comprehensive. If I knew everything in that packet, I would be fine.

A couple of pilots in our sister squadron at HMH-466 were also going to do NSI check flights. One day, Fifer and I were in the chow hall, and they came over to ask me if I was also doing mine. I replied that I was. One of the guys pulled out a gouge packet and told me I should make a copy of it. "This is the best gouge packet we've ever seen; you should study it, too."

I glanced at it and knew right away it was the one that I had made. I just told them, "Thanks, but I already have it." They asked for my source, and I replied, "I made it."

Fifer started laughing. No telling where they got it. I always shared my stuff with anyone who asked for it, so that gouge packet was already circulating. The learning exercise for me was making those packets. Once I made them, I had a pretty good handle on the information. From there, I reviewed it a few times until I had it all down cold. I had been doing that since flight school.

I felt ready for the actual flight, and our field grade officers agreed. I was allowed to be scheduled much like the NSIs were and often flew with copilots, even on low light level nights. With the number of hours we were flying as a point five, I was getting a lot of reps. Flying low light level out of Al Asad was a varsity event. All the trash on base was constantly being burned in a giant fire pit off the southwest corner of the airfield. At night, that orange blaze glowed brightly on our NVGs. I would typically glance in that direction as we flipped our position lights from flashing to steady, indicating that we were ready to taxi. I knew what I would contend with on the other side of that trash fire after takeoff.

We never listened to music on our night flights, but on take-offs, I could hear Metallica's "Am I Evil" in my head. The guitar riffs and James Hetfield's vocals seemed appropriate as we launched ourselves into the night. To do what we were doing, you had to at least partially believe that you were the baddest motherfucker alive. That song playing in my head got me in the right headspace.

It was almost always a left turn out off Runway 27 Right. As soon as we were beyond the trash fire in a left turn, we would immediately hit the inky blackness of the night. I sometimes got a mild case of "the leans" in that turn. As an aviator, I had to trust my training, stay on my gauges, and smoothly roll out on the correct heading at 300 feet AGL. It would often take a few seconds of being wings level before I felt like we were wings level again. I was amazed that we didn't have pilots getting vertigo and crashing right after coming off that runway. It would have been really easy for a Controlled Flight Into Terrain (CFIT) incident to happen there.

In early April, we were still doing a lot of what had become our usual general support missions, moving ass and trash around the battlespace. We often flew what we called the "Iron Triangle" over to TQ, down south to Mudaysis, then way out west to Korean Village. The little Forward Operating Base (FOB) at Al Qaim was also a frequent hit for us. They had a Forward Arming and Refueling Point (FARP) there that the skids often used. But the Marine Corps was also gearing up for the first battle of Fallujah, so most of what we were moving around was in preparation for that. It was called OPERATION VIGILANT RESOLVE, and we were all excited about it because it felt like we were finally getting on track to fight the insurgency.

They wouldn't let us fly in direct support of the fight in Fallujah, which was probably for the best. It was all Cobras and Hueys providing Close Air Support (CAS) and the CH-46E "Phrogs" executing Casualty Evacuation (CASEVAC). TQ was less than ten miles west of Fallujah, so every time we made a hit at TQ, we would listen to the action on the Direct Air Support Center (DASC) frequency. Fallujah looked like a giant strobe light at night due to all the tracers and small explosions. It reminded me of how Baghdad looked when I flew that low light level resupply to the outskirts there on our last deployment.

About a week after Fallujah kicked off, we found out that we might be able to do NSI checks in-country. A major on staff at the group had just come from being an instructor at MAWTS-1, so the MAWTS-1 CO had given permission for him to do the check flights. It made sense. That was a lot easier than sending an active instructor out to Iraq from MCAS Yuma, Arizona. There were a handful of pre-certification flights I had already done, but

I needed current dates on them. For the most part, we were able to integrate those with regular tasking.

On the night of April 14th, we were tasked with moving a couple of 16,000 pound shipping containers from TQ back to Al Asad. At that weight, it would be a pretty varsity lift, and those containers were always difficult to fly as an external load. Even when we used our dual point hook system to keep them stable, they tended to be difficult. It was like a giant barn door hanging off the bottom of the aircraft, and you could feel them pulling the aircraft around. I was flying with Cooter, which was great. It had been a while since he and I had flown together. For some reason, the load was rigged for a single point lift, so we decided to try it. It was a low light level night, and the fight over in Fallujah was going again. The night prior, an Air Force MH-53 Pave Low had been shot down, and several other aircraft had taken battle damage. It felt strange to be executing the movement of a couple of containers a stone's throw away from that fight.

I was on the controls, and we got our load off the deck with no problem. But predictably, it immediately started swinging all over the place, so we quickly made the call to set it right back down. After doing that, we talked to the Helicopter Support Team (HST) that had rigged it and asked them to re-rig it appropriately for a dual point lift. That would take a while, and our dash two was picking up an "Angel" to take back to Al Asad. "Angel" was our codeword for a deceased casualty. That made it an easy decision to fly back to Al Asad with dash two to burn down fuel while HST re-rigged the load. When we got back to TQ, the load was ready for us. I got back over the load and got hooked up again. From there, we were on our way. It was predictably still swinging a bit, but it was doable. We had to fly slowly, just under 80 knots, and the whole aircraft had a pronounced rock as the load swung in the wind beneath us.

Cooter tended to get airsick, and about halfway back to Al Asad, I noticed that he didn't respond to a question on our Inter-communication System (ICS). I looked over and saw that he had taken his helmet off and was rubbing his face. The motion from the container was making him sick. About two seconds later, our Aircraft Survivability Equipment (ASE) started kicking off our infrared (IR) decoy flares. We hadn't seen a MANPADS shot, but we had to assume it was in the air. I couldn't do much in the way of evasive actions since we were already at a low altitude with a giant container hanging off the bottom of our aircraft. But after a few seconds of excitement, we escaped unscathed.

The Arrival Airfield Control Group/ Departure Airfield Control Group (AACG/DACG) was set up at the east end of the flight line at Al Asad. We pronounced it as "Ag-Dag." The Marines there accounted for every inbound and outbound passenger and pallet of cargo. That was where we went to pick up and drop off everything, both internal and external loads. They had us drop the load off in the dirt adjacent to the taxiway, which was dusty as hell. At that point, it was 0345, and we headed to the fuel pits before calling it a night. Cooter and I laughed about that whole sequence after we shut down. It had been a wild night and one hell of a way to re-punch a couple of NSI precertification requirements.

The remainder of April was a grind. We continued to have mortar attacks on the base as well as losses of water and power. Any time one of the utilities was out for a few days was fairly miserable. Not being able to take a shower or having to sit around in the dark always affected morale. When that happened, I just reminded myself that it was still better than our living conditions at Jalibah the year prior. With Fallujah raging and all of our other tasking thrown in, we exceeded the CO's flight hour goal of 300 by 100 hours. Flying 400 hours on eight aircraft was too much, and we all knew that heading into May, we were going to feel the effects of that.

We had to take a few maintenance days at the beginning of May to let maintenance catch up. The logical way to follow a 400 hour month would have been to dial it back to about 250 hours. But the CO said hell no, we're going for 450! We all thought he had lost his mind. The CO had also made a couple of calls during the execution of the flight schedule that had left a couple of my peers feeling uneasy. They complained to our flight surgeon, who went to Cooter as the XO for help. That resulted in an All Officers Meeting (AOM) to talk about the CO as a safety risk. I honestly thought the whole thing was bullshit. The CO was aggressive, arguably too aggressive. He was also a liberty risk. But I would take that over too conservative any day of the week and twice on Sunday. It was combat, and we were all there to support the Marines on the ground. We owed it to them to be aggressive. We needed to play to win. I stayed quiet during the bitch session.

Cooter handled the whole thing like a pro. Everyone was heard then we went back to work. Get 'er done. Later a couple of my peers, who had been complaining, asked me why I didn't back them up. I told them that if they were waiting for me to get conservative and start whining about safety shit, they would probably be waiting until we died. There's a fine line between good Operational Risk Management (ORM) and just being soft. I wasn't ever going to land on the side of the latter.

It was starting to get hot, so the day flights, in particular, were brutal. There is no air conditioning in a CH-53E, and the cockpit is like a greenhouse. If it's 110 degrees outside, then it's 125 to 130 in the cockpit. When you are wrapped tightly in body armor, survival vest, and helmet, it pushes 150 to 160 degrees inside your gear. If you cook a pot roast at that temperature for 8 hours, it is done. But we did it to our bodies on repeat. All you could do was try to hydrate enough to keep up with it. Being in shape also helped a ton. I had a one hundred ounce Camelbak that I always hung on the seat next to me. On the days when we were out there for six hours or more, I would go through the entire thing. My body was just a 190 pound water filter.

On the night of May 12, 2004, I was still fresh off the wild flight with Cooter when I had another low light level adventure. I was flying with one of our most inexperienced copilots. He was barely qualified to even be on the flight. I was dash two to our CO, who was also flying with one of our copilots. It looked like a straightforward mission on paper. It was just standard ASRs that would take us down to TQ and back for a couple of runs. On the way back from the first run, the CO deviated off our route and took us by the outskirts of Ramadi. There was no reason to do that, but he tended to do it regularly. We all thought he was trolling to take fire for some reason. I was mildly annoyed by that, but I just stayed in combat cruise at about three rotors back on his left side so that he would at least be closer to the population center, which was on our right.

Once we were past Ramadi and back over the open desert, it was standard low light level. Pitch black with no horizon whatsoever. My copilot struggled to stay with the CO, and I was calmly giving him talkies to try and help him hang in there. I took the controls to demo a couple of things for him. Right when I took the controls, everything went fucking haywire.

We were cruising at 300 feet AGL when it happened. It felt like we crashed into something, but we were still flying. The CO's aircraft in front of us disappeared, we bounced violently, and our gauges also bounced all over the place. Our Vertical Speed Indicator (VSI) fluctuated wildly up and down, making it look like we were climbing and descending rapidly. My radar altimeter looked like it was bouncing between 100 and 300 feet. We were climbing and descending without any control inputs on my part, and it felt like we were on a fucking roller coaster with no track.

I realized we had run into a haboob. I had seen haboobs during the daytime, but this was my first encounter with one at night. Due to the absence of any illumination, we never saw it coming until we were in it. I could barely make out the CO's tail rotor in front of us, so I closed on him to less than one rotor. I was flying the tightest formation I had ever flown. I knew that was our only chance of staying with him.

Meanwhile, I had to keep a scan underneath my goggles on

our gauges to make sure we didn't get too damn low. I worried the CO would get disoriented and fly us both right into the deck, which could happen in a matter of seconds. I asked my copilot to keep me honest with the altitude. I could tell by the inflection in his voice that he was terrified, but he did a good job talking to me about our airspeed and altitude.

"Climbing 150 feet, 200 feet, descending, 150 feet."

Our aircrew in the back also chimed in where appropriate. It was a full crew coordination event.

Somewhere in there, the CO came up on the radio and asked, "Little sporty, you still with me?" I replied, "Yes, sir. Two is on board."

We were 20 miles from the field at Al Asad and had slowed to about 80 knots. It was going to take us about 15 minutes to get back. That 15 minutes felt like an hour. I had to work my ass off to stay with the CO, but I was able to do it. When we got closer to the field, we picked up a section instrument approach, and I flew off of him all the way down to the runway. Once the runway lights started to poke through the dirt wall we were fighting through, I knew we were good.

We made it back on deck, and the CO called over the radio that we were going to "shut down and re-assess." When we shut down, I was certain my copilot was done for the night and told the CO as much privately when we got back inside, but he wasn't having it. He wanted to let the haboob blow through, then get back out there and finish up the second run. After waiting for about an hour, we went out and turned back up, but thankfully the visibility was still too shitty to launch. The CO finally called it a night. After we shut down, my copilot looked like he'd seen a ghost. He had. He'd seen his own. The first near-death experience really fucks with some guys, and I knew he was feeling the full weight of that.

He told me, "I'm never doing that again."

I replied, "Yeah, I hope I don't have to, either."

He clarified, "No, I mean flying. I'm never fucking flying again."

I knew he was freaked out, but I didn't think he really meant what he was saying. I was wrong. He meant it. He flew another couple of times on the deployment, but he mostly just stood duty as our Operations Duty Officer (ODO). After deployment, he would ultimately submit for a transition to a ground Military Occupational Specialty (MOS).

As I realized how spooked he was, it made me think about myself. I had been sitting right next to him, living the exact same experience. The flight sucked. And yes, I knew it had been a close call that could have easily ended badly for us. But it didn't. That was the game. I hadn't lost an ounce of sleep over it. I even joked about how crazy it was with some of the other pilots in the squadron.

Was it different because I was on the controls and felt like I could get us home? Maybe not feeling that way himself made it worse for him? I wasn't sure. But the difference in our reactions couldn't have been more extreme. The experience had convinced him he never wanted to fly again. Never flying again couldn't have been further from my thought process. If I was being honest with myself, I knew I'd actually gotten a kick out of it.

It was one of the first times I remember wondering if I was fucking crazy. I knew my reaction wasn't "normal." The problem was, I didn't know what the fuck normal even was anymore.

The next day, we got final approval to knock out our NSI check flights. I was doing an initial, and one of our majors was doing a re-certification. The major at higher headquarters who had just returned from being an instructor at MAWTS-1 would be our evaluator. I just wanted to get it over with.

We found a flat spot out in the desert that we named LZ Wolf for the landings and planned to do externals on the parallel dirt runway at Al Asad that we called "27 Dirt." For about a week, we kept executing our normal tasking as a squadron while also working in a couple of dry runs for the NSI checks. Somewhere in there, we took the written exam, and I got 100% on it. Apparently, the gouge I had made was comprehensive enough. I just needed to nail the flight.

We finally executed the flights on May 19th. The dust at LZ Wolf made for a high degree of difficulty for a check flight, but it went fine. Our evaluator had been flying a lot less than we had, which helped. After a year of buildup, finally getting it done was anticlimactic.

The only thing left for me to do was to attend and graduate from WTI when we got home. Before that could happen, I needed to stay engaged and not get complacent. I always felt the beginning and the end of deployments were the most dangerous. The beginning because everything is unfamiliar. The end due to the potentially lethal combination of complacency and fatigue. I knew I needed to stay sharp.

The afternoon after the NSI check, we had an awards formation at the base theater to receive the Air Medals we earned on our first OIF deployment. The last thing I wanted to do that afternoon was participate in an awards ceremony. It just felt odd since so much time had passed since that deployment had ended. A few of us who had flown the Umm Qasr mission received Individual Action Air Medals with the Combat Distinguishing Device "V," and all of us who had flown in OIF I received Strike Flight Air Medals with numerals that represented total sorties flown in combat. We all went through the motions to get it done and then went right back to work.

During the NSI check the night before, our evaluator had asked me about our installation of the red lens cap on our right position lights. When I explained why we did it, he noted it was a great idea. That night he went to do NSI checks over at our sister squadron, HMH-466. They had copied our red light idea. The evaluator mentioned it to their CO, and he didn't know anything about it. His squadron had done it without telling him. Somehow, he had managed not to notice. Didn't he fly himself?

Regardless, he subsequently lost his mind and came to our

squadron to yell at our CO since the idea originated with us. It was a pretty hilarious scene that made for some good evening entertainment. Nothing quite like having two lieutenant colonels going at it in the passageway of the squadron spaces. Our CO loved every second of it.

A couple of days later, we got tapped to provide two aircraft for a big insert that was supposed to go into Rawah the next week as part of OPERATION RAWAH II. It would be a division of four, with two coming from our sister squadron, HMH-466. I was tapped to lead the division as part of a larger flight of 18 total aircraft. I had come out as part of our advanced party, and we were supposed to head home the third week of June. So, with less than one month to go, I was going to lead the biggest mission we had been tasked with on the deployment. It was good; I needed to stay as busy as possible.

There was a never-ending planning session for that mission. There must have been at least ten iterations of the details. It was painful. Still, I managed to get in a few flights with a couple of our copilots, trying to finish up their Helicopter Aircraft Commander (HAC) syllabus before the deployment ended.

I had been doing a lot of flying with Suit throughout the deployment, and he had been ready for a while. Some guys "get it" early on, and you know they will be players. Suit was in that group. My observation was that an average pilot starts to develop what we call "seat of the pants" somewhere around 700 hours. Until that point, you are totally dependent on what you see inside and outside the aircraft to fly it. I always considered "seat of the pants" as the point where the rest of your senses kick in, and you start being able to make control inputs based on what you "feel" before you can see it. You start to become one with the machine. Coming up on 500 hours, Suit was already getting there. Having flown a ton with him, it was cool to see. I realized early that I enjoyed teaching and instructing as much, if not more, as I enjoyed doing it myself.

We finally flew the big insert for OPERATION RAWAH II on

June 5th, 2004. I was in the lead with one of our majors as my copilot. Our squadron WTI and another major were my dash two. Dash three and four were both HMH-466 aircraft and crews. Our piece of the mission was to insert 3d Battalion 7th Marines into four blocking positions surrounding the city.

In total, there were 24 aircraft supporting the mission. We had everything from an EC-130 Compass Call, P-3 Orion, and multiple sections of AV-8B Harriers providing Imagery, Surveillance, and Reconnaissance (ISR). We had attached skid escorts for our piece of the insert and CH-46s airborne with the reserve platoon. After turning up at 0150 and knocking out radio checks, we took off and were joined by our skid escorts without incident. The CH-46s also joined on us to push to the objective area as one big package.

Shortly thereafter, things got a little rocky as both my dash two and dash three aircraft had to work through some minor issues. Both were resolved quickly, and we pressed on the route. It was a high light level night, so we could at least see. Our NVGs had plenty of lunar illumination to amplify.

As we approached the objective area, I was scanning five frequencies. There was a lot going on. Little skirmishes were breaking out around the city, and we could see some of the tracer fire when I called "IP Inbound" to let everyone know we were crossing our final checkpoint prior to the objective area and setting up to land in our respective LZs. At the Initial Point (IP), the 46s broke off to their holding area, and our flight of four CH-53Es split into two sections to hit our separate LZs. The 466 aircraft were hitting the north and east LZs. We were hitting the west and south LZs. I was pushing to the west LZ.

The major I was flying with was on the controls, and I had Fifer in the back. He and I had joked that the major would pass me the controls on short final, and he did. It was really dusty, but I had reference, so I took the controls and got us on the deck. He claimed that the calls from the crew chief opposite Fifer had caused him to lose reference. Whatever. I did a standard instrument takeoff due to the dust, but it worked fine, and we got the hell out of there. We re-joined our flight once clear of the objective area and pushed back to Al Asad without incident.

The big mission had gone off without a hitch. It was good for the squadron to fly at least one big named operation before wrapping up the deployment. After the slow start, the mission went a long way toward making a lot of our Marines feel like the return trip had been at least somewhat worth it. I spent the last couple of weeks flying general support missions with copilots and going over the things we would need to execute as the Advanced Party on our return home.

Fifer and I would depart with the Advanced Party just like we had on the way out. Seven months had passed since he had picked me up at my house to head to Okinawa in November. We had managed to cram a lot of shit into those seven months.

On the night of June 22, 2004, our Advanced Party took buses to the AACG/DACG to catch a KC-130 flight down to Ali Al Salem in Kuwait. We had a little awards formation there, and I was awarded a Navy and Marine Corps Achievement Medal for my performance on the deployment. It was my first personal award other than the Air Medals we had received a few weeks prior. It was a nice gesture from the command. But I was just ready to get the hell out of there. As we boarded the KC-130, I didn't even bother to look back over my shoulder at the flight line. When I got home, I would go to the WTI class as a student and officially take over as the squadron WTI. That meant I was going to deploy back here one more time. There was no need to look back at something I knew I would see again.

The return trip was long. We took off from Al Asad just after midnight. Then it was a bus ride from Ali Al Salem to Camp Victory. We dragged our bags into transient tents and hung out on cots, waiting for the chow hall to open for breakfast. We sat around at Camp Victory for about thirty-six hours, then took buses to Camp Doha. At Doha we received customs briefs and had to dump our bags out for customs to go through to make sure that none of us were smuggling rounds or any other contraband out of the country. That was always a good time. Then we re-packed our gear and took another bus ride to Kuwait City International Airport. Just after midnight on June 24th, we finally boarded our flight home. Forty-eight hours had passed since we departed Al Asad.

There was too much downtime in that process for me. The deployment had been a bit of a blur. Iraq round two by way of the Echo Chamber in Okinawa. It had all unfolded in such a way that I just did it without thinking about it too much. It was the first time since leaving home that I spent any time thinking about it. I had just been doing it.

Moving back to operations had given me an added sense of responsibility. I missed being in maintenance because I loved leading and working with the Marines. But jumping into my operations role had given me the responsibility to smartly build crews that could execute. And most importantly, to live to fight another day. I had developed a strong sense of personal accountability, and I pushed the copilots hard to do the same. I wanted them to understand the responsibility we accepted every time we strapped into the machine.

Every Marine who rode in the back depended on us to safely deliver them to their destination. I believed we had to own that responsibility entirely. As individuals, we could draw strength from wherever we deem appropriate. But it always came down to the fact that it was us with the controls in our hands. Our decisions and actions dictated the fates of ourselves and everyone else in our aircraft.

As I thought about it, I realized how much I had grown and evolved as an aviator over the course of those two deployments. When I flew that initial insert into Umm Qasr, I was a 750-hour boot Division Leader. I was now cruising past 1200 hours as an NSI headed to WTI. Over two combat deployments I'd started to evolve into the aviator I had hoped to become when I first checked into the squadron. I was scared when Browner and I took off for that Umm Qasr insert the year prior. On this deployment, I hadn't been scared at all. The crazy external flight with Cooter, punching into the haboob low light level with the CO, and flying the big Rawah insert hadn't phased me in the least. If I was being honest with myself, I liked it. Those flights had been a rush. Combat had officially become my drug of choice. And I still wanted more.

The flight home from Kuwait City was by way of Rhein-Main Air Force Base on the outskirts of Frankfurt, Germany, and then on to Bangor, Maine. Bangor, known for having a nice contingent of people at the airport to welcome us, was a great experience. From there, we flew to March Air Force Base just outside of Riverside, California. By then, March was a staging point for west coast units going to and from Iraq. Once off the aircraft at March, we grabbed our gear and loaded onto the waiting buses for the ride back down to Miramar. We had been traveling for just over 72 hours when we finally got home. It didn't matter at that point. We were home.

13

REALITY CHECK

MY HOMECOMING with our Advanced Party was a lot more low-key than the previous two. A bus ride from March Air Force Base down to Miramar was anticlimactic compared to flying right into Miramar and having a few hundred people waiting for us waving flags and signs on the flight line. The bus dropped us off at the armory on base so that we could immediately turn in our weapons, and our families were all waiting there on the other side of the parking lot. It was a small group, so finding Kerry and Tristen was easy after turning in my weapon. It was great to see them both, and I was glad to be home.

In those first few days home, I tended to rearrange the items in the refrigerator, which drove Kerry crazy. We were so happy to see each other, it didn't result in much more than a playful, "You don't need to do that; it was fine!" I knew little things like that could imply that something wasn't being done "right" while I was away, so I had to pick my spots.

Living together again was always an adjustment that felt like a mix between a honeymoon and re-establishing roles and responsibilities. Tristen was almost two, and I enjoyed our time together. It felt good to be a husband and a dad again. We had family that planned to visit during the coming month for Tristen's birthday. That would bring some natural stress, but I was happy I didn't have to deal with that right out of the gate. It was just the three of us for a little while.

I also knew this was another short-term stop that would be filled with me being gone a lot. We knew I would deploy again the following spring. I would have approximately nine months at home. But a significant portion of those nine months would be filled with me being gone for six weeks at WTI, three weeks for pre-deployment training, and a few other random training detachments. By the time it was all said and done, I knew I was looking at about four or five months of really being home. And that time was going to be broken up quite a bit. Kerry always said, "Gone is gone." It didn't matter if I was in Okinawa, Iraq, or just over the hill in Yuma, Arizona, for a training detachment. She was right. Gone is gone.

Back at the squadron, Fifer and I again found ourselves turning over aircraft. With both our squadron, HMH-465, and our sister squadron, HMH-466, deployed simultaneously, there was a surplus of aircraft on the flight line that HMH-462 and HMH-361 had been attempting to maintain. HMH-466 was still in Iraq, and HMH-361 would deploy in a couple of months to take over for them. We would then replace HMH-361. The go-forward plan was to indefinitely position a full CH-53E squadron in Iraq.

We had only been there, in addition to the full squadron from HMH-466, as a point five, because the Marine Corps wanted additional heavy lift in Iraq to get everything set up for this next phase of the war. Fifer and I busied ourselves accepting aircraft and getting everything ready for the remainder of our main body point five and our 31st MEU detachment, which we'd left in Okinawa. Our 11th MEU detachment had deployed later than we had, so we wouldn't have them back for another few months. At that time, they were moving forward into Al Asad, Iraq, off the ship to operate in-country for the next few months. Part of me wished I could have just stayed there and joined them.

Once those two groups returned, we occupied ourselves with the usual post-deployment routine. Marines checked out of the squadron, and new Marines checked in. It was saying goodbye to the seniors and welcoming the freshmen all over again. The toughest departure for me was Fifer. He was getting orders and moving on. He had been with me for all three deployments as a mentor, my favorite crew chief, and a great friend. I would miss him.

I had already completed three deployments, but since I was going to WTI, I would be sticking around for a fourth deployment. Before the war broke out, most company grade aviators spent four years in a squadron and completed two deployments on their first fleet tour. I was going to spend almost six years in the squadron and complete four deployments. My timing was either great or terrible, depending on your perspective. My buddy Dave "Apollo" Payne was the only other pilot in my peer group extending to deploy again. The rest of our peers were checking out and moving on to their B billets, getting out of the fight for at least a little while.

When our main body and 31st MEU detachments returned to Miramar in July, I was only a couple of months away from leaving for WTI. I was already in operations as the Pilot Training Officer (PTO), so I was doing a portion of the WTI job before I went to the school. I was busy. I was at the squadron ten to twelve hours a day, working on our operations training plan and flying. When I was home in the evenings, I spent most of my time studying to make sure I was ready for the WTI course.

I tried to make sure I spent time with Tristen every day. I took study breaks to play with her on the floor in the living room before and after dinner. When I had night flights, I made time for that in the mornings. Kerry and I tried to spend time together in the evenings, but due to my flying and study schedule, we mostly hung out on Friday and Saturday nights. We were there together and felt close, but our individual lives still felt separate. That feeling of being a transient visitor in my own house crept back in. Kerry and I made an effort to stay connected, but it was hard. We both knew I would be in and out until I left for deployment the following spring. We also knew our next real chance to return to something resembling normal wouldn't be until that next deployment ended. We tried to make the most of the time. Most days felt good. We talked, we laughed, and we had moments when we were able to stop thinking about what was in front of us and just enjoy being together again. Kerry and I held each other close every night. Still, a part of me longed to get back to the fight in Iraq.

Our 11th MEU CH-53E detachment was attached to HMM-166 Reinforced (REIN), the Aviation Combat Element (ACE) for the MEU. Two of my best CH-46E friends, Dave Wright and Kurt Hendrix, were also part of that squadron. By that point, they were established in-country and primarily operated out of Al Asad and a couple of other smaller Forward Operating Bases (FOBs) in Iraq.

On August 3, 2004, I got a reality check. I was at the squadron working in Ops when I received a call from Kerry. She told me that Hendrix's wife had just called her and told her that a Marine Corps Casualty Assistance Calls Officer (CACO) was at her house and told her that Hendrix had been killed in Iraq. She was really upset, and I was stunned.

I ran out of the squadron, jumped into my truck, and raced down the street to the Marine Aircraft Group 16 (MAG-16) headquarters building to see what I could find out. I got out of my truck and was walking into the building when I saw Cooter walking out.

He said, "Hey, I'm sorry; I know he was one of your good friends."

Cooter told me the initial notification hadn't gone well and that they might need my assistance. I was only minutes into processing at that point. I just told him I would do anything I could to help.

I proceeded into the building and got the brief. Hendrix's

wife was understandably devastated. I was asked to help as an unofficial liaison between her and the designated CACO. I immediately agreed. I drove home to change into civilian clothes before going to their house. I didn't want to show up in a uniform. I needed to be a friend, not a Marine.

When I got home, Kerry was extremely upset. When we were in flight school, Hendrix sat with Kerry in the kitchen, and they shared intellectual conversations about politics and Walt Whitman while the rest of us drank too much and acted like idiots. After he married, we spent a fair amount of time hanging out with him and his family. We'd even had our first kids at roughly the same time.

I had already lost some friends, but this was the loss of a close friend. It hurt. A lot. But this wasn't about me. I needed to be the best version of myself for his family. I let Kerry know what I was doing as I changed clothes. I then kissed her goodbye and went to his house to start several of the toughest days I would ever experience.

After returning home that night, Dalton came over and sat with Kerry and me at the kitchen table. We talked about how stunned we felt, and how much it hurt. We all knew the dangers of our lifestyle. Now, it was real. I had been fortunate to deploy to combat twice and not have our squadron lose a single Marine. But now that I had lost a close friend, anything resembling a streak of good fortune seemed to be over. The shit was real. And all three of us sitting at the kitchen table that night struggled to come to terms with the gravity of that reality.

A few days later, Dalton and I spoke at the memorial service at Miramar. Then we flew to his hometown to speak at the actual funeral. Dalton, Hendrix, and I had all been in the same platoon at TBS, so I reached out to our old Platoon Commander, Captain Randy Soriano. He also came to the funeral, despite being out of the Marine Corps and practicing law at that point. It meant a lot to us that he came. Dalton and I also spoke at the funeral. Afterward, we attended a reception at Hendrix's parent's house.

A local organization had erected a full flagpole in their front yard. We all went out front to raise his flag when a group of bagpipers came marching up the road playing. I remember standing in my dress blues on the outskirts of Hendrix's front yard, crying like a little kid while they played. It hurt so fucking much. I knew I never wanted to feel that level of pain ever again.

A few days later, on August 11, 2004, we got word that one of the CH-53Es from our MEU detachment with that squadron had caught fire and gone down. The pilots were injured but had lived. The crew chiefs had not been as fortunate. That one hit our entire squadron hard. I had a lot of Marines who were close with the aircrew that hadn't made it. They were all experiencing the same thing I had experienced eight days prior. Suddenly, death felt like it was everywhere.

I didn't have time to process any of that. I was less than a month away from checking into MAWTS-1 to go through the WTI course. I had been working towards that goal for years. I compartmentalized my emotions and focused on my final preparations to attend WTI. I had come too far and gone through too much not to make the most of my opportunity to finally become a WTI. I was also very aware that my squadron needed me to do this. The squadron provided aircraft and Marines to support the course so I could attend. They were banking on getting the best version of me back for this next deployment. I needed to deliver.

WTI was a welcome distraction. It is an intense three weeks of academics followed by three weeks of flying. It would leave me no time for idle thoughts. The instructors had all been hand selected to be there. The entire staff was considered "the best of the best." WTI is the Marine Corps version of "Top Gun," only the Marine Corps brings all type model series aircraft to WTI. Fixed wing, rotary wing, and all other elements of the Marine Air Ground Task Force (MAGTF) were present at the course. The intent was that the students come out of the course as true experts in planning and executing Aviation Combat Element (ACE) operations as part of the MAGTF. Students were also expected to be the Pilot Training Officers (PTOs) in their respective squadrons, where they would build and execute the squadron training plan.

It was a unique time to attend WTI as a student. The instructors were all senior to us, and most of them had left the fleet to become MAWTS-1 instructors before the war started. So my fellow students and I came to the class with more combat experience than the instructors. They still had more flight time and more expertise. But we all knew the students had logged a lot more "red time" in our logbooks than they had. We also knew that we were going right back to our squadrons to deploy to combat again. It made for an interesting dynamic.

My roommate for the course was a peer from my sister squadron, HMH-462. Captain Eric "TULSA" Purcell and I were a good match. TULSA was an acronym for "The Ugly Loud Stinky American." He was a big, tall guy with a booming voice. Great guy. We both worked hard in the building and studied hard in every minute of our off time. There was no real downtime. It would be a six-week sprint to the finish.

It was a challenging course, but I got everything I needed out of the experience. I completed my last two flight leadership designations as an Assault Flight Leader (AFL) and Air Mission Commander (AMC). I also finally earned the Weapons and Tactics Instructor (WTI) qualification. I had finally achieved the goal I had set for myself when I first checked into the squadron four years earlier. Now it was time to return home and put it to work.

Before going home, there was an actual graduation dinner with a guest speaker. Kerry and Tristen had come to visit me for a weekend earlier in the course, so we decided that she wouldn't come back out again for graduation. Tristen couldn't sit through the ceremony, and we didn't have any childcare options in Yuma.

Graduating from WTI had been a significant accomplishment for me that was four years in the making. The idea of celebrating without Kerry was difficult but I understood, although it added to my feeling that we were living separate lives.

At graduation, we finally let off some steam and headed out for a few beers. It had been a long six weeks. The instructors finally broke character and hung out with us. It was nice to see that side of them. A couple of them mentioned I might be a good fit to come back as an instructor after my next deployment. Flattering, to be sure, but I didn't know what I wanted to do after my next deployment. It was difficult to even think that far ahead. The next deployment loomed, and I would carry the most responsibility I had ever experienced. I was focused solely on that deployment, but I told them I would stay in touch and think about it.

When I got home, the calendar was flipping to November, and we were only three months away from sending the Advanced Party for our deployment to Iraq. We would be going as a full 1.0 squadron this time, so we didn't have any MEU detachments to CHOP. We would all deploy together.

A lot happened in the six weeks that I was at WTI. On our last deployment to Iraq, our CO had openly encouraged the whole squadron to have liquor mailed out to us and it had caught up to him. There had been an incident in the barracks during the deployment that turned into a sexual assault allegation. The fact that several Marines had been drinking came out in the investigation.

While I was at WTI, our CO had ultimately been relieved. The squadron didn't feel good about that. At all. He wasn't super popular, but no squadron feels good about having their commander relieved. When they relieved him a senior officer from 3rd MAW had come down and had a squadron formation where he proceeded to tell the entire unit that the behavior of the squadron had been a disgrace. It wasn't well received. I was glad to have missed that.

Our new CO, still inbound based on the timeline originally set for the planned Change of Command, was coming from the

Pentagon. None of us knew him. We would be without a CO for a few weeks while awaiting his arrival. In the meantime, we had what we needed to continue training and prepare for the deployment. We knew what needed to be done, and that was our focus, with or without a CO.

The next few weeks were a flurry of activity. Our 11th MEU detachment returned home. Our Detachment Officer in Charge (OIC) was flying the aircraft that went down, resulting in the two aircrew fatalities, so Krusty had taken over as the Detachment OIC for the remainder of the deployment. Krusty had just pinned on major's oak leaves, so that worked out. He already planned to transition out of the Marine Corps right away. Focker was also immediately checking out to do a B Billet that would also set him up to leave the Marine Corps. I had reached the point where my friends were actively working on departing the service.

Our new CO also checked in. We could tell right away that he was going to be challenging. He was coming to us from a billet at the Pentagon, but he had previously been in HMH-466 when he was a major. He had been out of the game for a while and hadn't been part of the war thus far. He had a lot of "good ideas" and talked a lot about some flying he had done in Somalia several years prior. But we needed to get him dialed in for the modern fight. And quickly. He needed to refresh on the entire flight syllabus, including a refresher NSI check flight with a MAWTS-1 Instructor. We would have to cram several training flights in for him on top of the training everyone else in the squadron needed.

There was a shortage of pilots to meet all the deployment requirements, so higher headquarters had resorted to playing a never-ending shell game of cross-decking pilots from one squadron to another to ensure that the next squadron scheduled to leave had enough pilots to deploy. We had already received two senior captains who had come to us after being in the CH-53D "Delta" squadrons out in Hawaii. Now we were getting another three senior captains from our sister squadron at HMH-466. They had been next door to us the last time we were in Iraq, but since we were now ahead of them in the rotation, they were coming over to deploy with us. They were an easy fit, though. We knew them, and they knew us. And since they already had some qualifications and experience, they didn't need much in the way of training. They were just instant help in the "middle" of our schedule. They could lead sections during the day and do Functional Check Flights (FCFs) on aircraft. I was thankful for that.

At the squadron, I was settling into the WTI role. I understood the responsibility and had wanted that role since the day I checked in. But I was also feeling the weight of the responsibility. It was on me to make sure we got everyone as prepared as possible for this deployment. Then, once we were in-country, I would play a significant role in every mission we executed.

At that point, the squadron felt more comfortable to me than home. At the squadron, things were simple. Work, fly, repeat. There was a ton to do, but I was so immersed in it that I didn't have much time to think about anything. The sense of urgency, risk management, and sometimes chaos were all welcome. It demanded my attention in a way that I didn't have the bandwidth to think about anything else. When I was at home, things slowed down. I had time to think. Definitely not a good thing for me at that point.

I sensed that I had something resembling an addiction to combat flying. I wanted to return to Iraq and get back in the air. I couldn't really explain why; I just did. Combat flying was my drug, and I wanted more. At the same time, I thought now about my own mortality in a real way for the first time. I'd had some close calls, and I was very aware of how close I had come to dying on a few occasions. Umm Qasr, fighting through haboobs with little to no visibility, and the random indirect fire attacks were all things I had escaped thus far.

It wasn't until Hendrix died that the thought of possibly

dying myself became real to me. Our 11th MEU aircraft going down and killing our crew chiefs further hammered that point home. I knew my chosen profession might catch up to me, too. I mentally wrestled with all of that. Strangely, I was okay with the thought of dying for myself. I understood, accepting that risk was just part of the deal. Perhaps dying was just the ultimate tradeoff for being able to experience the highs of being a combat aviator. But that came with many strings attached.

Hendrix dying also forced me to see what it does to the families in an up close and personal way. It also left me with newfound guilt about those thoughts in relation to Kerry and Tristen. Although I accepted the risk of possibly dying, I felt guilty about them having to navigate the reality of my choices. That felt heavy. But it wasn't something I could talk about or show in any way. I had to make them feel like there was no way that would ever happen to me. I was always going to come home. They needed to believe that. If I let Kerry know that I was at all thinking otherwise, it would only make it harder for her. I couldn't do that. At the same time, I was trying to find ways to cope with everything that was weighing so heavily on me. The invisible wounds slowly stacked up inside of me. And inside of us. They would have to be dealt with eventually.

Drinking had become my coping mechanism. I had been up for a good time, drinking with my friends since my college days. This was different, though. I was self-medicating, primarily on Friday and Saturday nights when I slowed down and sat on the couch. I couldn't just enjoy watching a game, a movie, or a show. I struggled to relax and be in the moment. I had always been a little bit that way, but this was different.

Every time I tried to relax, my brain raced at a thousand miles per hour. I struggled to fall asleep, and I started randomly waking up in the middle of the night. Work dominated my thoughts. It was always on my mind. I constantly thought about the upcoming deployment, the responsibilities, the mission, my dead friends, and my ability to maintain the edge I needed to survive and thrive in that environment.

I felt like there was a balloon inside of me that was always slowly filling with air. I didn't know exactly what that air was composed of, but I felt it steadily building up, a combination of stress, anxiety, and a constant hypervigilant feeling that I needed to be one step ahead of whatever near-death experience awaited me. Sometimes, I found ways to let some air out of that balloon before it popped. Drinking was my go-to. It temporarily let the air out of the balloon and calmed my thought process. It also allowed me to sleep.

That wasn't helping an already strained situation at home. Kerry saw my drinking as my way of checking out and avoiding everything. She wasn't wrong. She wasn't happy about it and didn't hesitate to say so. It became an additional source of conflict. But my gut instinct was that everything I was doing at that point was all tied together.

My life was like coexisting on two different planets. On one planet, I fought a war. On the other, I was a 30-year-old guy with a wife and a little girl in the suburbs of San Diego. When I was at home, I was supposed to be a different guy. Impossible. I lived in a combat mindset. Once I reached that place, I needed to stay there. It wasn't a switch I could flip when I walked out of the gate and drove home. Even if the collateral damage in my personal life was starting to pile up. The risk was too great. The personal fallout was better than the alternative, which was death. I believed that doubling down on being me was my best chance to keep myself and everyone else around me alive.

In the aircraft, I needed to be fearless and intuitive and without hesitation. Any hesitation could be fatal. When any bit of doubt or fear crept in, it had to be pushed out or squashed immediately. That led to the same mindset in my personal life. If I started to try and reel myself in at home, I was concerned that would result in me hesitating and second-guessing myself. And if I went down that road, it would carry over to the aircraft. I couldn't let that happen. Every second counts when you must be a half-second faster than death. I was living off instinct without hesitation. Just do.

I wasn't alone in what I was doing. There were a lot of us in the squadron navigating the same things in a similar fashion. Everyone pushed the envelope in their downtime. Mostly with drinking. It was the one legal outlet we all had available to us. In the military, there is a long list of potential vices that will end your career. In comparison to those, drinking was totally fine. To a degree, it was even encouraged, especially in a squadron. For the single guys, it was a little different. They could go tear it up in Pacific Beach on the weekends, and nobody cared. But the guys like me going home to a family in the suburbs were trying to do the same thing in our living rooms. It wasn't working out well. It was a bizarre form of purgatory, and we failed to navigate it well.

In early December, our squadron went to exercise Desert Talon 1-05 to complete our pre-deployment training. The year prior, the Marine Corps had tasked MAWTS-1 with providing pre-deployment training for all aviation units going to Iraq. This was going to be our first time executing that since it started. I had just graduated from WTI a few weeks earlier, so coming back with my squadron was a bit of an audition for how I was executing as the Squadron WTI.

It was almost three weeks of concentrated training that we needed. The proximity to the Yuma Range complex made it efficient to cram a ton of training into our flights for multiple pilots. It was exactly what we needed, and I was glad we did it. We returned to Miramar on December 18, 2004, and started our holiday leave blocks.

My in-laws came to visit for the holidays. That wasn't an easy transition for me. Trying to visit and talk about "normal" things proved to be difficult for me at that point. I focused on staying busy, helping with things around the house. Cooking and prepping for all things Christmas helped fill the time. My in-laws asked me what I thought about President Bush and the war. The truth was that I had no opinion on politics. It didn't matter. I also knew that line of thinking could be dangerous. My job was to fly and fight. And the primary reason I was doing it was for the other Marines around me.

It was good to get back to the squadron after the holidays and settle back into deployment prep. We were getting close to deploying, but we were still four pilots short of the number we needed to deploy. Someone at higher headquarters decided we couldn't pull four more pilots from any of the sister squadrons on the west coast. They decided to send them to us from one of the CH-53E squadrons on the east coast, instead. Marines on the two coasts were different and prided themselves on such. So culturally, we knew it might be challenging to absorb some east coast pilots into the squadron. It was awkward when they first showed up, but we all made a genuine effort to be welcoming and make it work.

On January 26, 2005, we got another sobering reminder about the risk of flying in Iraq from our sister squadron HMH-361. They were operating in Iraq but getting short while waiting for us to show up and take over for them. Their CO had been our OPSO and my boss on my first deployment with HMH-465. One of their pilots, Chris "Ahab" Alaniz, was a peer who was originally in our squadron for my first deployment to Okinawa. He was also one of only two other Marine Corps aviators I knew who had gone to college at my alma mater, Texas Tech. After our first deployment, Alaniz had cross-decked over to HMH-361. That night he was flying dash two in an HMH-361 section, making a run out to Korean Village. They had a total of 31 personnel on board that aircraft between the aircrew and the Marines that they were transporting.

It was a low light level night, with poor visibility, and "Tiger 60" in the dash two position had trouble maintaining visual reference on dash one. The situation was similar to the haboob I had fought through at night a few months prior. In this case, they didn't make it. Tiger 60 ultimately flew their aircraft into the ground, killing everyone on board. It was every CH-53 aircrew's nightmare. A Controlled Flight Into Terrain (CFIT) mishap.

Every one of us who had flown those night flights in Iraq knew how easily that could happen. The combination of it being one of our former pilots and the squadron we were about to relieve in-country ensured that we all felt it. A heavy loss, it put an exclamation point on what felt like a bad streak for me. Our younger pilots immediately started to show signs of trepidation about the deployment. The loss weighed heavily on our entire squadron.

As that was happening, I noticed something different internally. I felt empathy for the families left behind, and I felt empathy for the hundreds of Marines who mourned the loss. But my own grief response seemed to be gone. I had felt overwhelmed by grief when Hendrix died, but that didn't happen this time. I couldn't feel the pain. I was numb to it.

As a final bonding exercise in early February, we had our first Kangaroo court in a couple of years. At a Kangaroo court, any aviator in the squadron can "charge" another pilot with a "heinous crime" and recommend an appropriate callsign for the "guilty bastard." My buddy Apollo was the judge, and I was the prosecutor. In the events that unfolded, I was charged multiple times for the incident where I got caught drinking on the boat. I came out of that with the callsign "Whiskey." And it would be my callsign for the remainder of my time in the Marine Corps. At least I got a cool callsign!

But that wasn't the main event of the evening. The event was close to wrapping up when someone charged one of the new east coast pilots with something and our CO came to his defense. Somewhere in the course of a lot of back and forth, I told the CO that he was "fucking crazy." When I did, the room fell immediately silent, and he looked at me like he was going to kill me. I knew my comment was over the line, and I knew I would pay for it.

The majors quickly broke up the Kangaroo Court, and that was the end of the night. The rest of the captains and I ducked out the back of the Miramar Officers' Club to regroup and figure out how to get home. None of us were in any condition to drive. Kerry picked me up, and she was none too pleased about it. It was a fair reaction.

The next morning, I got a call from one of our majors, who was the OPSO, and my boss. After chewing my ass, he told me to call the CO and to apologize, which I did. When I called the CO, he smacked me around a bit, but he was super cool about it. He could have hammered me, but he didn't. The way he handled it gave me a shot of motivation that I welcomed going into the deployment. It reaffirmed my determination to give him and the squadron the best version of myself.

In the wake of the HMH-361 mishap, I knew I still had to keep pushing everyone to finish up the last of our pre-deployment training flights and stay focused. That was more important than it had ever been. We could not allow ourselves to become timid in any way. Our last month at home was focused on completing the last training flights and taking a little pre-deployment leave. At home, we officially reached the hard part. The last few weeks prior to deployment were always rough, but losing Hendrix and Alaniz had added a whole new layer to the reality of the situation for us.

I just wanted to leave and get on with it. Sitting around thinking about it was driving both Kerry and I crazy. It was time to go. Thoughts about my own mortality had crept back in. I remained strangely okay with it for myself, but my guilt about leaving Kerry and Tristen behind continued to escalate. Having to be there in the house with them and think about what their lives would be like if I were dead was getting to me. I felt a lot of guilt for something that hadn't even happened.

I jokingly said, "The Marine Corps is my abusive boyfriend that I can't bring myself to leave." There was a lot of truth in that statement. And I knew if I kept going, it might actually kill me, but there was nothing in the world I wanted to do more than execute that deployment. I knew how big it was for the squadron, and I was the squadron WTI. It was time for me to live up to the legacy left by great WTIs like Spooner. Until we completed the deployment, I wouldn't be capable of thinking about much else.

14

ROUND THREE

WE FINALLY LEFT for deployment on March 12, 2005. It had only been nine months since returning from the previous deployment, but it had been a very full nine months. As had become my custom, I said goodbye to Kerry and Tristen at home. One of our neighbors gave me a ride to the squadron. Saying goodbye hadn't gotten any easier, but I knew our only chance at "normal" couldn't start until the deployment was over. I was ready to get on with it and get it done.

My first two deployments to Iraq felt big, but this one felt monumental. Since our squadron had left Iraq the last time, the war had fully transitioned to a highly kinetic counterinsurgency fight. A lot was going on in Iraq, and we were going to drop right into the middle of it. We heard from our advanced party that, in the wake of the HMH-361 mishap, higher headquarters had temporarily stopped giving them night tasking. For the time being, that made it more difficult for the Marine Corps to execute the plan as a whole. They also let us know that there was an appetite to get us more involved in the named operations that were going on. I fully expected a busy deployment.

The trip itself felt routine to me at that point. On the first leg to Germany, I watched the movie *Friday Night Lights* again. That movie always reminded me of growing up as the son of a high school football coach in West Texas. It reminded me again of how far I had come. I was sitting on this flight with approximately three hundred squadron mates, all wearing desert utilities and carrying guns. I would have to be at my best for the next seven months to make sure we would all make the return trip.

The next leg took us to Kuwait City International Airport, where we grabbed our gear and loaded up on buses to Camp Victory, Kuwait. We arrived at Camp Victory just prior to midnight on March 13th. The officer helping us get settled in our transient tents in Camp Victory looked familiar, and I realized he had been in the rack next to mine at OCS. I said hello and asked how it was going. He said, "Aside from herding cats in Kuwait, it's going great."

He looked miserable. I did not envy him.

The following afternoon we made our final movement to Ali Al Salem Air Base, where we were flown on KC-130s to Al Asad. Unsurprisingly, the place looked the same. It was like we had never left. We were getting settled into our transient tents on Al Asad late that afternoon when our Intelligence lieutenant provided some comic relief. He couldn't remember the combination for the lock on one of his seabags. After a temper tantrum that included several failed attempts to break the lock open with a spastic flurry of karate kicks, someone finally found him some bolt cutters and just cut the lock off. We all laughed at him for hours over that.

The next morning, we went through our in-briefs. The war now had neat naming conventions that we all got a chuckle out of. Our first deployment to Iraq had just been "OIF." The second was "OIF II." Now we called our current deployment "OIF 04-06." Whatever that meant.

During the in-briefs, one of the officers briefing us talked about how we weren't allowed to have alcohol in-country and mentioned our last deployment as an example. He didn't realize he was talking about our unit or that our CO had ultimately been relieved. His comments resulted in several of our Marines coming out of those briefs extremely annoyed.

Turning over with HMH-361 was eerie. I had never seen a squadron look like they looked. As a group, they appeared somber and like they couldn't wait to get the fuck out of there. They had paused flying at night after the mishap, and their CO, who had been our OPSO on my first deployment, had also been sent home. Their new CO had joined them in-country. Highly respected and a great guy, he was the sole beam of positivity in their squadron spaces. It was hard to interact with them. Their presence was a constant reminder of how quickly you can go from feeling like you are winning to feeling like all has been lost in a combat environment.

Just like our previous deployment, our higher headquarters was MAG-26 from the east coast. My primary contact in MAG Operations was the Future Operations Officer (FOPSO) Major Doug "Bullwinkle" Glasgow. He was a former MAWTS-1 Instructor and CH-53E pilot on the short list of majors I really trusted, so I was happy to have him there.

We finished up the turnover with HMH-361 and assumed the mission a few days later. It was nice to take over the squadron spaces, as well as move out of the transient tents and back into our barracks. We were in the same spaces and barracks we had been in the previous year. Everything felt familiar.

The base was essentially the same, with the exception of adding something called "Green Beans Coffee." We had gotten smarter about life on Al Asad, so several of us ordered mountain bikes before the deployment and mailed them to ourselves. They arrived right on time, and after a quick bike assembly party, we again had our own means of transportation around the base.

Initially, we also had the CH-53E detachment from the 15th MEU hanging around in our spaces. They were from our sister squadron HMH-462, and my buddy Chris Dalton was their WTI. It was great to have Dalton around, but we weren't at all integrated with them. Their tasking was coming via the MEU and was separate from ours. They didn't have anywhere else to hang out, so they were in our spaces with us. Their Detachment Officer in Charge (OIC) was a character, but outside of that, we got along well with them, so having them around was fine.

Right out of the gate, MAG-26 started handing us night tasking again. I was thankful for that. Our young guys were spooked about flying at night in the wake of the HMH-361 mishap, but the best cure for that was to rip the band-aid off and start doing it. We needed to get everyone out there and remind ourselves that flying at night wasn't a big deal. Risk was everywhere; darkness was just a slightly higher degree of difficulty. There was nothing sane about strapping into a CH-53E and flying around in a combat environment. It was a school bus with a rotor on top of it and a juicy target for the enemy. The darkness provided additional safety against the threat, so flying at night was well worth the tradeoff.

We had our operations down to a science at that point. Instead of having individual pilots randomly flipping back and forth between a day and a night schedule, we had gone to a highly organized "swing schedule" that smartly rotated pilots with the right qualifications between a day shift and a night shift. That allowed us to ensure we always had the right qualifications on each shift to cover any tasking that came up. We also took billets into account so that we also had appropriate supervision in each department twenty-four hours per day.

Apollo and Suit were my primary peers in Operations, and between the three of us, we handled the heavy lifting for the department. I was in charge of our swing schedule and building the weekly schedule that assigned all the crews for the daily flight schedule. Consistently putting crews together that would be capable of the type of tasking they would receive was critical, so I always put a lot of thought into it. That had to be balanced with keeping flight time relatively even amongst the peer groups and simultaneously completing training needed in conjunction with actual tasking. There was a lot to it, but I enjoyed the responsibility of putting that puzzle together. That was my responsibility as the Squadron WTI, and I embraced the opportunity to finally do the job in an official capacity.

Before the deployment, we started working on a new tactical mission profile that the Marine Corps called "Snap Vehicle Checkpoint" (VCP). The basic premise was that we would insert Marines onto main highways to set up roadblocks and search vehicles. The intent was to ensure Al Qaeda learned that those searches would happen randomly.

Our first tactical missions of the deployment were all Snap VCP and leaflet drops, warning locals in places like Haditha that operations to eliminate Al Qaeda were imminent. Leading up to the deployment, I had prepared our squadron to execute the Snap VCP mission. I personally flew the first one we did to validate the concept. Despite being organized, and well executed, it still felt a little bit like something we drew up in the dirt. It was dynamic and fun to execute. It would be a nice change of pace mission for us to fly throughout the deployment.

About a week into our taking the mission, Apollo was leading our Quick Reaction Force (QRF) standby section one night and was tasked to take a group of special operators to chase down a high-level Al Qaeda operative near the town of Husaybah on the Syrian border. The special operators captured the target at a truck stop, and things went full ridiculous. The Battle Captain recalled Apollo's section, because they were coming up on six hours of night flight time. The call made no sense, considering they were only minutes away from going back in for the extract.

We ended up having to launch another section to execute the extract. That process wasn't fast, so it ended up causing a four-hour delay. In the end, the extract still got done. If nothing else, it at least felt like an overarching master plan was being executed to fight the insurgency. We felt like we were actually doing something, and that was good.

The following day Apollo took it upon himself to find out the identity of the special operators he had been flying. They worked out of a building about halfway between our squadron spaces on the flight line and our barracks on mainside. They had a wall around their compound, but you could see inside the gate. There were always jacked-looking guys with beards lifting weights and shooting the shit outside.

A few UH-60 Blackhawks and AH-6 Little Birds were also parked on the road next to their compound. At night we had seen them taking off a few times loaded with the operators. We knew the aircraft belonged to the 160th Special Operations Aviation Regiment (SOAR) "Night Stalkers." The 160th was the only aviation unit organic to Special Operations Command (SOCOM), and they exclusively flew named operations and other high-level tactical missions for assorted SOCOM units.

We quickly learned that this group of special operators were an elite unit composed of a mix of the most elite of America's special operations forces. Quite the crew. None of them wore rank or name tapes of any kind. They didn't even wear full conventional uniforms. They wore components of uniforms, but for the most part, it looked like they were all just wearing whatever the hell they wanted. Every now and then, we would see them at the chow hall, wearing hockey helmets with Night Vision Goggle (NVG) mounts on them. Most of them also had beards. As far as special operators go, they were about as "special" as it gets. We were intrigued about what they might be up to.

With a little more digging, we discovered that they were a special Task Force formed to hunt down a High Value Target (HVT) who was the leader of Al Qaeda in Iraq. As such, he was the number one coalition target. The Task Force was there specifically to get him.

A couple of days later, two of the Task Force guys showed up in our squadron spaces, looking for whoever was in charge of our Operations Department. Both Apollo and I just happened to be there. They introduced themselves by first names only and gave us the basics. They also told us they did indeed have support in the form of Blackhawks and Little Birds from the Night Stalkers, but they didn't have the MH-47 Chinooks that are organic to the Night Stalkers on this deployment.

Bottom line: they were looking for some heavy lift support from us. Your basic feasibility of support inquiry. They knew they would need to make an official request via our higher headquarters at MAG-26 to work with us, but they wanted an opinion from us about feasibility first. Otherwise, they did not need to waste their time with official requests.

They had several unique vehicles and wanted to know if we could internally transport them. Apollo and I weren't sure about a couple of the individual vehicles off-hand, so we asked them to bring them over to our flight line to take a look. A few minutes later, Apollo and I stood out on the flight line, watching them pull up in a short parade of cars. They had Toyota Hilux trucks, which we knew would fit inside our aircraft with no problem. They also had a dune buggy that looked like something out of a Mad Max movie. It didn't take us long to figure out that would fit, too.

The last one was tricky. It was a Chevy Caprice cop car that had been stripped down and modified. When they pulled up, it sounded like a race car. I asked the "team leader" how souped up it was.

He questioned, "You a gearhead?"

I replied, "Not really."

"Well, dude, I'll just give you the basics then." As he talked through the specifics, it reminded me of the scene in *The Blues Brothers* when Elwood tells Jake, "It's got a cop motor, a 440 cubic inch plant, it's got cop tires, cop suspension, cop shocks." That made me chuckle. It turned out that it did fit in the back of a CH-53E. You couldn't open the doors once it was inside, so whoever drove it into our aircraft would be stuck sitting in the damn car until they drove it out. But it was doable if someone up on high would sign off on letting us do it.

From there, we shook hands and agreed that we would both start running the requests up our respective chains of command. Apollo and I needed authorization to carry non-standard vehicles internally. We also had to get our OPSO and CO briefed on what we were up to. At that point, it was just a couple of captains making handshake deals that weren't ours to make. But the truth is, we really wanted to work with those guys. A shot at helping chase down the HVT they were after would certainly be an adventure.

We had to start by convincing our CO. He was initially annoyed we hadn't told him right away, but we wanted to see if it was going to be feasible before presenting it to him and our OPSO. A unique dynamic exists in Marine Corps Aviation where there is actual rank; then there are billets, then there are qualifications in the aircraft. In our case, I was a captain, but I was also the Squadron Weapons and Tactics Instructor (WTI). Neither our CO nor OPSO had the WTI qualification. They were my superiors by rank and billet, but when it came to flying and the mission, higher headquarters was going to ask my opinion. My job was always to advise my superiors in the squadron. To their credit, they were always receptive.

After I broke it down for them and answered a few questions, they were on board with providing support. Their only request was to meet and discuss the basics with the Task Force team leaders in person. Apollo and I jokingly referred to that as wanting them to come to kiss the ring.

Jokes aside, it made sense. Our CO would own the risk, so he wanted to be sure he understood what we were signing up for. We quickly arranged the meet and greet so that we could all get to work on the official requests with higher headquarters. I went straight to MAG-26 Operations to chat with Bullwinkle. He was also all about the Task Force integration, which helped put the wheels in motion.

As part of the initial proof of concept, we planned to exercise loading and unloading their vehicles and then flying some laps in the pattern at the base. We executed some practice landings with their assorted vehicles on board to the parallel dirt runway at Al Asad that we called "27 Dirt." It also allowed us to practice various forms of Initial Terminal Guidance (ITG). ITG encompassed multiple options for marking the Landing Zone (LZ) for us at night. We experimented with everything from laser pointers to laser marking provided by an AV-8B Harrier Lightning Pod. We jokingly referred to those nights in the pattern as the "700 level codes" since the actual training codes in our Training and Readiness (T&R) Manual stopped at the 600 level.

I also arranged to do practice drops of Battlefield Illumination (BI) with our resident KC-130 Hercules squadron. The Hercs could drop overt or covert illumination flares, making it easier for us to execute safe desert landings in low light level conditions. Once deployed out of the KC-130, the flares each looked like a giant ball of light hanging under a parachute. We went out one night and executed several line numbers, incorporating different quantities of flares and standoff distances until we found the sweet spot. Once that was complete, higher headquarters was finally convinced that we would be ready to execute with the Task Force when called.

In the meantime, we were still flying and executing missions around the clock. The named operations were picking up, which was good to see. It was forcing the entire squadron to dial in, and things were starting to click. The anxiety about flying at night eased, and typical squadron shenanigans resumed. That was also great to see.

I walked into the ready room one night to find a group of our copilots watching some ridiculous video of people doing aerobics to techno music. A couple of days later, one of our Operations Clerks lost his wedding ring in one of the porta johns. That turned into a bit of an event, but he recovered it. That's love. The HMH-462 15th MEU detachment also left us to head back to the ship, so it was back to just us in our spaces. It became evident that everyone was starting to settle in and relax.

On April 23, 2005, I was set to lead a section for our first insert of the Task Force. Apollo and Bullwinkle woke me up at 1400 to tell me I needed to get up to the squadron because I was going to lead the first insert that night. They had received short notice intel on the location of a different High Value Target (HVT), and the Task Force guys wanted to execute right away. The basic plan was to insert two Hilux trucks and their team just south of the Euphrates River. They would then drive up to the river, cross in rubber Zodiac boats, grab the HVT, and egress on the same route. The extract would also happen on the south side of the river. Overall, it sounded straightforward. We had Battlefield Illumination (BI) and ITG set up to support both the insert and the extract. I was excited.

The Task Force guys showed up on our flight line with two Hilux trucks loaded with the Zodiacs, a bunch of ammo, and homemade wooden ladders in the back. As we were loading those up, one of their guys and my copilot started to chat. We had seen him before and referred to him as "Tommy Lee" because he looked like the drummer from Motley Crue. He had sleeve tats and long dark hair, and on that night, he wore these huge clear glasses as some kind of a fashion statement.

He also wore an Oklahoma Sooners visor.

My copilot asked, "Hey, Tommy, what's up with the glasses and the visor?"

He answered, "I don't know, man. I just thought it was a badass look for kicking doors down and snatching this guy."

I couldn't decide what was funnier. His actual answer or that he answered to being called "Tommy" like it was his actual name.

We quickly loaded their trucks. Unfortunately, our aircraft did not share our sense of urgency. We had one of those nights during which my primary aircraft went hard down in the chocks, so we rolled to the backup, which also went down. By the time that was complete, we had reached our drop-dead time, so the mission was a scratch. The Task Force team was great about it. They thanked us for pushing to make it out on time despite our aircraft issues. I was pissed we had missed the opportunity to finally execute a mission with them.

Two days later, I had to swing back to the day shift. Apollo and one of our majors wound up flying the Task Force mission in the early morning hours of April 26th. It was a success, and they captured the HVT. A key capture, it would lead to our next big mission in support of them.

When I came in the next morning for my day shift, Apollo gave me the back brief on the mission. It sounded like all had gone well, and I was jealous I hadn't been able to fly it. I was on the schedule to execute a Functional Check Flight (FCF) on one of our aircraft that had just had some heavy maintenance done on it. I turned my attention to that. I had always loved FCFs, so I looked forward to spending my day on that.

Late that afternoon, I was out making the final run for adjustments on the aircraft when my copilot said, "Ummmm, Whiskey, you might want to look up."

I had been heads down on the instruments, plotting the engines to make sure we had them dialed in exactly right. When I looked up, I saw the biggest haboob in front of us that I had seen in-country to date. It resembled the wall of dirt from the movie *The Mummy*.

I immediately adjusted the speed control levers to normal flight settings and took the controls. I turned 180 degrees and accelerated back towards Al Asad. We were racing back to the airfield with the dirt wall chasing us. We landed and taxied off the runway just as it hit the airfield and violently shook our aircraft.

Getting back to our line and shutting down proved to be an adventure. Walking back into the squadron spaces was almost even more challenging. Even with desert goggles on, we could only see about a foot in front of us. We all looked like sugar cookies. Like the enemy, the weather remained a constant threat.

On April 29th, I was out executing a mission where we were

externally carrying pallets of water down to Al Qaim. We were about twelve miles away when our aircraft blew a main rotor damper. I knew exactly what it was as soon as it happened due to the unmistakable lateral shake. We always described a blown damper as feeling like you are in a washing machine tub that is totally out of balance. We handled the emergency in accordance with NATOPS and cautiously made our way to Al Qaim. After dropping off our load and shutting down, I knew we were going to be stuck there until we could get that damper changed and test the aircraft back up. That ended up taking a lot longer than any of us wanted. After camping out in the back of our aircraft for two nights, we finally made it back to Al Asad on May 1st.

The next day I was back out in the aircraft, moving external loads again. Only this time, I was moving the burned-out hulks of old Iraqi armored vehicles to Test Fire Area (TFA) North so that our crew chiefs would have actual targets to shoot at when we did weapons checks shortly after takeoff. The loads were around 20,000 pounds, so fun to execute. I had one of our copilots with me to give him a review flight for his upcoming Helicopter Aircraft Commander (HAC) check flight. Combat Camera also came out and shot a bunch of photographs in the pickup zone. One of those photos has consistently turned up in several random places over the years. Years later, I saw it on a Bank of America ATM in Washington, D.C., while grabbing some cash.

There was a little phone center on the base where we could stand in line to call home. I did that about once a month, but those conversations were always hard. Me being gone so much took a toll on Kerry, and she had her hands full with a toddler at home. I sometimes thought it might be better if I didn't call at all. At the same time, I occasionally tried to check in on my parents. That wasn't much better. They had a lot of their own stuff going on at the time. I knew there would be some shit to deal with when I got back home, but I lacked the capacity to think about it in depth. My personal life was one more thing I compartmentalized to prevent it from becoming a dangerous distraction.

On May 4th, our OPSO told me I needed to go to a planning session for a low light level battalion insert the Marine Corps intended to do in support of a Task Force mission to capture the HVT in charge of Al Qaeda in Iraq. He said that the mission fell under the umbrella of a larger Marine Corps operation called OPERATION MATADOR. He wanted me to lead a flight of four CH-53Es as part of the package for this insert. I was all about it. I quickly made the adjustments to our weekly schedule to put together the crews. With that completed, Apollo and I headed to the planning session.

The Marine Corps portion of the mission was led by HMM-264, the CH-46E squadron. They would provide the Air Mission Commander (AMC) and Assault Flight Leader (AFL). I had gone to WTI with both of them. Escort Flight Leader (EFL) Andy "Babs" Thomas had also attended WTI with us. The plan was to use six CH-46s and four CH-53s to insert 490 Marines into three Landing Zones north of the Euphrates River and the border town of Husaybah.

The mission of those Marines would be to provide a blocking position to keep any bad guys from fleeing Husaybah in an attempt to cross the Syrian border. It was really a Task Force mission to try and capture the HVT in the town of Husaybah, and the Night Stalkers were flying in direct support of the Task Force.

The intel had come from the capture of the HVT, which Apollo had executed with the Task Force just a few days prior. The Night Stalkers planned to have 21 aircraft in the air over Husaybah, using Al Qaim as both a pickup zone and a Forward Arming and Refueling Point (FARP). To try and simplify it for themselves, they put up a Restricted Operating Zone (ROZ) around both Husaybah and Al Qaim, which meant we would have to circumnavigate that airspace.

We were also told we would have to use Al Qaim as our Pickup Zone (PZ), which added a layer of complexity. Getting ten Marine Corps Assault Support aircraft in and out of there for multiple waves while the Night Stalkers aircraft were also coming in and out for fuel would be a clusterfuck. After several hours of planning, Apollo and I went back to our spaces to work on some of the specifics for our piece.

The next day we returned to HMM-264 to continue planning. Everyone always said the Marine Corps hadn't executed a successful battalion insert since Vietnam. The fact that we were trying this low light level still seemed like a strange call, given it was only a blocking position. Did a blocking position really require a battalion? It seemed excessive.

About halfway through that planning session, we learned the only thing the Task Force had requested was a fifty man blocking position north of Husaybah. That made a lot more sense. Our own higher headquarters had beefed it up to a battalion insert. I'll never know why, but our assumption was that the Marine Corps wanted to be as involved as possible with the big mission that was going to take down the HVT.

A couple of hours into that planning session, the HMM-264 XO announced the mission would likely be scaled back to the fifty man blocking position initially requested. At that point, Apollo and I left and returned to our squadron spaces to stand by for the final word. At about 0200, Bullwinkle called down from the MAG, confirming we would insert a single platoon of 48 Marines. We would execute with a section of CH-53Es and a section of skids for escort.

I was happy cooler heads had prevailed. Apollo and I headed over to the HMLA-269 spaces to quickly put together a final plan for what was now our mission with Babs providing escort.

We kept the plan simple. Babs would have a mixed section of skids. One AH-1W Cobra and one UN-1N Huey. They would join us en route to provide escort. Our route would circumnavigate the ROZ to the east. Once we neared the objective area, the skids would push ahead and drop chem lights on our landing zones for ITG. When we were on short final to landing, they would shoot IR flare rockets over the LZ to provide illumination for landing.

We took off to execute shortly after midnight on May 8, 2005.

Once away from the airfield lights, the extremity of the darkness settles in around us as we are outbound on our route. We can't see anything at all in the inky darkness. It feels as if we are flying into a black hole.

The Beowulf Platoon Commander comes up and sits on the jump seat between the OPSO and me. He is also equipped with NVGs, and I can tell right away he is confused. He takes a quick look around outside and says, "Sir, I think my goggles are fucked up. I can't see anything."

I glance at him and see the faint green glow being reflected on his eyes, so I know his NVGs are working just fine. I respond, "Your goggles are working. That's what low light looks like. You've just never seen it from a cockpit."

He then asks, "How are you guys going to land?"

I calmly tell him, "That's the interesting part." I can tell in the tone of his response that the young lieutenant isn't enjoying this.

"Sir, you fuckers are crazy."

I simply respond with, "Yeah." and we keep pressing to the objective area.

We skirted east of the ROZ, and our escort section joined us to the east of Al Qaim. We had intel on a terrorist camp along the Euphrates, and we were able to take about four miles of lateral separation to ensure that reality didn't become an issue for us either. We arced around to the north of the objective area to set up for a north-to-south landing as our escort section peeled off to sanitize the zone and drop our ITG chem lights. On final approach, the OPSO was on the controls as I ran through landing checks.

"Turns up."

"Gear is down. Three down and locked."

"Brakes are off… no light."

"Harness. I'm locked. Check yourself."

"ASE gear all set."

Our crew chief then came up with his portion, "Ramp up, tail skid down, all set in the back." On short final, I came up on the radio and called for "Sunshine," our codeword for the skids to fire the illumination rockets.

Babs delivered two perfect shots that resulted in the flares popping just forward of the landing zone. It was like turning on a light bulb. The landing zone was exceptionally dusty, so the degree of difficulty on the landing was still high. The OPSO lost reference with the ground at 25 feet, but I still had a ground reference from the right seat, so I took the controls and got us on the deck. Apollo had eaten our dust, so he had to wave off and go around. He got down on the second attempt with no problem.

Once the insert was complete, we pushed back out on our return route to Al Asad. As we skirted back around the ROZ, Husaybah looked like a strobe light. There was a hell of a fight going on over there. We returned to base without incident. We had successfully completed our portion of the mission. It felt like a win for the squadron, and everyone felt good about the fact that we had executed our portion of a mission that big.

The next morning, we learned that coalition forces had killed six insurgents and detained 54 more. None of them were the HVT. He managed to escape. The chase would continue.

On May 17th, I flew a night mission with one of the cross-decked HMH-466 pilots as my copilot. She was awesome and always fun to fly with. We exchanged a lot of banter back and forth about the fact that she usually smelled like strawberries when she would get into the cockpit. I would always tell her, "It's supposed to smell like hydraulic fluid, sweat, and JP-5 in here, so cut it out!" She would just laugh and tell me to "stop being a little bitch." Then she would usually light a cigarette. We weren't supposed to smoke in the aircraft, but she didn't give any fucks about that. I loved that about her.

Later that night, we were in the AACG/DACG and had just finished loading up when I looked up and saw three rockets launch at our two o'clock long. It looked to me like they were heading right for us. I immediately called for taxi and had just pulled power to start moving when the first volley of rockets hit. They were targeting the AACG/DACG, and one hit on Echo taxiway about 200 meters from us. Close enough for me to ask for an immediate takeoff from our present position to get the hell out of there. That request was granted, so I pulled power and got airborne and onto our route. Our crew chiefs saw the next volley of rockets landing on the deck behind us. Another close call.

A few days later, we had a section out flying, and they were redirected to change their tasking by the Battle Captain. It wasn't uncommon. The Battle Captain always watched everything that was happening and had the authority to change the tasking of any aircraft available. Those tasking changes would be relayed to the aircraft via the Direct Air Support Center (DASC). Despite that, our CO flipped out about it and called an All Officers Meeting (AOM) right away.

In that meeting, he told us that we could no longer change our tasking without his personal approval. I immediately piped up and reminded him that it didn't work that way. Once we launch, we work for the Battle Captain, and our tasking can change at any time. That's the Marine Air Command and Control System (MACCS). Nowhere in there is it written, "Get approval from your CO."

The CO's responsibility was to provide up aircraft and qualified crews. The actual tasking was always subject to change. It was the second time I openly challenged him in front of all the officers in the squadron. He was pissed off, but I was right. He still insisted we needed his approval, but we all knew it wouldn't work that way. To his credit, he called me down to his office for a follow on conversation. I appreciated that he did. He could have just summarily crushed me, but he didn't. We had a good conversation. It was development.

In June, I celebrated my third consecutive birthday in Iraq. I turned 29, 30, and 31 on three consecutive deployments. I celebrated by finalizing a decision about my future. I had been invited back to MAWTS-1 at MCAS Yuma, Arizona, to be an instructor. Becoming a WTI had been my goal since flight school. Being invited back to be an instructor felt surreal. At the same time, I had some serious family considerations.

Kerry and I had been struggling for a few years, and it would take a lot of work to put us back together. My other options were going back to Pensacola to be a flight school instructor or to apply to Marine Helicopter Squadron One (HMX-1), the squadron that flies the President of the United States. I liked my chances of being selected if I applied to HMX-1, but I knew VIP flights weren't my passion. I had grown to love tactics and combat flying, and I also loved teaching and instructing. MAWTS-1 was the best answer for me professionally.

I knew Kerry wouldn't be thrilled about living in Yuma, Arizona, but I was hopeful that the quiet small town would help us re-connect. I emailed MAWTS-1 and told them I would join the staff. That was my birthday present to myself. One less thing. With that decision behind me, I dialed right back in on finishing the deployment strong.

15

ADDICTION

AT THE BEGINNING OF JUNE, the Task Force experienced a personnel change and a name change. The mission remained the same. And they still wanted us to support them. They also now had a couple of Air Force MH-53 Pave Lows in support of them, making it look like they would need less support from us.

Then, on June 18th, the Pave Lows promptly crashed one of their aircraft in an LZ just to the south of the LZ where we had inserted the blocking position for OPERATION MATADOR. They had been extracting the Task Force when they browned out and had a hard landing. The aircraft was not flyable, and the Task Force asked the Marine Corps for help.

Bullwinkle called down from MAG to talk to me about putting together a feasibility of support. I knew sunrise would be the lowest temperature of the day, so I worked up the numbers based on the temperatures at that time. I determined that, if we could get the Pave Low down to about 22,000 pounds, we could externally lift it out of the LZ.

After some back and forth about how quickly we could execute, we set the lift for sunrise on June 20th. The CO wanted to do it himself, so I assigned him one of our strongest young HACs as a copilot to help increase our chances of success.

As the WTI, it wasn't always about executing yourself. It was about being willing to help build a plan for someone else to execute. I wanted to be very involved in the planning for the lift and hand it off to the CO in a pre-packaged way that would give him everything he needed to execute successfully. Thankfully, in execution, our math and planning worked out just right, and they successfully moved the aircraft back to safety at Al Qaim. That planning exercise would come in handy for me down the road.

On June 27th, our Commanding General (CG) came down to fly with us. He wasn't a CH-53E pilot, so one of us - a NATOPS Instructor and Standardization Pilot - would fly with him. The CO asked me to fly the CG myself. During the flight, he talked to me about us providing direct support to the Task Force. He told me they wanted a section of CH-53Es to be in direct support of them 24/7. That would mean we would execute whatever tasking they requested without our Marine Corps chain of command being involved. I was all about that idea and told the CG as much, but I could tell he was hesitant to give up any of his assets to another command. If anything went wrong, he would have to answer for that decision. He was much more comfortable with the individual Assault Support Requests (ASRs) running through his chain of command. I understood why he felt that way.

On the 4th of July, we had a cookout at the squadron, which was a nice slice of something resembling normal until another haboob rolled through. There is nothing quite like eating a hot dog in a sandstorm that made the street lights come on. The irony of the fact that I had grown up in Lubbock, Texas, where similar events happened every spring, was not lost on me. Halfway around the world, I was still getting that same lovely experience. I just had to laugh.

The next day Apollo and I continued to work on the relationship with the Task Force. Shortly thereafter, we completed a couple of night inserts with them. We were on pace to do significantly more named operations than any other CH-53E squadron had done in Iraq on a single deployment. Thankfully, I had started keeping a detailed log to track them all at the beginning of the deployment. I added that to my daily routine of journaling.

Apollo and I were roommates in the barracks, but we were rarely on the same shift. We had a few days in July where we overlapped, and both happened to be in the room asleep when an indirect fire rocket landed right outside. It was probably twenty feet away from where we were sleeping. Thankfully, it hadn't come through the roof. We both woke up and spent a few minutes bitching about how ridiculous the situation was, then we just said the hell with it and went back to sleep. If we were going to get taken out by indirect fire, there wasn't a damn thing we could do about it.

As we pushed into July, the pace of the raids continued to pick up. We were regularly executing raids with the Task Force and still doing some with the resident Marine Corps Battalions, 1st Force Reconnaissance, 2nd Anglico, and the 155th Brigade Combat Team (BCT). The requests for us to support them on assorted named operations and tactical missions were steady. Suit was out on an extract one day when some guys piled out of a mud hut and started to open fire on them. They had skid escorts that immediately rolled in and suppressed with a combination of guns and rockets, allowing them to get out of the LZ and back on their egress route. The fight was getting more kinetic, and we were right in the middle of it.

On August 18th, I was on to execute a raid with the 155th BCT in support of OPERATION STOCKPILE. The 155th BCT was a Mississippi National Guard unit that had fallen under the command of II Marine Expeditionary Force (II MEF) with us and the rest of the Marine Corps units in-country. As a guard unit, they operated differently than the Marines and Special Operators we normally worked with. They also worked with AH-64 Apache helicopters from the 151st Aviation Regiment for their

Close Air Support (CAS), which meant we would also use them for escort, vice our usual Marine Corps Cobras and Hueys. The 151st was also a reserve unit out of South Carolina. They referred to themselves as the "Gamecock" squadron, but their tactical callsign in-country was "Ghost."

Planning with the 155th BCT and 151st, I was able to work out the minor differences and put the plan together. The most significant difference was that our Marine Corps escorts always established Battle Positions (BPs) as deconfliction measures in the objective area. The 151st preferred to use what they called a "Line of Death." They would stay on one side, and we would stay on the other. Like us, they added some altitude separation as a second measure of deconfliction. At the end of the day, it was still a raid. It really didn't matter whom we supported or worked with.

We picked up the 155th Soldiers at Forward Operating Base (FOB) Iskandariyah, and Ghost was launching out of FOB Kalsu, so we executed an airborne rendezvous for the insert. We inserted the Soldiers and had just gotten established in our holding area when they called for extract due to a casualty. As we pressed back into the objective area, they clarified that the casualty was the target of the raid himself. When they kicked in his door to grab him, he apparently had a heart attack. As soon as we were on deck, they carried him out and strapped him to the floor in the back of my aircraft. I took off as quickly as possible to expedite getting back to FOB Iskandariyah, which had the nearest medical facilities. We didn't make it in time, and the target died in the back of our aircraft.

Throughout the deployment, we executed raids and pulled High Value Targets (HVTs) out of little houses and compounds in the middle of the night. It always felt a little eerie when you looked in the back of the aircraft and saw them being dragged on board bound with flex cuffs and blindfolds. We would typically get them on board, and the spooks that were part of the raid force would start working them over on the way back to what we called "The Slap Factory" at Al Asad, where they were detained and questioned.

This was the first time one of them had died on board one of our aircraft. I was a little surprised that more of these HVTs didn't have heart attacks when we were conducting raids. Having forty-eight warfighters pile out of two CH-53Es in your front yard to come kick your door down and drag you out of bed and into the night has to be a max-stress event.

We were entering the home stretch of the deployment. We were supposed to have the Advanced Party from HMH-466 arrive in mid-September and then turn the mission over shortly after October 1st. The last few weeks of the deployment were always dangerous. Everyone thinks they have everything figured out, so it is easy to get complacent. I personally made a concerted effort not to let that happen.

On base, we were still taking indirect fire regularly. Every time it happened, the CO would tell us he heard the shots from miles away when they were fired. "I heard it coming out of the tube!" became the favorite CO quote amongst the company grade officers in the squadron. The CO was a character. We all got a kick out of all the crazy shit he said. We all knew the deployment had gone well to that point, and everyone felt good about it. We just had to keep it going for a few more weeks.

Little things helped everyone stay sane. We had a couple of PlayStation 2 consoles and the "NCAA Football" video game. We had endless tournaments to fill our limited spare time back at the barracks. Video games were a popular way of passing the time. Everyone shared DVDs and books as well. My sister mailed me a copy of the Motley Crue autobiography, *The Dirt*. That was the most popular book in our barracks. Those guys were insane!

It seemed like every other week, we would lose running water for a couple of days due to insurgents endlessly blowing up the main water line running into the base. I had gotten smart after our last deployment and brought a camp shower that endlessly came in handy. The electricity also went out frequently, and we all got used to life with a headlamp on our heads. It was ridiculously hot again and the crappy air conditioning going out was worse than dealing with the darkness. Regardless, it was still better than living in tents at Jalibah as we had two years prior.

At the same time, everyone was tired and irritable. On occasion, tempers flared. One night two of our captains almost got into a fistfight over a Red Bull that was in the fridge in our Operations office. The rub was that one of them was calling it "his" even though everything we had originated from the chow hall. Nobody bought anything. A few minutes after we broke up that scuffle, the OPSO came in and told one of them congratulations. We had just gotten word that his wife had given birth to a baby girl. Two minutes later, he was outside smiling and smoking a cigar. It was a fucking ridiculous way to live.

In the early morning of September 11th, I was on Quick Reaction Force (QRF) standby, allowing me to sit in the ready room and watch the University of Texas play Ohio State in football on the Armed Forces Network (AFN). I had always enjoyed watching college football, so it was a nice little piece of something normal. As the sun came up, Texas was driving to win the game when the CO came into the ready room and ordered us out onto the flight line for a Foreign Object Damage (FOD) walk. Every aviation unit in the Marine Corps does a FOD walk every morning to ensure there isn't anything on the flight line that can get sucked into an aircraft and cause a problem. I understood the utility of FOD walk but always found it ridiculous that we did them in Iraq. We typically just picked up tiny pebbles and threw them 10 feet into the desert right next to the concrete pad where the aircraft were parked. It seemed like a total waste of time.

I asked the CO if we could wait a few minutes to watch the end of the game. He refused and told us all to get outside. I was totally annoyed, but I knew I had already challenged him in front of the ready room two more times than I should have survived, so I decided not to push it. After picking up a handful of pebbles on FOD walk, I got back into the ready room to see that Texas had won the game on that last drive.

I forced myself to shake off my annoyance and think about everything that had happened in the last four years. Four years prior, on that same day, I was drinking beer and talking shit with my squadron mates in the Echo Chamber when the world changed. Now, I was in Iraq for the third consecutive year, fighting the war that had followed. Thinking about that helped me get over the fact that we had missed the end of the game. In the grand scheme of things, a football game really wasn't important.

On September 13th, I was back out executing another raid with the 155th BCT and the Gamecock Apaches. This time the plan was for us to pick them up at FOB Kalsu and then go back to Kalsu to hold one deck for approximately one hour while waiting for the extract call. When we reached Kalsu for the pickup, I left my copilot on the controls and climbed out of the aircraft to talk to the 155th BCT team before we loaded up.

Several of them had gone with very non-traditional camouflage paint on their faces, utilizing black and white paint. One guy had painted his face white and had black "X's" over his eyes. Another had painted his face like a skeleton. I thought to myself that all those guys were probably out hunting all the time when they were back home. Between them and the Gamecock squadron, it was like giving a bunch of guns and Apache helicopters to a big group of Southern boys and telling them to go get it. They were fucking wild.

The objective area for the mission was only a few miles away from FOB Kalsu, so it was a quick flight. On insert, everything went smoothly, and the Apaches were able to perfectly sparkle our landing zones with lasers for ITG. That made for an easier landing and quick offload. We then headed back to Kalsu to wait on deck for the extract call. The extract call took 15 minutes longer than expected, but we took off and pushed back into the objective area without incident. But once we were on deck, I could tell right away it was a shit show. Our passengers were scattered all over the zone and needed more time to be ready to go.

I was watching the clock while calling them on the radio, telling them they needed to board the aircraft quickly. It was a vulnerable position to be in just sitting on deck, turning in the objective area, so we always wanted to limit that time to the shortest window possible. This was going to take way too long. We were getting the last passengers on board right as we hit minute ten of being in the zone. At that exact moment, I saw two insurgents come out of a building at my 10 o'clock with what looked like a Rocket Propelled Grenade (RPG).

I quickly slewed my FLIR towards them to verify the RPG as I radioed the Gamecock Apaches for help. "I have two guys right outside the building to my 10 o'clock with what appears to be an RPG."

I watched one of insurgents lift the RPG to his shoulder right as one of the Apaches rolled across my nose and came hot on them with rockets. The threat was instantly neutralized. We'd been just seconds away from taking an RPG shot right into the nose of our aircraft. As soon as our passengers were strapped in, I called "lifting" and got the fuck out of there.

When we landed at Al Asad and shut down, my copilot commented to me about how unphased I seemed about the flight. "You are like a fucking robot."

It wouldn't be the last time someone would say that to me. On my first deployment to Iraq, I started out a little bit scared and excited, just like everyone else. Somewhere in there, I became desensitized to anything resembling fear. I was very aware that I liked that crazy shit. The RPG sequence was as exciting as hell for me. It was a dopamine hit, and I was totally addicted to it. I wanted to go right back out and do it again. The risk of combat flying was my dragon, and I relentlessly chased it.

I also had what I called "getting into character" down to a science. Once it was time to brief and fly, I could completely block everything else out and totally focus. It didn't matter what else was happening in the squadron or at home. It was like flipping a switch for me. Once I was in that zone, I didn't feel any emotions at all. I always believed the ability to do that was critical to mission success and staying alive.

At OCS and TBS, they taught us about the OODA Loop and the decision-making process. OODA is an acronym that stands for Observe, Orient, Decide, Act. The basic premise is that you must make decisions faster than the enemy to gain and maintain the advantage in the engagement. That allows you to stay "inside their loop" and dictate the outcome. To do that, you must be willing to make decisions quickly without all the information. A mediocre decision made quickly is better than a perfect decision made too late.

In the cockpit, that loop needed to move at hyper speed. At any given moment, you are flying, navigating, monitoring over 100 gauges, listening to and talking on multiple radio frequencies, and also communicating with your crew and your flight. It is the ultimate in multitasking, and you must be ready to make split-second decisions all the time.

Emotions slow down your thought process and make that impossible. I liked to say that in the cockpit, "if you get excited, you get dead." In an environment where one second could be the difference between you and twenty-eight other people dying, there was no place for emotion. We used to brief, "no fast hands in the cockpit," and often said, "smooth is fast." Those were just different ways of reminding ourselves to stay calm and keep thinking. When I was relaxed and totally dialed in, it felt like everything was happening in slow motion. I could see, hear, and feel everything. It allowed me to make decisions at whatever speed necessary while ensuring that it felt deliberate and totally under control.

Things back home were testing my limits, though. I only had

a few weeks to go, but it felt like things back there were bad. Kerry was maxed out. At that point, I had been gone for the better part of three years, and we had a little girl I barely knew. It was fair for her to feel the way she did. I could also tell my parents were not in a good place. I wasn't sure where any of that was going, but the cumulative effect made me feel like I didn't have a support system back home.

As much as that annoyed me, there wasn't a damn thing I could do about it from Iraq. The squadron had become my support system. If I could have done whatever I wanted, I would have just stayed there to keep fighting and flying with them forever.

Late in the afternoon on September 20th, I arrived at the squadron spaces ready to brief my flight for that night. I was on to lead a section raid in support of OPERATION CLEAN SWEEP. When I walked into the squadron, it was buzzing. I found Apollo in our operations shop with two of our majors, trying to hash out something on the whiteboard. I asked what was going on, and they explained being tasked with a day battalion insert of the 82nd Airborne for OPERATION DIABLO the next day.

They were trying to determine how to execute it with four CH-53Es and four CH-46Es. I asked where the Pickup Zone (PZ) and objective area were. The PZ was Al Asad itself, the objective area a short flight away. It was the exact type of thing I enjoyed being able to help with as the squadron WTI.

The PZ being at Al Asad made that piece easy. We would put two officers in the PZ to maintain positive control and account-ability of each stick as they loaded. We put together ingress and egress routes that essentially set up a counterclockwise flow from Al Asad to the objective area and back. I suggested they go in and land as sections, then return to Al Asad as sections in trail. That would keep the lines moving in the PZ for subsequent waves. It only took a few minutes to help them work it out, and they had it.

I got back into character and briefed my section for the night. We executed our raid for OPERATION CLEAN SWEEP without incident; the next day, the 82nd Airborne insert for OPERATION DIABLO went off without a hitch. Just like we drew it up on the whiteboard. It was great to see the squadron execute that well.

On September 24th, I went out for one last raid in support of 2nd Force Reconnaissance (FORECON). We were close to the finish, and I was certain this would be the last tactical mission I would fly on the deployment. Maybe my last tactical combat mission ever. It was a straightforward raid in the vicinity of a little village called Jubbah. Originally requested a couple of weeks prior when it was still low light level, MAG-26 had put it on ice to wait for high light level. It was now time to execute.

I was in dash two of three, and our XO was leading the flight. The insert LZ was a field that had been flooded, which we didn't realize until we were on deck. I was trying to keep the aircraft from sinking into the mud, so I kept a little power on the main rotor head while offloading the Marines. On takeoff, my crew chief let me know he couldn't get the ramp to raise back up. It should have been a non-event. We had a panel on the overhead console in the cockpit where we should have been able to raise the ramp with the flip of a switch. Only that aircraft was missing that specific panel.

There was a workaround, but for the life of me, I couldn't remember what it was. That had never happened to me before. I knew the systems cold. But in that case, I couldn't remember! I was getting pissed off, which violated my rule to stay calm and keep thinking. My emotions were clouding my thought process. I finally calmed down and figured it out. And I realized that the ramp hadn't come back up on deck because, when I pulled in that squeak of power to keep us from sinking into the mud, I had disabled the weight on wheels switch. The answers were obvious all along, and I was pissed at myself for not remembering them sooner.

Despite that, the extract went off without a hitch. When we

returned to Al Asad and shut down, I knew I had hit the wall. Three consecutive combat deployments had caught up to me. It was a seemingly little incident, but it told me everything I needed to know about where my head was. It was time for me to take a break.

I flew my last flight in Iraq five days later, on September 29, 2005. It was a standard "ass and trash" night flight, knocking out a pile of ASRs. My last landing outside of the wire was at FOB Duke. That was the FOB where Hendrix had died just over a year earlier. Somehow, it seemed appropriate that it would be my last stop on my last flight in Iraq.

I thought about him while we sat in the zone, offloading and loading. I felt a lot of guilt that he hadn't survived this place, and I was on the cusp of surviving it for a third time. There is a randomness to death that fucks with you. It isn't fair. It takes the best people at the most inopportune times. Why him? Why not me? He was probably better than I was at all of this shit. Those of us who survive the experience live with the guilt that we didn't die.

When we got back to Al Asad and shut down, several of our pilots, aircrew, and maintainers came out to greet us. It was over. We had set a new high-water mark for named operations, executing sixty-eight of them on this deployment. I didn't think any CH-53E squadron would ever beat that. It was also my third combat deployment where we didn't lose a single Marine. We were bringing everyone home again. That was more impressive to me than the sixty-eight named operations.

We had about five days to kill while preparing for our trip home. On the very first day, I got an email from my Dad asking me to email him when I had flown my last flight. I replied that I had finished up the night before. He then revealed that he and my Mom were splitting up, and he asked me to come home to Texas to see him. I felt like I needed to do that, but I knew it wouldn't play well at home if I got off the plane and then took off to Texas. There was no right answer.

I had been away from home for twenty-two of the last thirty-three months. Tristen was thirty-nine months old. I had missed one Christmas, one Thanksgiving, two wedding anniversaries, Tristen's birthday once, Kerry's birthday twice, and my birthday three years in a row. I had been living off sketchy chow hall food, MREs, Power Bars, and endless bottles of Kuwaiti and Jordanian bottled water. Who knew Nestle made bottled water in Jordan?

The things that kept me going were an endless combination of Copenhagen, gum, and toothpicks. I was ready for some consistent creature comforts like climate control, hot water, and functional toilets. The thought of eating real food and drinking a few beers sounded like paradise. But a part of me already missed being there. I knew it might be my last combat deployment. Hell, I thought it might have been my last deployment, period.

Someday I would look back on these three years as the time of my life that shaped whatever I would become. It had all happened so fast, I hadn't had much time to think about it. And when I did have time, it sometimes fucked with me in a way that I hadn't really figured out how to deal with yet. I knew that, at some point, I would need to acknowledge the insanity of it all and find a healthy way forward. But I wasn't anywhere near that point yet. I was leaving Iraq, but my mind would remain there for a very long time.

We loaded up on our first flight headed home at the Al Asad AACG/DACG at 0900 local on October 5, 2005. I did stop, turn around and look across the Al Asad flight line one last time. That time, I said goodbye. That time, I felt certain I was never fucking going back.

16

WARFIGHTER WITHOUT A WAR

IT WAS another long ride home from Iraq. We left Al Asad on a KC-130 flight to Ali Al Salem Air Base in Kuwait, where we caught a bus ride to Camp Victory. Thankfully, we only stayed at Camp Victory long enough to get accountability before jumping on another bus ride to Kuwait City International Airport. By the time we were airborne for Frankfurt, Germany, I was ready to sleep. I had too much on my mind to sleep longer than a few hours, though. The fact that the deployment was over had begun to settle in, and I wasn't sure how I felt about it.

Everything I had done up to that point was to prepare me for that deployment. Now, it was over. I had just played the biggest game of my life and felt like we had won. Now, what?

Some of the close calls from the last three deployments were cycling through my mind on fast forward. Part of me was amazed I had made it to another flight home. Another part of me didn't want it to ever end. Over those three deployments to Iraq, I had turned into something I would have never imagined I could become. A warfighter now without a war to prosecute. I didn't know how to reconcile that. I also had a ton of difficult personal shit to wade through when I arrived home. I looked forward to seeing Kerry and Tristen, but I dreaded having to sort through the mess the last three years had made of our lives.

We made our last fuel stop at Baltimore/Washington International Airport at 0300 local time on Thursday, October 6th. The CO gathered all of us up for a formation. We thought that the CO would make his remarks about the deployment so that when we got back to Miramar, we would just be released to our families to start a 96. We were wrong. He formed us up to tell us we had to come into the squadron on Friday, October 7th, so that the MAG CO could talk to us. Then, we would be released to start our 96. We were all pissed off.

I understood why a senior commander would want to thank us for a successful deployment. But to make the entire squadron come in the day after getting home to do so just made me mad. I added it to my list of things never to do if I ever ended up in command of anything.

We landed back at Miramar just after 0700 local time in San Diego. When I approached Kerry, she was holding Tristen. Kerry handed Tristen to me, and that three-year-old girl clung to me like she never wanted to let go. She was crying, and she told me they were tears of joy. That hit me hard. Had I not lost the ability to cry, I would have in that moment. I had been off fighting a war for most of her life. Sometimes, kids epitomize resiliency.

I was home for a day, and those first 48 hours were as good as the first couple of days of a homecoming always were, despite me having to run up to the squadron for the ridiculous formation with the MAG CO. Then I took off to Texas to deal with what awaited me there. My Mom was already out of the house, so I stayed with my Dad. We spent a couple of days drinking too much while he caught me up on everything that had transpired. I wasn't really surprised; it had been trending that way for a long time. But it was still a mess, and whether I wanted to be or not, I was somewhat in the middle of it. I had my own shit to figure out, so I had to make some decisions about how to prioritize things.

After a couple of days, I flew back home to San Diego and started to sort through it. I had only been home for a couple of days when Kerry asked me to run to the grocery store to grab something for her. A standard mindless errand. I was always happy to help with stuff like that, so I jumped in the truck and headed to a grocery store close to our house. I wasn't thinking about anything in particular, but as soon as I walked into the store, it hit me like a ton of bricks. In a matter of seconds, I went from feeling perfectly fine to feeling lost and pissed off.

What the fuck was I doing there? On the other side of the planet, there was a war going on, and I was no longer there to fight it. HMH-466 was fighting and flying in the same CH-53E aircraft I had flown a couple of weeks earlier. At that moment, I wanted to return to Iraq. Immediately. As I scanned the store, I was beyond furious at everyone in the building. Oblivious to what was happening, they went about their day like the war was a non-event. They all mindlessly roamed around a grocery store, reading cereal boxes like there was anything at all fucking useful written on the goddamn boxes. I grabbed what Kerry asked me to and headed for the register.

When I got to the line at the register, the lady in front of me was leafing through a copy of the *National Enquirer*. It was too much. The fact that I had to look at a person even remotely interested in the *National Enquirer* was more than I could take. I set my stuff down and walked out of the store with nothing. I went out to the parking lot and just sat in my truck for a few minutes, trying to come down from adrenaline flooding my system.

I felt on the verge of exploding, and I didn't know how to stop that feeling. The balloon inside of me would soon pop. I couldn't let it out. I didn't know what the fuck to do. After a few minutes, I pulled myself back together. I went back into the store, picked up what Kerry asked for, and got out of there without talking to anyone.

When I got home, I was quiet. I didn't tell Kerry what had happened because I didn't know how to explain it. I just did what I always did and had a few beers. It was the only way I knew to let the air out of that balloon. A few years later, the movie *The Hurt Locker* depicted a similar scene in a grocery store for the main character. That scene resonated with me. I had lived it.

A couple of days later, I returned to the squadron, relieved to get back to work. We had sent Suit home early to go to WTI as a student, and he would take over in that billet when he graduated from the course in late October. I would spend a couple of months helping him get settled in, and then I would go to the Spring WTI class to be an Augment Instructor, the latter giving me a head start on the assignment before I officially checked in to be a MAWTS-1 instructor in May.

At the end of October, I went to MCAS Yuma, Arizona, for Suit's WTI graduation ceremony. I put together a party in the back of the Dos Rios Inn on base, and all of the CH-53E guys there came. Dalton had been an Augment Instructor for the class, so he was there, too. It was a great way to blow off some steam. It was also cool to see MAWTS-1 again, and it got me excited about being assigned there as an instructor. If I couldn't fight the war, at least I could train the best of the best to make sure they were ready to fight it.

At home, we had a relatively low-key holiday season. My Dad came for Christmas, then Kerry, Tristen and I went to Texas for the New Year to see both of my parents. The whole thing felt beyond depressing. Once we headed home to San Diego, it finally felt like we had a little time to try and settle back in as a family. It didn't work.

Kerry and I were still living on two different planets. We had spent way too much time apart. My head remained in Iraq, fighting a war and in the very early stages of trying to reconcile my experiences. She still struggled, because she had spent most of the last three years alone and raising our daughter. We both knew there wasn't going to be enough time to make much headway before I left to augment the WTI class in March. We agreed to try and be as amenable as possible until we moved to Yuma, Arizona, in May. We decided that when we got there and settled in, we would start trying to sort it all out. I was certain it would be one of the hardest things I had ever done.

Augmenting the spring WTI class ended up being a great experience. I hadn't particularly enjoyed my time as a student, but I realized I would love being an instructor. During my entire time in the fleet, MAWTS-1 instructors had a reputation as asshole evaluators. I was excited about the opportunity to change that perception. I wanted to be a real teacher and instructor. Someone that squadron COs were glad to see in their squadron spaces. Augmenting that class gave me a great head start on getting my arms around everything I needed to do and understand. It also gave me a chance to look for a place for our family to live. Kerry came out for a couple of weekends so that we could look for houses together. We ultimately settled on a neighborhood we liked and made an offer on a home as the class wound down.

My return to San Diego signaled it was time to move. We sold our little starter house, and we were in escrow on the new Yuma house. I only had a few days to get checked out of the squadron before the movers arrived. We had a standard "hail and farewell" for the officers in the squadron, where Apollo and I received our going away plaques as part of the farewell group. Apollo was heading to the 20th Special Operations Squadron to fly the MH-53 Pave Low.

The work that we had done with the Task Force in Iraq had set him up for an exchange tour with them. We purposely got the CO hammered that night in hopes he would provide maximum entertainment. He did not disappoint. The CO had been good to me, and we'd had a great deployment as a squadron. I appreciated that.

A couple of days later, the other company grade officers in

the squadron had their own going away party for me. It was in one of the guys' backyards, and it was a blast. It was nice to have a few beers with those guys one last time before I left. As the senior captain in the squadron, I had been there when every single one of them had checked in. I had played a role of some kind for each of them. While still in Iraq, we had all ordered Omega watches to commemorate the deployment. I had never bought a nice watch in my entire life, but I figured if I was ever going to do it, that was the reason to do so. After almost six years in the squadron and four deployments, I wanted to have something tangible to keep.

That night as we were drinking beer, they gave me my watch. They also gave me the check I had written to pay for it. They had all pitched in and bought mine as a "thank you" for everything I had done for them. They joked that they had done it because I'd had the guts to stand up to the CO on multiple occasions. They recounted those stories in a way so funny, I couldn't stop laughing. The back of the watch was engraved with the squadron patch, my name, and the words "From the Warhorse Company Grade." Over the course of my career, I received a lot of plaques, gifts, and mementos. To this day, that watch remains the most meaningful because it came from my peers.

The following week, I secured the last signature on my checkout sheet and walked out of Hangar 4. I stood in the parking lot across the street, looking back at the hangar for a few minutes. I had walked into that building five and a half years prior as a nobody lieutenant with the goal of becoming a squadron WTI. I was leaving as "Whiskey," a salty captain and combat veteran headed to MAWTS-1 to be an instructor.

I hoped to return to Hangar 4 for fleet support as a MAWTS-1 instructor. Beyond that, I wasn't sure what the future held for me.

Would Kerry and I make it? Would I continue in the Marine Corps? Would I ever return to Miramar to be a member of one of those squadrons again?

I had no fucking clue, but I felt good about what I had accomplished. I gave everything I had to give and then some. I had zero regrets. There were many strings attached to what I had done and experienced that still might get me. But my sense of accomplishment was such that I was okay with any possible consequences. It had been one hell of a run.

17

MAWTS-1 "HEAVY METAL"

MAWTS-1 HAD BEEN INTIMIDATING as a student. Walking in the door to officially become an instructor was slightly more intimidating. Despite everything I'd done up to that point, I knew that every other instructor in the building had also been hand selected to be part of the staff because they were the best of the best. The expectations couldn't have been higher. We were all expected to be experts in our respective areas, and we were all expected to look the part. No detail too small.

When I checked in, the Flight Equipment Marines informed me that none of my flight suits or flight gear would suit a MAWTS-1 Instructor. It was all too worn and beat up. They gave me brand new flight suits, helmet, helmet bag, gloves, everything. The Marine Corps was all about looking good in uniform. MAWTS-1 took it to another level.

MAWTS-1 conducted the semi-annual Weapons and Tactics Instructor (WTI) course every Fall and every Spring. At that time, MAWTS-1 also hosted a semi-annual pre-deployment training exercise called "Desert Talon" for all the squadrons slated to deploy to Iraq in the next rotation. When those courses were not underway, the instructors traveled to conduct fleet support. There were certain upper-level qualifications like

Night Systems Instructor (NSI), where the exam and certification flight could only be administered by a MAWTS-1 Instructor.

Most fleet support requests were for those certifications, but the instructors would also often teach classes and fly other standardization and certification flights on those trips. Being on staff would provide me with the opportunity to fly with all the CH-53 squadrons in the Marine Corps, which excited me. I hated being out of the fight, but teaching the best of the best graduate-level aviation tactics they could take back to their squadrons to help prepare them for combat was the next best thing.

It was an exciting time to be checking into the squadron. The Marine Corps had been executing Cold War tactics for a very long time. OEF and OIF had changed that. We were back to fighting an insurgency. As a result, the academic curriculum and flight syllabus for the WTI course needed to be formally updated. Those of us checking in as new instructors were all coming from units that already employed some of those revamped counterinsurgency tactics in combat. It was now on us to update the curriculum. I considered it the perfect assignment for me.

The CH-53 shop supported the CH-53E squadrons on the west coast at MCAS Miramar, the east coast at MCAS New River, and the CH-53D squadrons in Hawaii at MCAS Kaneohe Bay. Since every Type Model Series (TMS) aircraft was represented at MAWTS-1, we had an Assault Support Department (ASD) for the rotary wing instructors and a Tactical Air (TACAIR) department for the fixed wing instructors.

Internal to those was a "shop" for each TMS aircraft. Each TMS had a callsign we used for the class. In the CH-53 shop, ours was "Heavy Metal," which was appropriate in multiple ways. Since I had come from a CH-53E squadron, I wasn't qualified in the CH-53D. As a result, my first order of business was to travel out to MCAS Kaneohe Bay in Hawaii for a few weeks to complete an abbreviated CH-53D conversion syllabus. I would fly both the CH-53D and the CH-53E as an instructor at MAWTS-1.

Kerry, Tristen, and I were still settling into our new house. It was a newer ranch-style with a pool in the backyard. At the time, I thought it would be the nicest house we would ever live in. It was almost twice the size of our little 1200-square-foot starter house in San Diego. And we thought having a pool in our back-yard was the greatest thing ever. Most houses in Yuma had pools, a fringe benefit of living in the Arizona desert. Tristen and I were out in that pool every evening after dinner. It was a great way to spend time with her.

I headed out to Hawaii to knock out my CH-53D transition. The predecessor to the CH-53E, the CH-53D was an older aircraft with two engines and far less power. My primary takeaway was that I understood why the Marine Corps had upgraded to the CH-53E. Regardless, learning to fly the "light twin" was a great reason for me to spend three weeks in Hawaii. Kerry and Tristen came out during my final week, which was nice for all of us.

In early June, I returned to Yuma and dove into re-working our academic classes and flights to prepare for the fall WTI class. In the CH-53 shop, we worked long hours that first summer to ensure that everything would be perfect for the upcoming fall WTI class. In the MAWTS-1 building, we were also making the decision to have the rotary wing squadrons go from flying low-altitude to medium-altitude tactics in Iraq.

Our Aircraft Survivability Equipment (ASE) had received a significant upgrade that could better counter the Man Portable Air Defense System (MANPADS) threat, which would allow us to fly at slightly higher altitudes while in transit to reduce the odds of hitting power lines and other low-level obstacles. The idea felt strange to me after flying low-altitude tactics throughout all three of my combat deployments, but I also really liked the idea of never having to spend another low light night cruising at 200 feet AGL.

At home, we ran out of excuses to keep avoiding it, so Kerry and I entered counseling. We were working to find some common ground and get back in sync with one another. It wasn't a question of whether or not we still loved each other. We had just gone through an extreme experience, with a lot of time apart, and we were both carrying a lot of baggage.

On June 7, 2006, I was still settling in at MAWTS-1 when I heard we had finally taken out the HVT I'd helped try to capture in Iraq. I had spent an entire deployment chasing that bastard all over Iraq. We had finally given up on trying to capture him and just dropped a bomb on his ass. It was a fitting end to the saga.

Later that summer, MAWTS-1 hosted a Desert Talon pre-deployment training exercise. The first group coming through that summer would include my former squadron, HMH-465. They had a new CO, and their new OPSO had been one of my instructors when I came through MAWTS-1 as a student.

Suit was now their squadron WTI and most of the company grade who had gifted me the watch were still there. It was cool that my first real instructor duty was helping prep my former squadron for another deployment to Iraq. I enjoyed the hell out of flying with them again.

I quickly settled into all things MAWTS-1. I had been assigned to teach several academic classes and to lead a few of the WTI syllabus flights. The CH-53 shop had also undergone a significant turnover. The only instructor remaining in the CH-53 shop from the previous year was Major Dennis "Dolf" Sampson. Dolf had grown up as a member of the HMH-464 "Condors" on the east coast, and he was a Marine's Marine. After deploying to both Afghanistan and Iraq, he established himself as an aviator and warfighter with a great reputation.

Dolf was jacked, had a flat top, and often had a dip of Copenhagen in his mouth. He could have been equally successful as an infantry officer, something you couldn't say about most aviators. He loved the CH-53, the mission, and the Marine Corps. He had an intellectual understanding of the Aviation Combat Element (ACE) and the Marine Air Ground Task Force (MAGTF) as a whole. He was exactly the guy the Marine Corps and his fellow Marines needed him to be. His great sense of humor complimented the fact that he was also just a good dude. Despite that, nobody fucked with Dolf. Not. Ever. He was the last person on earth any of us wanted to get crossways with. Everything about him shouted future General Officer, which made him the perfect CH-53 Division Head for the tasks ahead of us.

The other four of us were all new check-ins. From the west coast, it was me and my former WTI roommate Eric "TULSA" Purcell. He and I had already hit it off as students, so I knew working with him would be great. From the east coast, it was Brian "Kramer" Laurence and Scott "Dimes" Silvia. Kramer was very together and the quietest of all of us. Dimes was laid back like a west coast guy. He lived off quesadillas and Diet Coke. We quickly became fast friends, amusing ourselves by talking endless shit to one another about one thing or another. Who was the best pilot, which coast bred the best Marine Corps aviators, and what college football team was the best? It didn't matter. The banter was non-stop. We also had two crew chiefs on staff, including Ron "Ski" Strzalkowski. Years prior, I had done my first walkaround on a CH-53E at HMT-302 with Ski. I loved all those guys from day one.

In the building, it was all professional all of the time. The first time I was supposed to be at a meeting, I arrived ten minutes early. Nobody was there. When it got to be two minutes before the meeting, I started to get nervous that I was in the wrong room. Then about one minute before the meeting was scheduled to begin, everyone showed up all at once, and the meeting started right on time to the second.

The guy sitting next to me leaned over and asked, "Hey, new guy, you got here ten minutes early, didn't you?"

I nodded. "Yes."

He replied, "Don't do that. You wasted ten minutes."

That was MAWTS-1 in a nutshell. Maximum efficiency. On time, on target.

The best thing about MAWTS-1 was the people. Not just in the CH-53 shop, but the whole building was full of accomplished officers who also happened to be great people. Not surprisingly, they also had great spouses. There was nothing else to do in Yuma, so we all just hung out with each other. Every weekend someone had a get-together of some kind. We invited each other to every birthday party, anniversary, or anything else we could dream up. We would make up another reason if there wasn't an actual occasion to celebrate.

A real community, I loved everything about it. My job was awesome, our house was awesome, I loved being a MAWTS-1 instructor, and I had eighty or so built-in friends just like me. Perfect for me.

It wasn't quite as perfect for Kerry. She was always a city girl, and living in a tiny town like Yuma wasn't her jam. The desert wasn't her jam, either. The only saving grace for her was that there were a lot of other wives in the same boat with whom she became fast friends. The people at MAWTS-1 would ultimately become lifelong friends for both of us.

I thrived in that environment, but I still wasn't sure what I wanted to do long term. When we left HMH-465, I felt like the only real chance we had at normalcy would be for me to leave the Marine Corps. Going to MAWTS-1 was counter to that. The Marine Corps expected MAWTS-1 instructors to stay in and become squadron COs. When that didn't happen, it was the exception. But I still wasn't sure. Things at home felt better, but they still weren't "good." Kerry and I continued to try to work our way back to that.

During my first year at MAWTS-1, I was put in charge of a major evolution for the spring WTI course. That was typically reserved for a more seasoned instructor, so I worked hard to make the most of the opportunity. As part of the WTI course, we conducted a Non-Combatant Evacuation Operation (NEO) evolution in the cities of Yuma, Arizona, and Brawley, California. I was in charge of that NEO, and one of my duties was to brief the city councils for each city on how we would safely conduct the evolution. Our CO attended those meetings with me, but I gave the brief. That spring, my first evolution as the lead instructor went well. Overall, it had been a great first year in the building.

On October 1, 2007, I was promoted to major. As a captain, I had maintained a general distrust and dislike for all majors, so I was slightly torn about the promotion. I had become one of them! I low-key hated myself on general principle. Fittingly, I would end up holding the rank of major longer than any other rank I held during my Marine Corps career. Karma.

After my promotion, I rolled right into my second turn as the lead instructor for the NEO evolution for the fall WTI course. When I went to brief the city councils, I brought our current CO and soon-to-be new CO with me. Apparently, those briefs went well. Shortly thereafter, I got tapped to be the Assistant Operations Officer (AOPSO) for the entire squadron - a job no one wanted. The MAWTS-1 OPSO was known for working 20-hour days during the WTI course, and his AOPSO lived a similar life. My fate was sealed when our current and incoming COs attended those city council briefs with me.

Initially, I wasn't happy about it, but I grew to love that job. I had to quickly become an expert in every TMS aircraft in the building. I got read into the Top Secret aspects of all the other aircraft. I had to understand everything they were doing to review and approve the overall flight schedule during the exercises. I also lined up the milestones for every WTI and Desert Talon exercise to ensure all the planning for those exercises went off without a hitch. It was a huge job that required a ton of detailed work and coordination. I loved everything about it.

At home, we were still working on all of the usual things. Being as busy as I was at MAWTS-1 helped, but I was still coming down from a combat stress level. I wasn't totally out of the woods, and I knew it. I regularly awakened in the middle of the night. My thoughts raced, and I felt like I was simultaneously running from and toward my combat experiences. It had changed me, but I still craved more.

My only solace was flying during the WTI classes and Desert Talon. It wasn't combat, but it was the closest thing to it. And it fed the inner beast. I still felt compelled to chase the dragon, but I didn't talk about any of that with anyone. I feared getting pulled off of flight orders or something else equally fucked. My expectation for myself was to just deal with it. I didn't have it that bad. Other guys had seen a lot worse.

I loved everything about combat flying. It had almost killed me a few times, but my head was still in Iraq. Flying low light level combat missions. In the shit. Kerry was asking me to come back down and meet her on planet Earth, but I couldn't. I was still there. When I started feeling maxed out and couldn't turn my brain off, I let the air out of the balloon by drinking. I used it as the reset button that would help me keep running.

In early 2007 we had only been in Yuma for about eight months, but Kerry and I had figured out some things. It was far from perfect, but it was progress.

I was in my office one night, trying to start writing version 1.0 of this book. I had my journal, and I wanted to do something with it, but I was struggling. It was still too close. I kept getting bogged down as I relived my flights. Every close call. Each memory hurled me right back into a combat stress level. I wasn't ready.

I was sitting there trying to write one night when Kerry came in and started chatting with me. The conversation led to her saying she thought we should have another baby. Talk about being caught off guard. Tristen's entry into the world had been so traumatic, I just assumed we wouldn't try it again. Kerry was adamant that we should. I asked her to think about it for a few weeks. And a few weeks later, she came back and told me she was certain she was ready.

Things continued to settle down for us at home. As the tension eased, we got back to being close again. MAWTS-1 was busy, but it wasn't anything at all like the consecutive deployments had been. When I traveled on fleet support, it was typically only for a few days at a time. I was home a lot more than I had been previously. We were all able to eat dinner together most nights. We spent a lot of time in our backyard, cooking out, and spending time in the pool with Tristen. The stress level slowly eased, and Kerry and I settled back into something that felt a little bit healthier for both of us. Things felt good.

A few months later, Kerry was pregnant with a boy, but I still wasn't sure what we were going to do. The four deployments with HMH-465 had been hard on us, so I was still seriously considering leaving the Marine Corps when my time at MAWTS-1 was complete. One evening, I was in our kitchen, prepping food for our dinner, when Kerry walked in and sat at the bar. She looked at me and said, "I think you should stay in the Marine Corps. We are at war, and you are really good at what you do. It's important."

I was shocked. It was the most selfless thing I had ever seen her do.

I asked her if she was sure.

She said with certainty, "We'll figure it out."

The following Monday, I asked the adjutant for a bonus package. At the time, the Marine Corps was offering a bonus to aviators who would commit to an additional six years of service. I signed that bonus paperwork and turned it in on the same day. I didn't want to give myself a chance to second-guess the decision. It was done.

Our son Dalton was born in February of 2008. Because the doctors knew Kerry's history, they were able to keep her going longer than they had with Tristen, but it was still dicey. She was in and out of the hospital for the last few weeks, but she got Dalton to 37 weeks. He was five pounds fifteen ounces at birth and didn't require any NICU time. After Tristen's entry into the world, we took that as a win. It was a few days before the spring WTI course was about to start, so I was on my Blackberry the whole time we were at the hospital, ensuring everything was set for the course. It was classic Isaac and Kerry. Having a baby was still competing with the Marine Corps.

Shortly after Dalton was born, his namesake, our good friend Dalton, planned to be married in San Diego. He had transitioned out of the Marine Corps and was attending law school. The rehearsal dinner was at the University Club in downtown San Diego, and somehow, we ended up in a cab with Dalton and his soon-to-be wife. They asked us the secret to staying married. After everything we had been through, it seemed crazy that they were asking us. But I will never forget Kerry's answer. She turned around, looked at them, and said, "Don't quit."

At the end of our second year in Yuma, Fifer also got orders to Yuma and moved into a neighborhood about a half mile from ours. It was good and bad. I love that guy, and in a roundabout way, we were one another's support system. He would strap a wheeled cooler to the back of his bike and ride over to our house. He didn't even call first. He would just come in the back gate and sit down at our patio table on the back porch next to the pool. Anytime he did that, Kerry would always see him first and say, "Your boyfriend is out back." Her way of saying goodnight, and it was accurate. He and I would sit out there drinking and talking until it was time to go to bed. It was the closest thing we had to therapy.

One of my favorite things about MAWTS-1 was going out to fly with squadrons on fleet support. Since I had come from Miramar, I especially enjoyed visiting the squadrons on the east coast and in Hawaii. I loved being with the fleet squadrons, seeing how they functioned and talking to the Marines. I always had to do an in-brief and an out-brief with the MAG CO and the Squadron CO. I learned a ton from those conversations. Mostly about what not to do. It was a great look behind the curtain at how squadrons and Marine Aircraft Groups (MAGs) functioned.

I also ended up really enjoying my time as the AOPSO. Since

I took that billet in the middle of my second year, I kept it through the end of my third year when my time in the squadron concluded. I didn't mind at all. I had grown to love that job. In that role, I also got to fly several other helicopters, including the Mi-24 Hind, which always came out as an adversary for the WTI class. Flying as the adversary for our students was always a good day. During my time at MAWTS-1, I learned a ton and made several great friends. It had been the perfect tour at the perfect time for me and my family.

In the spring of 2009, my time at MAWTS-1 was coming to a close. I wanted to return to the fleet and get back into the fight immediately, but the Marine Corps had other ideas. I was selected to attend resident Command and Staff College to earn my master's degree.

I was annoyed, but I understood. Coming out of MAWTS-1, I was likely now "on track" to be a CO. The Marine Corps wanted me to stay on track, and going to school for a year was part of that. The upside was that I would probably have my choice of duty station on the back side. Since it was a condensed one-year master's program, I would get back to the fleet without having to refresh on all of my aircraft qualifications. It wasn't a bad deal.

I requested to attend Marine Corps University at MCB Quantico for the program. I didn't care for living in northern Virginia, but if we were going to move somewhere for one year, at least we would be close to Kerry's family. That would allow the kids to spend time with their grandparents, aunts, uncles, and cousins. I could deal with the weather and traffic in Northern Virginia for a year.

MAWTS-1 was a great reset for our family. We said goodbye to our friends, although several of them were heading to school with us, too. We rented our house out in Yuma and headed back to Virginia. My Mom made the trip with Kerry to help with the kids. I hadn't been to Quantico since I completed TBS over a decade prior. We rented a house just north of the base and set up shop for a year. It was a nice little break.

Command and Staff College was like a college with a significant military twist, and I enjoyed all the discussions with my fellow students and working on my master's thesis. I wrote that paper on OPERATION EAGLE CLAW, and how those guys had developed tactics we were still using in the current war. I even tracked down and interviewed two of the pilots, which I enjoyed. But the whole time I was in school, I itched to get back to the fleet and back into the fight.

That spring, the monitor reached out and told me that multiple inbound COs to the west coast were requesting me by name. He asked if I wanted to go back to Miramar. My answer was a resounding yes. San Diego and Miramar had become home to our family during my first tour there, and we wanted to return. Kerry immediately started to look at houses in San Diego.

Doug "Bullwinkle" Glasgow was slated to take command of HMH-361. The same Bullwinkle who'd been invaluable to me as the MAG-26 Future Operations Officer (FOPSO) when I was a captain WTI in Iraq in 2005. HMH-361 was slated to deploy to Afghanistan in the summer of 2010. Eric "Dobie" Gillis was slated to take command of HMH-465, my former squadron. He had been our Operations Officer at HMH-465 when we went to OIF I in 2003. HMH-465 was slated to send a detachment to Afghanistan for deployment with an east coast unit. That combined squadron would take over for HMH-361 in January of 2011. Both were great options, and in either case, I would likely be the squadron OPSO for a deployment to Afghanistan.

Eric "TULSA" Purcell would also head back to Miramar. One of us was going to go to HMH-361, the other to HMH-465. TULSA ended up getting the orders to HMH-361, and I received orders to return to HMH-465. With that settled, Dobie let me know that I would be the squadron OPSO and lead the squadron detachment to Afghanistan.

I loved the idea of working for Bullwinkle, but the HMH-361 timeline meant I would check in and deploy within weeks. The HMH-465 timeline sounded much better to me. It would give me six months to train everyone and get to know the squadron before we left. I also savored the idea of going "home" to HMH-465 as a major.

Kerry reached out to the realtor in San Diego who had sold our starter house, and then she flew back to meet with her and look at neighborhoods. When she came back to Virginia, she was certain she wanted to live in a community in the San Pasqual Valley that had a great K-8 school for the kids. The housing market was a mess at that point, so we just started writing offers on every house in that neighborhood. All of the houses were short sales, so most of those offers just disappeared into bank hell. But our realtor eventually got a lead on one that wasn't a short sale, and we wrote an offer on it sight unseen. The sellers accepted, so I flew to San Diego the following weekend to do a walk-through and had a flooring guy meet me to measure everything in preparation for a quick facelift. We were almost set.

I graduated from Command and Staff in May of 2010, but Tristen still had a few weeks of school left, so I pushed to San Diego, and Kerry and the kids stayed in Virginia to finish school. I picked up my Dad in Texas, and we went to the new house to do a bunch of work. I had guys install new flooring, but we did a lot of painting and other cosmetic work. We slept on air mattresses for a week while we gave the house a makeover. Dad went home a couple of days before Kerry arrived with the kids. My mother-in-law drove across the country with them. As we settled into San Diego again, I started to think about how quickly I would return to war.

I hadn't flown in combat since the fall of 2005. I was maxed out at the end of my last combat deployment to Iraq, but now I would return as the Detachment Officer in Charge (OIC) and the OPSO. A new level of responsibility. I was ready, but I was also slightly concerned that I would immediately go back to that combat stress level I'd felt so acutely at the end of my last deployment. That thought really weighed on me.

When that started to weigh on me, I dealt with it the way I always had. A few beers always helped me turn my brain off and get some sleep, despite being an unpopular decision at home. When I was at MAWTS, Dimes and I often went on fleet support together. We always bought Coors Light and Swisher Sweets cigars. At some point, he would tell me, "Just keep being you, man. Just keep being you." It was his way of re-affirming the way I functioned, and I loved him for it. He wasn't judging. He understood.

I still hadn't dealt with what I had become or experienced on my first round of combat deployments. MAWTS-1 just let me keep being "Whiskey" the CH-53 pilot without having to address any of that. But it was still there under the surface, and I knew it. For the time being, I needed to keep being that guy. It kept me and everyone around me alive. I had no idea how it would come home to roost, but I knew I would eventually figure out that part. Until then, I busied myself with the move back to San Diego and checking into HMH-465 as a major. I was about to be tested on an entirely new level.

18

BACK IN THE FIGHT

AFTER THREE YEARS of instructing at MAWTS-1 and one year of reading and writing in Quantico, I was finally back home. Hangar 4 sat there on the flight line at Miramar, waiting for me to walk back in the door. I would return to the squadron in which I had grown up, which was cool. Only one problem. The squadron was a shell of its former self. After I departed four years earlier, the squadron had been pulled out of the combat deployment rotation. Suit and those guys had completed one more deployment to Iraq, then higher headquarters decided it was time for Warhorse to take a breather.

I was walking back in the door as a major to be the OPSO. I had grown up generally disliking most majors, and now I was one. I wanted to own that leadership level and be effective like the few I had really respected during my first fleet tour. I needed to be competent, demonstrate common sense, and take great care of our Marines. That was the goal. It would be on me to get half the squadron ready to deploy to combat in six months. With one exception, none of the other pilots going with me had ever deployed to combat before. We had another major a bit junior to me who had done it as a CH-46E pilot and then transitioned to the CH-53E. But none of the company grade officers possessed an ounce of combat experience. It was going to be all new to them.

There were a few staff non-commissioned officers (SNCOs) downstairs in maintenance I had grown up with in the squadron. They had just returned for a second tour, like me. I would need them to help me make it all work. Having deployed with them before would help a ton. They knew what needed to happen for us to get ready. I checked in a couple of weeks before the Change of Command.

Dobie was coming in to take over, but the outgoing CO wasn't a fan of mine. I didn't know him, but when I checked in, he made a point to tell me that he didn't care for MAWTS-1 instructors. Whenever I was on the receiving end of a conversation like that about MAWTS-1, I always assumed the speaker had not had a good experience as a student. It happens. Regardless, I was only allowed to start writing the training plan Dobie would sign off on after the Change of Command, and I was okay with that. I had a ton of shit to figure out, anyway.

I was slated to be the Detachment Officer in Charge (OIC) for the deployment. I would take half of our squadron and deploy to Afghanistan, where we would join half of an east coast squadron. The difference is that they were bringing their CO with their flag. The squadron was HMH-461 "Ironhorse." When we mashed the two halves together into one squadron, we would all be wearing the HMH-461 patch, and I would be working for their CO. I hadn't met him before; I only knew of him by reputation, which was highly competent but high-strung. I knew it would be challenging. Not for personal reasons, just cultural differences.

Marines are all deadly serious about warfighting, but Marines on both the east coast and west coast maintained negative stereotypes about one another. East coast Marines believe that Marines on the west coast are less disciplined. West coast Marines tend not to be quite as rigid with things like haircut regulations, uniform standards, and civilian attire. The perception is that those are things you can get away with when you are "further from the flag." Like most stereotypes, there were grains of truth sprinkled into their perceptions.

In reverse, west coast Marines found east coast Marines to be extremely rigid on an array of "little things" and believed they weren't as good at operating in "the dirt" of the desert because they were on the east coast surrounded by trees and greenery. That thought was especially prevalent in the west coast CH-53E squadrons. West coast squadrons trained year round in the desert around MCAS Yuma and Marine Corps Air Ground Combat Center (MCAGCC) Twentynine Palms. The east coast units could only do that when they deployed to the west coast for training detachments. The west coast units had also spent more time in Iraq and Afghanistan at that point in the war, and they felt their additional combat experience was a differentiator. The east coast Marines disliked that perspective. As a result, those perceptions around proficiency at operating in the desert and overall warfighting capability represented the most pronounced points of conflict.

Unit culture was always critical to unit success. We were being asked to create one fully functioning squadron by mashing together two culturally different squadron halves from opposite ends of the country. Both might be Marine Corps CH-53E squadrons, but this little experiment could go sideways in a hurry if those in leadership positions didn't handle it correctly. We were all highly annoyed about the fact that it was happening this way at all. The brass would never do something like that with two infantry battalions. But fuck the 53 guys; we'll make them do it. I was more than a little bit concerned that the arrangement was set up for failure.

Our squadron had a highly motivated captain WTI named Teddy "Aflak" Hart. Aflak was from the Bronx, New York, and he had played baseball at the Naval Academy. He had a big personality, was a great dude, and I was immediately a huge fan of his. Aflak had already earned the trust and respect of the squadron, which I appreciated. He was going to be a critical player to us pulling this off. But before I started to build a training plan with Aflak, I needed to get my ass downstairs and bring the SNCOs on board with the training plan I intended to build. Our squadron aircraft readiness had diminished over the last few years while out of the combat deployment rotation. To pull off the blending of two squadron halves, aircraft readiness needed to be fixed quickly. The training plan I was about to write would be worthless if we didn't have aircraft to fly.

The SNCOs were happy to see me and quickly gave up the goods. They were all disgruntled because, from their perspective, they hadn't had a solid operations training plan to support in quite some time, and they were sick of maintaining aircraft to simply burn holes in the sky. It was a perspective common to squadrons out of the deployment rotation for a while. I reminded them we had a combat deployment a few months away, and assured them I would have a solid training plan in short order, but I needed improved aircraft readiness for us to execute it. They said they were on board. We all went to work. It was a handshake contract, but it would be critical for all of us to honor it. We needed every flight hour we could get to whip our pilots and air crews into shape for what would be a varsity level deployment.

When Dobie finally took over, I had version 1.0 of the training plan ready for his review. We only had June through November to work with. December would be a lot of pre-deployment leave and last-minute stuff. All the real training needed to be done before that. We were also supposed to do our final pre-deployment training with the contingent from HMH-461 at an exercise called Enhanced Mojave Viper (EMV) at MCAGCC Twentynine Palms in November. That would be our one chance to work together as a combined squadron for a couple of weeks before meeting up in Afghanistan.

I was told I would be the OPSO for the combined squadron, which I appreciated. I wanted to be driving the fight, but that meant I also had the lead on ensuring that both squadron elements got to Afghanistan with all of the requisite pre-deployment training complete. I reached out to their OPSO, Stu "Thurston" Howell. Thurston was a former HMH-466 west coast guy, a bit junior to me, and he had gone through WTI when I was an instructor. He had a unique combination of intellect and candor that I appreciated. The plan was for Thurston to work with me as the Assistant Operations Officer (AOPSO). I knew immediately I would have him be my mirror once deployed. Meaning, we would always be on opposite shifts, because I knew he was more than capable of handling anything that came down from higher headquarters or the CO when I wasn't around.

I asked him to send me an estimate of what training his HMH-461 crews would have completed when we all converged at EMV. Aflak and I were already finalizing our version of that for our HMH-465 crews. Based on those projections, we would know exactly what training the combined squadron would need to have available at EMV. Building that entire plan was a big job, but I enjoyed it. A few days later, Aflak and I headed out to MCAGCC Twentynine Palms for the EMV planning conference to represent both squadrons. Since we had figured out the details on what training we needed, we knew exactly what to ask for. We needed a lot of gun shoots for our enlisted aircrew and a lot of night externals for the pilots. Thankfully, both would be readily available at the exercise.

During the planning conference Aflak and I spent our nights sitting at a table out by the pool at a shitty little hotel in Twentynine Palms, drinking Coors Light and writing the details of one of the most aggressive exercise training plans I had ever been a part of. Mashing together the pilots and aircrew from separate squadrons for the exercise was a good warm-up for what would be required of us all when we reached Afghanistan.

As soon as the planning conference ended, we headed back to Miramar and dove into executing our squadron training plan.

We were running what we called a two-turn-two at least three if not four days per week. That meant we sent out a section of two aircraft to train during the day and then handed those two aircraft off to different crews to go out and train at night. As Night Systems Instructors (NSIs) and WTIs, Aflak and I served as the instructors for most of the night flights. Dobie flew a lot of them, as well. The fact that we were putting everyone else through their paces made me feel a little bit better about our chances. But we needed to get a lot better in a few short months.

I took a training detachment out to Naval Air Facility (NAF) El Centro, California, to expedite the process and get everyone more reps. Being there next to the training ranges eliminated transit time and allowed us to get everyone a bunch of landings and external training in the dustiest parts of the desert where we trained. That detachment went well. When we returned to Miramar, the time flew by. Once we reached November, I felt confident our aircrews would be ready to go.

At home, we celebrated Thanksgiving two weeks early since I was going to be at the EMV exercise during the Thanksgiving holiday. Adjusting things like holiday celebrations had become commonplace for our family, but for the first time, our daughter Tristen was old enough to notice. She was in the third grade. She didn't know where Afghanistan was, but she knew that it didn't sound good when adults talked about it. She knew we were having Thanksgiving early because Dad was getting ready to deploy there. It was a lot of weight for an eight-year-old kid to carry. But she handled it like a champ.

Dalton was only two, so he was oblivious for the time being. Following the early celebration, I said goodbye to the family for a few weeks, and on November 17, 2010, we launched a flight of five CH-53Es to MCAGCC Twentynine Palms for the exercise. It was time to mash this thing together with HMH-461.

The initial integration was as rough as I expected. In fairness, the CO had every right to be nervous. He was being handed half of a squadron he didn't know, and like all O-5 Commanders, he would own all of the risk. If we got to Afghanistan and started fucking it up, he was going to be accountable for it. It was a tough position for him to be in, and I was empathetic to that. He was also a vintage east coast Marine. Extremely professional but rigid and very formal. It was like he was speaking a language our detachment from the west coast couldn't quite understand. I expected culture shock from both sides, but we needed to start working through it.

It was stressful, but we initiated the plan and knocked out the needed training. The common ground between the two halves of the unit: everyone knew it was a priority to be as technically and tactically proficient as possible. We would all be interdependent, not only to execute at a high level but to survive the experience. At Twentynine Palms, we always slept on cots in these shitty little Quonset huts out at Camp Wilson near the Expeditionary Airfield. There was nothing out there besides those Quonset huts, the flight line, and a lousy little chow hall. The shitty living conditions were perfect. When you cram everyone together in a place like that, the shared adversity can be a bonding agent for the unit.

On Thanksgiving Day, I treated myself and drove over to mainside to eat at Carl's Junior. I ate a Superstar double cheese-burger and looked out the window across the desert training area and the water treatment facility called Lake Bandini. I just sat there, looking at it and thinking about what we were about to do. I thought about my deployments to Iraq as a captain. The flying had been equal parts amazing and stressful on those deployments. My combat stress level was high by the end of my third deployment to Iraq. I thought about how it had taken me a couple of years after that one to come back down and reset. I wondered if I would instantly go back to that stress level when we arrived in Afghanistan. I wasn't sure how I would feel about it once we got there and took the mission. It felt heavy.

As a former MAWTS-1 Instructor and the OPSO for the combined squadron, I was in a significant leadership role. I knew that everyone else would take their cues from me. The more comfortable I appeared, the more comfortable everyone else would be. Keeping my stress level down and being the calmest motherfucker in the room would be critical to our success. It was a hell of a thing to think about as I ate my Thanksgiving cheeseburger alone.

We wrapped up the exercise on December 10, 2010, and both elements headed home. I felt good about the training that had been completed. That piece was very productive. But I was still concerned about the unit culture. We had made a little progress over three weeks, but it didn't feel like a single cohesive squadron. There were still two very distinct sides.

As soon as we got home, we started our pre-deployment leave blocks. We were slated to depart shortly after the New Year and didn't have any required training left to do. We flew the aircrews that weren't on leave a little bit to stay current and buttoned up our final administrative requirements. But everyone got a chance to take some leave and spend Christmas with family. Getting into the holiday spirit isn't easy when you know you are deploying to war a couple of weeks later.

All the familiar thoughts came back to me. Would this be my last Christmas with Kerry and the kids? If I don't make it back this time, will they be okay? Those thoughts weigh on you. And it isn't easy to watch *Christmas Vacation* and bake apple pies when you have that shit on your mind.

I played it off the best I could and tried to live in the moment. But there were a couple of late nights when I drank too much, just trying to stop thinking about the idea of never making it back home. I was ready to just get on with it.

Everyone was back at the squadron on January 10, 2011. We had a few days to get all our aircrews one last warmup flight before leaving. Our bags were packed. We were just waiting for a ride. The morning before we left, I was up early and grabbed a cup of coffee. Our kitchen had a nice little view of a portion of the San Pasqual Valley. In the winter, the marine layer tends to settle into the valley in the mornings, making the view a little more peaceful. I thought about how I was looking at one of the most peaceful valleys on the planet. And in a few days, I would be flying around in the Sangin River Valley, arguably the most violent and dangerous valley on the planet at the time.

It was a hell of a contrast. I was slowly getting into character so that I would be exactly who I needed to be upon arrival. That morning I was just a guy looking out his kitchen window in the suburbs of San Diego. In a few days, I would need to be the best combat assault support aviator I could be in order to make sure we brought all our Marines home again. It weighed heavily on me.

Then I sat down and put together a folder for Kerry on the computer in my home office. It was a ritual I completed before every deployment. Some of it was regular day-to-day stuff about our finances and the house. Some of it was things to do if I didn't make it back. I had completed that exercise prior to every deployment, but it always felt heavy. With that task complete, it was time to go.

We deployed on January 17, 2011. It was Kerry's 37th birthday. For a present, I said goodbye to her and the kids at 0545 and left for Afghanistan. It was the second time I had left for a combat deployment on her birthday. I have to give her credit. She didn't give me an ounce of shit about it. I had my Marine Corps buddy, and Dalton's namesake, Chris Dalton, pick me up and take me to the squadron. He had recently moved back to San Diego to start practicing law. I appreciated him doing it. Saying goodbye was always brutal, but I preferred doing it privately at home. Kerry had made the kids these "Daddy dolls" that had a photo of me in a flight suit on them. Tristen was eight, and this was the fourth time I was deploying to combat since her birth. Thankfully, she didn't remember the first three.

It was my first time to deploy since Dalton had been born, though. Thankfully he wouldn't remember this one. Saying goodbye to them while they were clutching those dolls and crying was brutal. Dalton only knew that I was going away for what seemed like forever. Tristen was old enough to know that not only was I going away, but I was going somewhere extremely dangerous. Walking out of your house, wondering if you will ever see it or your family again, is always a heavy experience. I had a 25-minute car ride to Miramar to let that go. I was the Detachment OIC. When I walked into the hangar, my demeanor needed to put everyone at ease. I knew they would all take their cues from me.

Once I was in the car with Dalton, I got into character quickly. It was time. Bring on the terrain, the shitty weather, and the fucking Taliban. I was going back to the show. By the time we got to Miramar, I was ready.

I thanked Dalton for the ride, grabbed my gear, and headed into the hangar. A few hours later, our detachment was on board a World Airlines charter headed for Manas Air Force Base, Kyrgyzstan. We had 142 Marines from HMH-465 on board and another 40 from Marine Aviation Logistics Squadron 16 (MALS-16), who would support higher-level maintenance. We also had some combat replacements for the 3rd Battalion, 5th Marines. They looked uneasy, and their presence reminded us what the stakes would be upon arrival.

Before getting to Manas, we stopped at Biggs Army Airfield in El Paso, Texas, to pick up some Army interpreters. Our next fuel stop was in Bangor, Maine. They still had a nice contingent of people at the airport in Bangor to welcome us as we moved into the terminal for an hour during the fuel stop. On the way home, the greeting from those people felt great. On the way out, it felt a little bit eerie.

We finally arrived at Manas at 0230 local on January 18, 2011. It was below zero outside, so sorting out our bags and getting the Marines settled in transient tents was a little rough for some of our first time deployers. Several of them experienced an obvious "What the fuck did I sign up for?" moment. We had about 24 hours to kill while waiting on our C-17 flights to our final destination at Forward Operating Base (FOB) Bastion, Afghanistan. It was a long 24 hours.

On the morning of January 20, 2011, we made our final movement to FOB Bastion. The British had originally built Bastion in 2005 with a little camp and a decent-sized helipad. From that point, it had expanded significantly. By the time we arrived, the airfield had an 11,000-foot runway 01/19 and a full flight line on the east side of the field.

The original Camp Bastion and helipad were on the west side of the runways, and Camp Leatherneck had been built onto the southwest side of that. Camp Leatherneck was originally constructed to house the I MEF Expeditionary Force in 2009, and it had been occupied by Marines ever since. It was a sprawling piece of desert that looked like a sea of "cans" that housed the Marines. There was also a mainside of Camp Leatherneck where the Marine Corps higher headquarters worked. Our Wing (Forward) Headquarters was located there, as was Regional Command (RC) Southwest. Interspersed in all of that were shower trailers, laundry facilities, dining facilities (DFACs), and everything else Marines needed for a seven-month deployment.

For the first 24 hours on deck, it was all logistics. Getting the Marines settled into their cans on Camp Leatherneck, showing them where the DFACs were, getting familiar with camp rules, and making sure everyone knew how to catch the jingle buses to the squadron spaces on the flight line so that we could all start work the next day. The jingle buses were janky little buses the local drivers tended to decorate with all kinds of random hanging shiny objects and fuzzy balls.

We were going to be taking the mission from our sister squadron HMH-361 and their east coast contingent from HMH-366. Like us, they were also a combined squadron from both coasts, but HMH-361 had brought the flag and their CO. My counterpart as their OPSO was my old WTI roommate and fellow MAWTS-1 instructor, Eric "TULSA" Purcell. Their CO was LtCol Doug "Bullwinkle" Glasgow. At the very least, I knew I would get a great turnover from them.

We still had a little over 24 hours before our counterparts from the east coast were expected. I wanted to take advantage of that time and get everything as organized as possible before the CO arrived with the other half of our combined squadron. TULSA and I went to work right away. I started on a combat schedule, so on January 22nd, I met up with him at noon. We spent a solid 14 hours together that first day. He was already using the same methodology I planned to use to maintain the appropriate number of pilots and aircrew on two shifts to support all tasking.

As he took me through everything they were doing in operations, he said one thing that jumped out at me. They had executed over seventy named operations. When we finished my last OIF deployment in 2005 with sixty-eight, I didn't think I would ever see another CH-53E squadron do that many named operations in combat. But they had just exceeded that total. That told me everything I needed to know about the pace of operations we should expect to experience.

The HMH-461 contingent and our CO landed at 0228 on January 23rd. I could tell right away that the CO was keyed up. I would have to be on my A game to help him get comfortable. The next morning, we had everyone together for our Reception, Staging, Onward Movement, and Integration (RSO&I) briefs. Once those briefs were complete, we would be cleared hot to start doing Familiarization (FAM) flights with HMH-361 and making final preparations to take the mission. My initial conversations with the CO were good. He seemed to be acclimating well, but I knew he faced a delicate situation. He'd just been handed half a squadron that he didn't know for a combat deployment, and I knew he wasn't comfortable with it.

The next day I briefed the CO on our swing schedule, which would systematically move the right mix of crews back and forth between what we called the evening shift and the morning shift.

The evening shift was 1300 to 0100, and the morning shift was 2200 to 1000. So the evening shift would take off late afternoon and fly into the night. The morning shift would start in the middle of the night and fly until after sunrise. Most of the named operations would happen on the morning shift, so the crews needed to be stacked appropriately. We also had to keep a couple of crews on a normal day shift to execute Functional Check Flights (FCF) for our maintenance department. That would primarily be mid-grade captains who were Functional Check Pilots (FCPs), along with a couple of young copilots.

The CO was good with the overall plan and the way we split the crews up. Everyone who was a Night Systems Instructor (NSI) had a "mirror." A person who would be on the opposite shift. The CO and XO were obvious mirrors. Myself as the OPSO and Thurston as the AOPSO were also obvious mirrors. We also split up the company grade WTIs and NSIs. I also had to take billets into account. We had to have officer coverage on both shifts in the departments as well. With 24-hour operations, there was always something going on, so we had to have the right people in the right places at all times. It was a well-thought-out and well-orchestrated plan. It had to be right. The CO was good with the plan and appreciated the level of thought and detail we had put into it. We got the blessing we needed from him to take off and run.

On January 25th, we started flying our warmup flights with HMH-361. We had aircrews from both squadrons in the aircraft for every flight as part of the turnover. In doing that, we were able to simultaneously complete the tasking while getting our aircrews familiar with the Area of Operations (AO) and punching current fly days in the aircraft. My first flight was a day into low light level general support flight with one of the captains from HMH-361. We ran some fuel blivets up to Kajaki dam and dropped those right before sunset. We were goggled up by the time we hit Delaram 2, Sangin, and Lashkar Gah. It was good to see a few of the FOBs in person. The low light level wasn't quite as extreme as I remembered it being in Iraq. I assessed that the general support missions should be quite doable for the majority of our aircrews. I knew the named operations would have to contend with some nasty Landing Zones (LZs) with heavy brownout. We would make sure we had NSIs and WTIs in each aircraft for those.

The actual Transfer of Authority happened on February 1, 2011. We officially had the mission. When we published our flight schedule the night prior, our Operations Chief sent it out on the Non-classified Internet Protocol Router Network (NIPR) as instructed by the Wing. The CO came down to my office and went off. He thought we had released a classified document on an unclassified network. It took us a bit to convince him that was the procedure directed to us from higher headquarters, but his reaction indicated the degree to which he was feeling the stress.

We had a little ceremony on the morning of February 2nd that we all found to be a ridiculous waste of time. We didn't need to get out on the flight line with the Commanding General (CG) making remarks to know we had the mission. For the next 180 days or so, we knew we would be out there every day making the mission happen. We just wanted to get on with it.

At home, our callsign in HMH-465 was "Warhorse." HMH-461 was "Ironhorse." For this deployment, the combined squadron was assigned the tactical callsign "Mongol." It was a curious choice given where we were. While "Mongol" would take some getting used to, I preferred having a single callsign for the deployment rather than the randomly assigned callsigns we used to get in the early days of OIF. When the tactical callsigns changed every day, it was confusing for everyone.

The first few days were predictably rough. Our maintenance department wasn't in a groove yet, and the aircraft got a vote. It was exacerbated by the fact that our sister CH-53D and MV-22B squadrons had supposedly "flown too many hours," so the 3rd MAW Forward (Fwd) operations staff was loading us up heavy right out of the gate. The weather sucked the first day we had the mission, which was a blessing in disguise. It gave us a little breathing room to get our shit together. But it turned out we needed more than that.

We started knocking out tasking on both shifts but had a string of bad luck in the process. One of my maintenance Marines fell out of his rack and started having vision problems, so he was sent back home. One of my captains had a Things Falling Off Aircraft (TFOA) incident where he somehow lost a fuel cap. Then one of the HMH-461 majors lost 300 rounds of .50 caliber ammo off his ramp.

Each of those incidents required the CO to go up and brief the Wing with an 8-Day Brief. That brief was basically, "here's what happened and what we are doing to make sure it never happens again." He got his ass handed to him on all of those, which just increased his stress level. While I understood why the process existed, I always thought it was overkill in most cases. Shit happens. To top it off, our maintenance department continued to struggle, and we had to get Wing to cancel our tasking on a couple of occasions to try and get caught up and get the aircraft healthy. Hence, a rough start.

Shortly thereafter, things started to settle. Just a little bit. Maintenance started getting into a little bit of a groove, and our Operations team did as well. We had a solid plan, and we were executing. But in the wake of the rough start, the CO was stressing everyone out about all kinds of shit. He was all over the majors in general, but as the OPSO, it felt like I was at the top of his list. The other majors and I had several conversations about how intense it was. He was trying to make a point about how important it was for us to nail the details, but we already knew that.

The east coast and west coast integration was also still going a little bit rough. My captains never missed an opportunity to bitch to me about something or other that a field grade officer from the east coast had said or done. It was mostly meaningless attempts to bust balls and establish authority, but it wasn't going over well. The one thing I heard that annoyed me was that a couple of the HMH-461 field grade officers had been commenting about how tired they were. I had no patience for that shit. We weren't even two weeks into a 180-day marathon at that point. We all needed to be setting the example for how to set and keep the pace.

Some of the other majors did similar things when it came to eating chow. Our schedules weren't conducive to sitting down at the DFACs and eating three times per day. We had breakfast, lunch, dinner, and midrats, all being served in our little flight line shack and the DFACs on mainside. But often, we could only make it to one or two of those meals. That was especially true when we were in the aircraft for six to ten hours. Some of those guys had been calling the Operations Duty Officer (ODO) to get them to bring food out to them when stopping back through the fuel pits at Bastion. That made me insane. We weren't airline pilots. Take some CLIF bars and eat what you can when you can. I ate so many CLIF bars in the seat of a CH-53E that, to this day, the mere sight of a CLIF bar grosses me out. But as far as I was concerned, that was the only way to do it. We weren't there to eat. We were there to fight and fly.

Somewhere in there, I flew our first named operation. It was a four aircraft insert in support of Marine Forces Special Operations Command (MARSOC) with some Afghan security forces. They had Afghan interpreters with them, and I stopped by to say hello to them before we turned up. One of the Afghan interpreters was saying all kinds of crazy shit in broken English. Perplexed, I looked at the MARSOC Marine who stood next to him, and he just shrugged. That was my cue to strap in. The insert at least went well and helped us start to settle in a bit more on the flying. A few days later, I made a hit at FOB Delhi, and some old Marine with stark white hair was standing just outside the landing zone, staring at us expressionless the entire time we were on deck. He had that hollow, slightly crazy look in his eyes like Colonel Kurtz from "Apocalypse Now." Someone needed to get that Marine the fuck out of there.

On February 18th, I started swinging to the morning shift. When we executed the swing schedule, we always "swung to the right." Swinging to the right meant that you would adjust to the other shift by staying up later and sleeping later. It was much easier than doing the opposite and sleeping very little or not at all. I had been on the same shift as the CO, so I had been riding from the cans to the squadron with him every day in the little pickup truck he had been given as a personal vehicle. Now that I was on the opposite schedule, I rode the jingle buses with everyone else. I enjoyed that because it always gave me a chance to chat with some of our young enlisted Marines. It was a nice break, and I was excited about swinging to the morning shift. I had our Operations Department on track, and I was ready to do some serious flying. The morning shift is where the action was, and I was ready to dive back into it.

The next morning Aflak and I were on the bus back to mainside and drove by this little spot on the flight line where the Third Country Nationals (TCNs) waste truck drivers pumped out the black water waste from the heads. The black water flowed out through a ditch into this field outside the wire and served as fertilizer. The field was this little area of vibrant green surrounded by the lifeless brown desert. As we were looking at it, Aflak said, "It looks like the Masters over there. Weird." That random patch of green did look very out of place.

Getting onto the opposite shift from the CO, I also started to get a better feel for the other HMH-461 guys. Without him around emanating stress, they were different people. Their Maintenance Material Control Officer (MMCO) was a salty Chief Warrant Officer (CWO) 3 named Jake Lewis. I hadn't worked with Jake before, but he had an excellent reputation, and I immediately liked him. He was extremely competent and no-nonsense. To say he had zero tolerance for incompetence or any form of bullshit would be a gross understatement.

I knew that for the squadron to have a chance at functioning in a healthy way the relationship between the Maintenance and Operations Departments needed to be good. A hard goal to accomplish in any squadron. It would be a bitch in this mashed together squadron from two different coasts. I knew Jake and I would be essential to that working, so I started making a point to go over to Maintenance Control and visit with him every day. I wanted to ensure he knew I understood maintenance and how to run operations in a way that would make life easier, not harder, for his Marines. We hit it off right away. Together, we immediately started solving problems over a cup of coffee on my daily visits to his office.

I was doing something similar with all the HMH-461 majors. As abnormal as the whole arrangement was, we would all need to work together to try and help the CO stay even-keeled and bring everyone together. In the beginning, I think they thought I was crazy for trying.

The squadron continued to settle into a better groove. I flew another couple of named operations and felt like we were starting to get into a rhythm. At the same time, our higher headquarters at 3rd MAW (Fwd) was starting to turn over with their replacements from 2nd MAW (Fwd). So there was a lot of churn happening above us. I had to work closely with our operations officers to try and dampen out some of that churn to ensure the squadron didn't feel it too much. We needed that higher headquarters transition to be transparent to our Marines.

The outgoing 3rd MAW Future Operations Officer (FOPSO) was a lieutenant colonel I had served with at MAWTS-1. He had been the Assault Support Division (ASD) department head my first year there. As the FOPSO, he was the primary person I interfaced with about our assigned tasking. Great communication between his team and my team in our Operations Department was essential. I loved working with him and hated to see him leave, but I was comforted by the fact that the incoming 2nd MAW FOPSO would be Lieutenant Colonel Larry "Sniper"

Brown. He was an MV-22 pilot, but I had known him as Captain Brown when he was a CH-46 pilot and WTI on my first deployment to OIF. Like his predecessor, Sniper was highly competent and just a really good dude. I knew he and I would have a great working relationship.

Just as things started to settle a little bit, two of my captains decided to procure bikes instead of riding the jingle bus to and from the flight line. They got busted for cutting across the end of the runway on their way to the squadron one night. Turned out to be the straw that broke the camel's back for the CO. He lost his damn mind.

It didn't help that those captains of mine had already grown out their "war staches," and their mustaches were totally out of regs. The CO hated shit like that, which made it even worse. The Wing Chief of Staff was an over-the-top asshole who loved to go off on people. I was the senior officer on deck when he called down to the squadron to summon the CO up to Wing for that ass chewing. As soon as I got on the phone, he yelled, "Get your fucking CO and those two fucking captains in front of my desk right now! Every minute that passes between now and then, they are in even deeper shit."

Senior officers like that were my favorite. I knew that would only throw gas on the fire for the CO.

After I got off the phone, I had to send someone down to the CO's can to let him know, and I took another couple of our guys to plan a big named operation we had on tap for early the next morning with the Brits. I didn't have any time to sweat the next round of ass chewings that I was inevitably going to be due for later. I needed to get into character for this planning session. But I did feel bad for the CO. Our guys had fucked him on this one, and there would be a little bit of hell to pay.

Our British Liaison was a captain who worked in Wing Future Operations. When we went over for the planning session, he broke down the players on that side of the flight line for us. He told us British Joint Helicopter Force Afghanistan were pros that we would enjoy working with. But they weren't the only ones on that side of the base. He said the Danes were "pretty good" because they understood British Tactics, Techniques, and Procedures (TTPs). But then he tossed in that the Norwegians were clueless, the Tongans were only good for base security, and the Italians "do nothing but drink wine." They had fucking wine! Bastards. We weren't allowed to have any alcohol in-country.

Planning with the Brits was a pleasure. They were so laid back about it. The operation we were planning was called "TORA ZHEMAY." It was an insert of 250 British and International Security Assistance Force (ISAF) troops into Nadi-Ali. The plan was to do it with a single hit of eleven Assault Support Aircraft. Four British Chinooks, three British Merlins, and four of our CH-53Es with escort from two British Apaches and two Marine Corps AH-1W Cobras. It sounded cool, but I walked into the planning, expecting a total clusterfuck of a planning session.

After some intros, we quickly learned that the Brits' idea of planning was just standing around a map, drinking tea, and listening to the Ground Combat Element (GCE) scheme of maneuver. Then, they briefly discussed potential LZs that they called "Helicopter Landing Sites," and we slapped the table on those. From there, we quickly hashed out the load plan for the pickup zone, the route, the objective area, and the wave off plan. The entire planning session took all of 90 minutes. If that was a Marine Corps Operation, we would have been planning that shit for two days. I liked their style. The only downside to knocking it out so quickly was not getting a chance to eat at the British chow hall. They supposedly had way better food than we did, and I wanted to check it out. Shepherd's pie would have to wait.

When I returned to the squadron, the CO was waiting to talk to me about "my guys." It was yet another, not fun, one-way conversation. As much as I didn't like it, I just took it. It was my job to be the buffer. Better him going off on me than everyone else. As he was laying into me, I was thinking about how I was pissed at myself for not trying to buy some wine from the Italians. I don't even like wine, but I could have used a drink.

The next morning, February 27th, I bounced right back, and we flew Operation TORA ZHEMAY. Execution went off without a hitch. As we rolled on final for insert, we had all the assault support aircraft in Combat Spread, which put us into one big line, all side by side, ripping across the desert floor. I remember thinking it must have looked like that helicopter scene in "Apocalypse Now." We executed quick stops to a landing and inserted the British and ISAF troops. Then, we pulled pitch and got the fuck out of there. The whole thing got my blood pumping in a way that it hadn't in a long time.

I had an all HMH-465 crew that day. My copilot was Tom "TITS" McKeon. We had one of our staff sergeants in the back with a couple of our other young crew chiefs. We had just executed a giant insert into one of the most violent places in the AO in broad daylight. The mission was ballsy to the point of being borderline stupid, but we had pulled it off. It was a good day. Our son Dalton had recently celebrated his third birthday, so I carried an American Flag for him in my helmet bag. I would put it into a plaque for him with a certificate signed by the crew after I returned home.

When we returned to the squadron, the CO grabbed me to tell me he wanted my captains, the ones who'd gotten his ass chewed for the bike incident, to put a class together on bike safety. In the grand scheme of things, that was a win, and I didn't let it phase me. I was in too good of a mood from the flight. Afterward, we all went to the chow hall to grab lunch before we crashed for the day.

TITS McKeon, who had been my copilot that day, was with us, and he was a character. TITS was the kind of guy you only meet in the Marine Corps. He was a small guy with dark eyes and a knack for saying the craziest shit. On a training detachment to Vegas a few months prior, he had challenged me to a whiskey shot contest in front of everyone. His callsign "TITS" was an acronym for "tanked in two shots." My callsign was "Whiskey," so I knew it was a bad idea for him. But he wouldn't back down.

After trying to talk him out of it a few times, I finally relented. After each shot, he would look at me and yell, "I'm 140 pounds of don't quit, Whiskey!" We were all cracking up laughing. That contest didn't end well for him, but the mere fact that he had done it cemented his status in the squadron. Everybody loved him.

TITS was from Queens, New York, and had crazy stories about how he used to drive around drinking 40's while delivering cigarettes and candy for some shady guys when he was growing up. But TITS was best known for leaving notes in guys' helmet bags that read "You've been owned by TITS McKeon." The connotation was that he had defiled their helmet bag. The fact that he left those notes used to crack everyone up. At the DFAC that day, he was eating everything in sight. He started with three chocolate Otis Spunkmeyer muffins and six cartons of white milk. Then he got a couple of scoops of mint chocolate chip ice cream. While eating it all, he kept saying, "I can't believe this is free." We were all laughing our asses off. There is nothing in the world more entertaining than Marines. Having guys like TITS around for levity was always welcome.

On March 9, 2011, 2nd MAW (Fwd) officially took over as our higher headquarters. I was ready to quickly settle into that transition. Sniper made that easy, which I appreciated. At the squadron, things still felt strained, but we were functioning better. We had a Command Climate Survey, and everyone was buzzing about filling it out. I knew the results were going to be bad, and the CO was personally going to get roasted. As soon as I saw the survey drop, I knew I could start the clock for what would likely be some serious drama.

But the flying was good. On March 13th, I took off at 0300 for what was supposed to be a four-hour flight. After continuously getting re-tasked and having our crew day extended a couple of times, we landed at 1345. Ten hours and forty-five minutes of banging around a combat zone in mostly daylight was not for the faint of heart. But I enjoyed it. On the morning of March 15th, I finished up what should have been another short flight when we got a call from the Tactical Air Command Center (TACC). They needed us to external some fuel blivets from FOB Payne down to LZ Wolfpack. The Marine Corps Light Armored Reconnaissance (LAR) Battalion was in a fight down there, and the AH-1W Cobras supporting them needed more fuel. It was on us to get it there.

I led the section, so we bustered (hauled ass) down to FOB Payne, where we found two bundles of 3 x 500-gallon fuel blivets waiting for us to pick up as external loads. We quickly made our picks and pushed out to LZ Wolfpack with the fuel blivets. I hadn't been to LZ Wolfpack yet, but I expected it to be dusty. When we got close, I switched over to LZ Control and called inbound to "Nomad."

The voice on the other end of the radio sounded familiar. He came back with, "Is Whiskey flying today?"

I replied, "You've got him." I recognized a master sergeant whom I had served with at MAWTS-1.

"I was hoping it was you, Sir, because where I need these blivets to go, the brownout is extreme."

I had one of our more senior crew chiefs in the back, so I liked our chances. I shot the approach right to where they had the Forward Arming and Refueling Point (FARP) set up for the skids. At twenty-five feet, I was fully in the "brown house," but I kept pushing and used the hoses and pumps on the ground for reference once I started to pick up the ground again around 10 feet. That was right about the time the load touched the deck. Our crew chief released it. It was a perfect drop. Once I was on deck, the Master Sergeant came up on the radio and said, "You've still got it."

It was a nice compliment coming from him. My dash two

took a couple of attempts, but they finally got their load on deck as well. Once on deck, we loaded their empty fuel blivets and got out of the way. As we took off, the skids that needed to refuel were on short final to land. It was a full-on MAGTF effort. Missions like that always felt good.

The next morning at the squadron, the CO got the results of the Command Climate Survey. He had swung back onto the morning shift with me at that point, so there was no avoiding him. We knew that he had the survey results and assumed that they were bad. Nobody knew what to expect next, but the officers were anxious. That night, the CO called me down to his office and started a conversation with me about unit culture.

We both knew that, because I was the senior guy from the west coast and the Operations Officer for the overall squadron, I was best positioned to help him bring everyone together. We had a long conversation that night and another one the next night. Those conversations were challenging. But I give him credit. He didn't have to talk to me. But because he did, those conversations ended up being very productive. I knew that, despite our style differences, we both wanted the same things for the squadron. We just had different ways of going about getting there.

The primary differences were delivery and demeanor. He was high-strung and formal. I was the opposite. In many ways, we epitomized the respective coasts we came from. Coming out of those conversations, I was clear on what I could do to help. We needed balance, and I was committed to helping us find it. As I thought more about it, I also hoped I could find something for the whole unit to rally around. Something that would force everyone to get on the same page. I didn't know it yet, but that's exactly what we were about to get.

19

IT'S A TRAP!

IT WAS JUST after 0100 on March 19th when the phone rang in my office. I had been on what we called the morning shift for over 30 days, doing a lot of night flying. Our morning shift typically came in at 2000, briefed, took off around midnight, and flew until shortly after sunrise. The majority of our named operations happened on this shift so that we could benefit from the cover of darkness.

I liked the morning shift, but after a month or so, it would start to wear on me. I was only a few days away from swinging back to the day shift and having Thurston swing back to the morning shift. On that particular night, I wasn't flying; I was in my office working on the squadron swing schedule and overall plan for our aircrews to ensure we had everything covered. I answered the phone to find a very excited Sniper on the other end.

"Whiskey, I have one for you, and your boss isn't going to like it."

I knew that meant we were about to be handed a high-risk mission.

He told me that an Army Chinook helicopter had crashed out on the Pakistani border. The Army had requested a Tactical

Recovery of Aircraft and Personnel (TRAP). It wasn't just any Army Chinook. This Chinook was an MH-47G that belonged to the 160th Special Operations Aviation Regiment (SOAR). The "Night Stalkers" had been executing a hard hit raid on some Haqqani network targets when the pilots browned out and rolled the aircraft over on landing. That told me everything I needed to know about how nasty the brownout had been in the LZ.

If the Night Stalkers browned out and rolled it, the zone had to be varsity. It also told me that this mission would receive a lot of attention. The Night Stalkers don't exist and can't leave any trace, so this aircraft either had to be removed or destroyed. It was a thirty-million dollar problem, and Special Operations Command (SOCOM) hoped we could solve it for them.

The real question from Sniper: would it even be possible for us to externally lift the damn thing out of there? I immediately knew that if the math worked and the actual lift was possible, this would be my most challenging mission yet. But the first question that needed to be answered was, would we have enough power to execute the actual lift?

It was a math problem, and that calculation had to be perfect to answer the feasibility of support. The only real information the Wing had for me at that point was a grid coordinate for the crash site and an estimate that the Air Force Downed Aircraft Recovery Team (DART) put together about the weight of the Chinook. The DART team estimated they could get the Chinook down to 25,000 pounds. It was enough information for me to get started. I hung up the phone and went to work. Having planned the MH-53 Pave Low lift in Iraq back in 2005 came in handy. I knew exactly what I needed to do.

I walked across the hall, jumped on one of our Portable Flight Planning Software (PFPS) computers, and quickly plotted the location. As expected, the aircraft was in a really shitty spot. The area immediately surrounding the crash site would make for a nasty LZ right in the middle of some cruddy little village called

Orgun-e-Kalan, which was way the hell out to the East in Paktika Province, and about twenty miles from the Pakistani Border.

Just south of Khost Province, at the base of the Spin Ghar mountains, Orgun-e-Kalan was at approximately 7,000 feet of Pressure Altitude (PA). The air is thinner at higher altitudes and warmer temperatures. Both of those atmospheric conditions decrease lift capability. The altitude for this mission would make this lift even more difficult. To help compensate for the high altitude, we would need the outside air temperature to be as cold as possible.

I had our S-2 reach out to weather to get an estimated Outside Air Temperature (OAT) for that grid coordinate at sunrise, roughly 0600. That is always the coldest time of the day, so our overall lift capability would be maximized. Executing the actual lift right after sunrise would be our best bet. The forecast OAT at that grid coordinate, the PA, and the calculated Density Altitude (DA) gave me what I needed to quickly calculate both the power required to execute the lift and the power our aircraft would be able to produce.

By the book, my power available needed to give me a 5% margin above the power required to execute the mission. That margin provides a safety buffer. My quick math told me that if we could strip about 5,000 pounds of weight off our aircraft and get that Chinook down closer to 21,000 pounds, we could likely pull it off. But there was a catch. We weren't going to have the required 5% margin. We would have no margin for error at all.

At 5 degrees Celsius and 7200 feet PA, our DA would be 7900 feet. The charts in my NATOPS pocket checklist told me that the power required would equal the power available at 109% torque. I quickly did the entire calculation two more times just to make sure. I got the same answer every time. No margin for error.

Having no power margin meant the planning math had to be perfect, and the flying execution would have to be perfect as well. I also knew planning calculations never work out quite that perfectly in execution. We would do a final power calculation in the LZ, but a host of variables could swing that equation in one direction or the other. Actual engine strength based on en route power checks, a slightly warmer outside air temperature, or even a slightly different than expected PA could make the lift impossible to execute at the last minute. Regardless, this mission was too big to walk away from. I was hell-bent on giving it a shot.

I then ran over to the maintenance hooch and talked to our MMCO Jake Lewis. I told Jake what was going on and asked him how much weight he could strip off one of our aircraft. I told him the goal was at least 5,000 pounds, and he was on it immediately. Jake was back in my office within a few minutes, saying we could do it. The only caveat was that I would have to be okay flying an aircraft with no armor or guns. He would remove all our Ballistic Protection System (BPS), and we wouldn't have our standard loadout of 3 x .50 caliber machine guns in the crew doors or on the ramp. We would enter a high threat area naked. We would also need to remove the troop seats, cargo winch, Forward Looking Infrared (FLIR), the refueling probe, and a few other miscellaneous items to make weight. The final measure was that we would also have to remove our auxiliary fuel tanks before executing the actual lift. That meant I needed to take a primary aircraft to execute the mission, a flying backup in the same stripped-down configuration, and a normally configured aircraft carrying maintainers and bomb carts to drop my aux tanks in the field just prior to taking off to try and execute the actual lift. Nothing about this operation would be simple.

Since 2nd MAW (Fwd) had just taken over, I knew the Commanding General (CG) would likely have serious reservations about executing this shortly after taking over the mission. I called Sniper back and told him I had run the feasibility of support. We would be able to execute if the Air Force DART team could get the aircraft down closer to 21,000 pounds.

"That's with a margin, correct?"

I answered, "No margin."

He replied, "Damn."

I could tell by his tone that he knew the CG wouldn't like the odds. My boss would not like them, either. I told him I was about to brief my CO, as well as start building a quick brief for the CG. He said he was already working on setting a time for us to present our plan to the CG shortly after sunrise. I said, "Roger that." I then headed down the hall to brief the CO.

I was pleasantly surprised when our CO didn't push back as hard as I thought he would. We were fresh off our conversation that had followed the Command Climate survey. We both understood that the combined squadron was at a critical juncture. I knew he didn't like it, and the idea of doing it made him uncomfortable. But I have to give him credit. I also know he understood the significance of the situation and what it would do for the sake of the overall mission and the squadron itself. He asked me to do it myself. I agreed but asked him to be the flying backup. For multiple reasons, I thought it needed to be one of us over that load when it came down to it. He agreed.

I went back to my office and started putting together the brief. The mission was all about the actual execution of the external lift, but a ton of other details needed to be figured out quickly. We knew where the aircraft was, but we were going to need somewhere close to that where we could land, drop our auxiliary fuel tanks, and do some final preparations. The objective area was roughly 300 miles away and well out of Regional Command (RC) Southwest, our Area of Operations (AO). We would have to coordinate crossing RC South and into RC East. Taking our own rotary wing escorts wouldn't be an option due to the range. We would transit without escorts and hopefully pick up some escorts into the objective area from the Army. I also wanted the DART team to rig the aircraft with special long slings.

The CH-53E is equipped with a hook system that allows external loads to be picked up with either a single hook and pendant or a dual hook and pendant. The dual hook system provides greater stability for bigger external loads that need to be very stable in flight. This was going to be a dual point evolution. The normal pendants we used for the dual point system were just shy of 8' long and required a low hover just above the load to allow the Helicopter Support Team (HST) Marines on the ground to attach the pendants to the actual load. The combination of the height of the Chinook and the brownout conditions in the landing zone were going to make those normal pendants unfeasible. The Air Force DART teams also carried long slings that were 65 and 75 feet in length. Utilizing those would allow me to land next to the Chinook and have the HST Marines hook up the load while we sat on the deck. It would be a much safer evolution with a higher probability of success if we could do that. I added the request for long slings to my list of pending questions.

Shortly thereafter, I had my answers. Sort of. Coordination to cross the other AOs was still in work, but the Army would provide us with Apache escorts into the objective area from a Task Force they had in the area. There were still a few questions left to be answered, but I knew that Sniper and the entire Wing Operations staff were working on those in earnest. The biggest lingering question was identifying a Forward Operating Base (FOB) near the objective area where we could safely deliver the Chinook. We would also need that FOB to drop our aux tanks before the lift, reinstall them after the lift, and refuel after completing the TRAP. Sniper thought there was a FOB we could use about 25 miles to the west, but we still needed to verify. If it was there, it wasn't on the map. Based on my calculations, 25 miles was about as far as we would be able to fly the Chinook. At that distance we would land right on our NATOPS minimums for fuel.

My brief for the CG was ready to go by sunrise. From there, it was just waiting on Sniper to confirm the time for us to arrive and brief him. It took longer than I wanted, but we finally got summoned to brief at 1100. At that point, it had already been a long day. I gave the brief to the CG with my CO sitting next to me, and the CG was flanked by his principal staff to include Sniper and his boss. As expected, the CG hated that I wouldn't have a power margin. He asked me if I was comfortable executing without one, and I told him I was. He left us by saying that he needed to think about it. We walked out of there, still not knowing if the mission for the next night was a go.

We made a quick stop at the little chow hall we called "the sandwich shop" and grabbed something to eat. We finalized the plan and the flight schedule, assuming we would launch for the mission. It would be easier to turn off at the last minute than it would be to turn on. When we got back to the squadron, it was a ghost town. It always was around lunchtime since our two shifts overlapped closer to midnight.

When I walked in, our S-2 had found the Unmanned Aerial Vehicle (UAV) feed of the crash site. I stood there and watched it for about a minute. The Chinook was there, on its side in the LZ. Just waiting for me to come and get it. I had left a detailed pass down for Aflak and Thurston on our Secret Internet Protocol Router (SIPR) email. If this thing was a go, I would need them to finalize the details of our plan during the day shift. With that email sent, I finally left the squadron spaces and headed back to my can on mainside to try and take a nap.

I laid in my rack and couldn't stop thinking about it. I wrote in my journal and then tried to read for a while. I finally fell asleep around 1800. I had been awake for almost 24 hours, but that didn't matter. Too many thoughts raced through my head.

It felt like I had only been asleep for about five minutes when someone started pounding on the door to our hooch. I got up and opened it, and it was Aflak.

"Boss, pack your shit for three days; you guys are fucking going!"

I quickly glanced at my watch and saw that it was 2100. I had only been asleep for three hours, but that was enough. I was wide awake, my adrenaline already pumping. I asked why I needed to pack for three days? Aflak said there might be a follow-on movement.

I asked, "What follow-on movement?"

Aflak said, "I'll tell you in the truck."

I always had a "go bag" packed with a couple of skivvy rolls and a spare flight suit, so all I needed to do was throw a few extra warming layers in there, and I was ready to walk.

The CO had brought his truck down so I could avoid the slow ride over to the squadron spaces on the jingle bus. When I jumped in the back seat of the CO's truck with Aflak, he was talking a thousand miles an hour.

Word was, our 2nd MAW (Fwd) CG and RC Southwest CG, both Marines, had pushed up to higher headquarters that they didn't want to execute the mission due to our having no power margin. Both had been overruled by the overall commander of U.S. and coalition forces in Afghanistan. The commander of U.S. forces, an Army General who was senior to them in rank and billet, wanted us to give this aircraft recovery our best shot.

Aflak and Thurston had finalized every last little detail. They had built me a six-part folder with every piece of information I could ever need. I flipped on the blue light I always wore around my neck and leafed through the folder as Aflak talked. The final details were all there. Aflak and Thurston had been busy, and they had done an amazing job.

The FOB that wasn't on the map wasn't an accident. It was there, but it was the FOB that the Army Task Force called home. They had also confirmed that the Chinook belonged to the Night Stalkers, and that was also their home base. Hence the secrecy.

The FOB would be our staging point and drop off point for the Chinook. The Night Stalkers had been operating out of there in support of an elite unit of special operators and intelligence personnel working to eliminate the remaining Taliban forces in the peaks and valleys of the Hindu Kush mountains on the Pakistani border. Aflak then briefed me on the follow-on movement. The Army asked us to take the Chinook an additional 50 miles to another runway where it would be easier for a cargo aircraft to load it internally for transport back to the U.S. I knew right away that would be a no-go. The way the math worked out for the lift, I would be running on fumes just flying it the 25 miles to the initial drop off at the FOB. There's no way I could take it 50 miles. The CO, who had been quietly driving us, piped up and said he would take care of making that follow-on movement go away. He ultimately delivered. Our only job would be to get it to the FOB.

When I got to the squadron spaces, I had about 40 minutes to finalize prepping my brief that was scheduled for 2200. The 2nd MAW (Fwd) CG was actually in our spaces, waiting for me. After a quick greeting, our CG personally told me, "If it doesn't look right or feel right, don't try it." I said, "Yes, sir," but there wasn't any way in hell that was going to happen. If I made it to the objective area with a good aircraft, we would either recover that Chinook or die trying. There was no middle.

Thurston hit me as soon as that conversation was complete, talking a thousand miles per hour. He was a walking database of all things military. Thurston knew where every unit in the country operated, where they were based, and what assets they had available. That knowledge had come in extremely handy on this one. He had tracked down Points of Contact (POCs) and had already coordinated ramp space for us at the FOB to drop the tanks. He set us up for billeting, chow, fuel, and everything else we would need to pull it off.

We would be out of crew day once the recovery was complete, so we would need to bed down there before flying back home to Bastion. Thurston had also gathered all the frequencies and airspace information we needed to cross RC South and into RC East. Finally, we talked about the actual external lift.

He had passed the word that we wanted to use the long slings to avoid having to hover over the load. The DART team planned to use 75 foot slings on the forward transmission and 65 foot slings on the aft transmission since it was taller. The aft transmission was taller, but not 10 feet taller, which meant the aft end of the aircraft would break the deck first when tension came onto the slings. That would be an important detail for me to remember. I couldn't have asked for anything more from Aflak and Thurston. After all of the work they had put into the details of the plan, I was sorry they weren't going with me.

As Thurston and I finished up, Jake Lewis came over and handed me a cup of coffee. He asked if I needed anything else, and I thanked him and told him that he and his Marines had done enough. They had stripped our two strongest aircraft of approximately 5,000 pounds. Both had T64-GE-419 engines, which were a little stronger than the T64-GE-416 engines typical of most of our aircraft. My aircraft also had no Integrated Mechanical Diagnostics System (IMDS). That meant that the aircraft wouldn't be recording any flight data.

I would also need to manually catch any overspeed or over-torque conditions that might happen to our engines during the lift. We would go with two enlisted aircrew vice three in the back of the aircraft to stay as light as possible. The maintenance Marines had stripped everything off the two primary aircraft that we had agreed upon. They had done all that in the last four hours after the official "go" order came down. It was an amazing squadron effort.

In addition to Maintenance, Aflak, and Thurston, the rest of the squadron labored all day to get this mission ready to go. The place was buzzing, and every Marine was on it. At 2200, some of our other pilots had the map up on the wall for me in the ready room, and it was time to brief.

I kept the brief straightforward and simple. I wasn't too concerned about anything but the lift of the Chinook itself. Everything else was just one big movement to the objective area to get me over that load. As I kicked off the brief, my abbreviated Concept of Operations highlighted exactly that. We would launch as originally planned as a flight of three CH-53Es. I would be in the lead aircraft, stripped down and configured for the lift.

The CO would also be configured for the lift as a flying backup in dash two. Dash three was a normally configured aircraft carrying some Combat Camera Marines, as well as bomb carts and maintenance Marines to remove my auxiliary fuel tanks when we got to the staging point. We would not be taking escorts with us. We would pick up Apache escorts into the objective area from the Army once we got there. From there, I gave a very condensed Division Brief off the map with the Tactical Pocket Guide. I hit everything I needed to and skipped everything else. Several items fell into the Standard Operating Procedure (SOP) category, so I briefed "SOP" to the max extent possible and didn't even bother briefing the objective area. We would have about an hour to hash that out with the Army when we got to the FOB. Time to go.

I headed to flight equipment, grabbed my gear, and walked to the aircraft. As I was walking out onto the flight line, Aflak was walking back in. He and a few other pilots had gone out and pre-flighted the aircraft for us. The standard good luck thing to say in Naval Aviation is "don't fuck it up." Instead, Aflak kept it light and laughingly said, "the legend of Whiskey is about to grow."

I chuckled and replied, "Or this is going to be my last flight." I knew this one was going to be dicey.

My co-pilot was Justin "Shakes" Smith. He was one of our best Functional Check Pilots (FCPs), and I needed someone that could expertly manage the engine Speed Control Levers during the lift. Shakes was perfect. My aircrew in the back were two guys I had been flying with for years. Staff Sergeants Shawn Mitchell and Rob Torres had grown up with me in HMH-465. We had already deployed together several times, and we were exceptionally comfortable flying together. I gave those three a quick final crew brief, then we started strapping in and getting ready to turn up. It would take all four of us having our best day to pull this off.

As we were strapping in, I briefly thought about Kerry and the kids. They were probably enjoying a typical Saturday morning back in San Diego. Meanwhile, I was strapping into a stripped-down CH-53E to fly halfway across Afghanistan in the middle of the night to try and recover a downed Army Chinook. I turned the thoughts of home off and got back into character. It was the mission every CH-53E aviator wants to fly in combat. It was long-range, heavy lift, high altitude, high threat, and a nasty landing zone. Everything I had done up to that point prepared me to execute that one mission. It felt surreal.

Roughly twenty-four hours after the first phone call from Sniper, we were conducting radio checks. All aircraft were up, and everyone was ready to go. We taxied down to the fuel pits to top off with fuel before taking the runway to launch. At 0130, we were outbound on the route. We pushed east across the Green Zone and checked out with "Overlord" as we crossed Checkpoint Horse. We were officially out of our AO, and the next 210 miles were all unknown.

Since my aircraft and the CO's aircraft had been stripped for weight, we had no FLIR. As a result, we put dash three in the lead for the transit to the FOB. His FLIR would allow him to ensure that we avoided the terrain and any other obstacles in our path. In our aircraft, I had Shakes fly while I sat in the left seat, reading through all of the documents Aflak and Thurston had put together for me. The moon was up, so it was a bright, high light night, and the scenery was pretty incredible. The further we went northeast, the more it looked like the Afghanistan I had pictured. The elevation slowly climbed from Bastion's 2900 feet, and the mountain peaks grew steadily taller. The lower Hindu Kush mountains were on our left, the desert floor sprawled out to our right. It looked amazing.

As we continued to push east and climb, the temperature steadily dropped. It was really cold outside and in the aircraft.

By the time we reached the FOB, we had climbed to 7400 feet, and the 10,000 foot peaks surrounding us were all snow-capped. It looked like a postcard. Too bad it was a combat zone.

We landed at 0330 and shut down on a fixed-wing ramp right off the approach end of the runway. The Night Stalkers had a couple of their pilots pick us up and take us to the Army Task Force Headquarters. They were nice enough to let us use their spaces. One of the Night Stalkers pilots was a guy who'd been a CH-46 instructor at MAWTS-1 with me prior to his departure to fly with the Night Stalkers. It was a random place to run into him, but it was nice to see a friendly face.

We quickly hashed out the objective area with the Army Task Force. I got a call sign and frequency for the Fires Net, and I was told that a section of AH-64 Apaches, callsign "Tigershark," would be on station for detached escort. The Joint Terminal Attack Controller (JTAC) "Stryker 39" was already on deck with the security force in place to protect the aircraft.

I also confirmed that the load would already be rigged for the lift. As planned, the DART team had attached 75 foot slings on the forward transmission and 65 foot slings on the aft transmission. I was also told the aircraft was upright. Initially, it had rolled onto its right side, but the security force had righted it with a Mine Resistant Ambush Protected (MRAP) vehicle. That was a relief for me. I was concerned about trying to pick it up on its side. But they also confirmed that they had rolled it over after browning out on landing again, confirming how nasty the zone was going to be.

Once that was complete, I quickly briefed our crews on the objective area. The Chinook was oriented due south, and there was about 75 feet of space between the aircraft and a 15 foot compound wall on the east side. On the west side, there was more like 150 feet between the Chinook and a little house with a short wall around it. I wanted to land next to the Chinook on the west side and hook the load up on the deck. The CO would hold airborne out to the west. Dash three would then come in and land to drop off our HST team and Combat Camera. Once HST verified the rig was good, they would hook up to us and get out of the way. I would then lift and do the pick. There was nothing left to cover, and it was time to get on with it.

The Task Force guys gave us a ride back to our aircraft. Our maintainers were done dropping our auxiliary tanks, and everything was ready to go. I strapped back into the seat at 0515. At 0540, we were airborne. The sun was rising, and we had already de-goggled as we approached the objective area.

It was a quick twelve-minute flight into the objective area. I had comms with Tigershark and Stryker 39 almost as soon as I switched off the tower frequency. Tigershark called the winds at 270 at 30 sustained. Not good. It was a straight crosswind as the Chinook was oriented due south. Stryker 39 then called the winds 150 at 15. Tigershark came back and overruled him. I quickly discovered Tigershark was correct. Coming into the objective area always looks a little different than you imagine it would with a map study. When I first saw the Chinook, it looked huge amid all those little mud hut compounds. The overall objective area also looked small. We were almost right on top of it when I saw it.

I quickly overflew the LZ to see if there was room to land on the west side of the Chinook. As expected, there was room on the west side but not the east. But on the more open west side, it looked like there was debris of some kind all over the LZ, and the Army Rangers from the security force were running all over the place. I came up on the radio and told Stryker 39 he needed to clear the zone for me to land. I swung around to the right and set up for a landing aft and right of the Chinook.

On final approach to landing, I quickly discovered that both the dust and the crosswind were no joke. I wanted to land on the same 180 orientation the Chinook had just to get a feel for the winds. It was a varsity landing, even with the available light from the sunrise. The degree of difficulty was quickly going from highly difficult to fucking ridiculous. We were on deck just before 0600.

Sitting there in the LZ, I quickly knocked out my "Quick and Dirty" in zone power computation and determined that Power Required did equal Power Available. As I had planned, we would be right on the line with no margin for error. The 30-knot crosswind added an additional layer of complexity. I sat there in the seat for a few minutes, mulling it over. The DART, HST, Rangers, and Staff Sergeant Mitchell were crawling all over the Chinook to verify it was rigged properly. I was still thinking through the last details of how I could pull this off.

The first thing I thought of was how big the damn Chinook looked. It was about the same size as our aircraft. And we were about to try and pick it up. Just to the south of the Chinook was an Afghan graveyard filled with tall sticks with flags on them for grave markers. That made the whole scene even more ominous.

I also thought about how many people would be watching this live via the UAV feed. I couldn't see the UAV, but I knew it was up there. This had to be the event of the day in-country. The commander of U.S. forces and his staff were probably watching. Hell, every general officer in the country was probably watching. Not to mention all the randoms sitting around in secret rooms back at the Pentagon. If I fucked this up, there wouldn't be any debating it. They were all going to see it live. I liked our chances, but I also knew there were no guarantees. A lot could go wrong.

I had been watching Staff Sergeant Mitchell as he walked all over the zone. He knew I wanted to move forward and land on the immediate right of the Chinook. He came over and hooked back up to ICS from outside. He told me the right side where there was room to land wouldn't work. He said the debris lying everywhere were the fiberglass splinters of the Chinook rotor blades. When the Chinook rolled over, the blades had completely come apart. If we hovered over and tried to land on that side of the Chinook as planned, all that debris would get sucked up through our rotor system and cause all kinds of damage. Then we would have two aircraft down in the zone. I had also put myself in the left seat, thinking that the Chinook would be on our left. We were going to have to hover on the left side of the Chinook, which would be to our right, and I wouldn't be able to see the Chinook at all.

At that moment, I knew I had enough reasons to call it off. We had no power margin, the crosswind was making it harder, and now I was going to have to get the load hooked up with a traditional hover in a brownout on the left side of the Chinook with my fuselage between the compound wall and the Chinook. The scenario was fucking ridiculous. But I also knew how awesome it would be for the entire squadron if we pulled it off. We had come too far not to give it a shot.

I was also acutely aware that the vast majority of aviators would have already called it off by then. There was a fine line between good Operational Risk Management (ORM) and simply playing that card because a pilot was scared. I refused to take the out to call it off in the name of ORM. I thought of it as simply having the guts to try. As I sat there thinking about that, I experienced an epiphany. At that moment, my confidence spiked, and I knew we would pull this off.

We had no margin, but that power available calculation was based on hitting your 10-minute T5 limit of 829 degrees Celsius. The "momentary peak" limit for T5 is 900 degrees Celsius. So I knew the engines had a little extra juice if I needed it for a few seconds.

I was going to do the actual flying for the lift, and Shakes would manage the Speed Control Levers. His job was to tell me how much more power I could pull and work the Speed Control Levers to ensure we didn't overtemp or overspeed any of our three engines. I reminded him that we had 900 degrees Celsius on the temperature for a few seconds if we needed it but that an overspeed would ruin an engine and the mission.

In the fifteen minutes or so that we had been sitting there, I also came up with a last bit of strategy. Once the load was hooked up, and tension was on the slings, if I could turn the Chinook about 45 degrees to the right, I could gain a partial headwind component out of that 30-knot crosswind. Instead of fighting it as a full-on crosswind, I could use it to our advantage. But I was going to have to turn the Chinook to do it. It was a very non-standard move.

HST wrapped up their final preparations, and Staff Sergeant Mitchell climbed back on board our aircraft. He plugged into the ICS and got in the hole to call me over the load. He said something to the effect of, "Let's fucking do this." Everything was set. It was go-time. I quickly briefed Mitchell and Torres on my plan to try and turn the Chinook into the wind when we brought tension onto the slings. I looked over my shoulder at Mitchell, who gave me a skeptical look. It was a fair reaction on his part, but I was still going to try it.

I picked up into a hover and slid over the aft end of the Chinook to get on the left side. The sun was coming up over the mountains to the east, and that was right in my face. The sand on the aircraft's left side was ankle-deep talcum powder, so the brownout was as extreme as I had expected. I couldn't see much of anything at all, and it was instantly understandable that the Night Stalkers had rolled the Chinook over on landing in the first place.

I used Mitchell's calls to hover forward into the spot between the Chinook on my right and the compound wall on my left. I could barely see the top of the wall to my immediate left, so while listening to Mitchell, I used that for reference. As Mitchell called me down to hook up, I lost that reference and was strictly executing off his calls and my radar altimeter.

The dirt was going out and away, hitting that wall to our left and cycling back at us. It looked like a tornado lying on its side, which made the brownout conditions that much more difficult to contend with. Torres kept me honest so that I didn't drift into the Chinook on our immediate right. I knew the aft right side of our aircraft was very close to the Chinook. That right crosswind also made a precision hover difficult, especially as light as we were. If you could see it from the front or rear, our fuselage was nestled down in between that wall and the Chinook. Our blades were above both of them on each side. It was tight in there.

It felt like it took forever, but we got hooked up in about 60 seconds. Mitchell then called me to come up for tension. I wasn't used to using the long slings, and I felt like I was really fucking high before tension was even on the line.

I remembered that with the sling lengths, the aft end of the Chinook would break the deck first. When it did, I would try to execute the rotation to the right. I turned my nose slightly to the right before tension was on the line, hoping to slowly start pulling that aft end around as tension came on and lifted the back end. It worked out even better than I could have possibly imagined. I got the Chinook turned about 45 degrees to the right - quickly and easily. When I started turning it, Mitchell yelled, "Holy shit! It's fucking working." on the ICS. Now it was moment of truth time. I had to get that thing up off the ground and flying.

I started gently milking our aircraft forward and steadily pulling power. My final in-zone calculation had given me Power Required equal to Power Available at 106% torque. As the Chinook broke the deck, I kept squeaking in more power and trying to get some forward airspeed going. My inputs on both the cyclic and collective were tiny at that point. The Chinook was barely off the deck, and our radar altimeter was stuck at 75 feet as the signal bounced off the top of the Chinook.

My altitude was a guess at that point, but based on what Mitchell was telling me, the load was about 10 feet off the ground. I needed forward airspeed and some additional lift immediately, or it wasn't going to happen. There were compounds all around us, so I was also concerned about slamming that Chinook into a wall or one of the mud huts.

Shakes gave me great calls on where we were with the power as I kept squeaking in collective. When he finally said, "No more power," I looked down and saw just shy of 120% torque and just shy of 900 degrees Celsius on our T5 gauges. Our aircraft was giving us everything she had, but I only had a few seconds to get it flying and reduce the power requirement.

We crept forward, slowly gaining momentum. I could also feel our tail rotor struggling to keep up, which was an indication that we were right on the brink of power required exceeding our power available. At that point, I instinctively made a light right pedal input to reduce the torque on the tail rotor. This kept us from losing tail rotor authority and gave me a tiny bit of power back for the main rotor. That allowed me to start an accelerated slip forward with my nose canted a little to the right. Getting into that slip further reduced our torque requirement, let me pull a squeak more power, and ultimately allowed us to pick up some forward momentum more quickly.

It all came together after a few seconds, and we started flying. The Chinook probably cleared the first walled compound in front of us by about 10 feet. It was close, but we made it. I started an easy climbing right turn to get the fuck out of Dodge. The Chinook was bouncing all over the place in the wind and was pulling us around. It was like having a giant 21,000-pound sail attached to the bottom of our aircraft. We were flying, but we felt every movement. Shakes went to throw our dual point hook switch from Load/Unload to 2pt Flight, which was our standard procedure. In 2pt Flight, the no-load sensors on the hooks would open to drop the load if it felt the weight removed from either hook. The way that the Chinook bounced made me worry it would happen right away, so I told him to stay in Load/Unload. It was a snap decision, but I decided the risk was worth it. After all of that, I didn't want to drop that Chinook in the middle of the desert.

Once we got out of the crazy wind in that valley, I was able to accelerate to 80 knots, and the Chinook smoothed out. It was still the longest 25-mile flight of my life. Going back into the FOB was much easier than the pickup had been. I made a left downwind for runway 14 and shot a slow precision approach down the length of the runway. They wanted me to sidestep to the "Victory Pad" on the right side of Runway 14, where the Night Stalkers normally park their aircraft. It was cake compared to the pick. I gently set the Chinook down on the spot, Mitchell and Torres released the hooks, and then we hovered forward to land.

Once we were safe on deck, we all just sat there quietly for a minute. No one said anything. I think we were all still in a state of shock that it was over and we had pulled it off. After a couple of minutes, Mitchell asked if that's where we were going to shut down. He was so fried, he couldn't remember. I told him this was it, so he jumped out front so we could shut down.

When we got our aircraft shut down and went cold, Shakes looked pumped. He looked right at me and said, "Awesome job." I told him the same.

It was over. We had fucking pulled it off!

After we shut down, I got out of the aircraft, and the CO was already almost there. He ran up and hugged me with tears in his eyes. We felt like we had just won our version of the Super Bowl. When the CO walked away, I looked at Shakes and said, "I think he's probably done giving us shit in Ops now." Shakes just laughed.

After a short celebration, we snapped a few photos with the Chinook, and a couple of the Night Stalkers started bitching at us for taking a picture with a secret aircraft. We laughed it off and headed to the chow hall. It was the most festive chow hall meal I was ever part of. We spent the rest of the day sleeping it off in some tents at the FOB, then got back up shortly after sundown to prep for our flight back to Bastion. It was close to 2200 when we made it back to Bastion, and the whole squadron was pumped. The mission represented a huge team victory. When I walked back into the building, the other officers in our Operations Department had made a poster with a picture of

Admiral Ackbar from *Star Wars*. Of course, it read, "It's a TRAP!"

In addition to our CH-53E squadron being at Bastion, there was also a CH-53D squadron from MCAS Kaneohe Bay in Hawaii. About ten days prior, HMH-463 "Pegasus" had taken the mission for the D's. Their OPSO was my former fellow CH-53 Instructor from MAWTS-1, Dennis "Dolf" Sampson. Shortly after getting back to our squadron spaces, Dolf came over and gave me a huge hug. He was every bit as pumped as all our Marines were. He knew how big it was for our CH-53 community and for the mission at hand. It was going to kick the door wide open for the type of tasking we would all be getting for the remainder of the deployment. It was going to be game on from that point forward.

In that moment, I knew I had jumped the shark as an aviator. Everything I had done to that point had prepared me to execute that one mission. I knew it was highly unlikely I would ever fly a mission that big again. As the fatigue finally hit me, I still felt like we had just won the Super Bowl. In that world, we had. It felt great.

20

THE GUTS TO TRY

Two days after executing the TRAP, the 2nd MAW (Fwd) CG came to our squadron spaces for an awards formation. Our entire crew was awarded Individual Action Air Medals, and several of the maintainers who went along with us were awarded Navy Achievement Medals. It was a nice gesture from higher headquarters for the entire squadron.

In the wake of the mission, the unlikely happened. The squadron started to click. What had previously felt like a terrible arranged marriage between two very different units began to feel like a cohesive and highly functioning squadron. The overall attitude had changed, and everyone started working together well. Our Maintenance Department hit its stride, and we had our battle rhythm down in operations. The supporting departments were also dialed in.

We had proven to ourselves and everyone else in-theater that we could execute on a high level. More importantly, it instilled a lot of confidence that we could do this together. My primary takeaway was that it was all tied to the fact that we had the guts to try. Our higher headquarters was hesitant to let us attempt the mission in the first place. At multiple points, our CO or I could have called it off. We didn't. Our willingness to simply give it a shot had changed the perspective of the entire unit.

Right after the mission, I swung back onto the evening shift. It was mostly going to be boring general support missions for me for a few weeks, but I was good with that. I wanted to make sure I had our master operations plan wired. I also knew I would have a little more time to work out on the evening shift. I felt like that was needed to help manage my stress level. On the nights I didn't fly, I would go for a run along the fence line. I always thought it odd that we didn't man all the guard towers. It was eerily quiet and dark out there, so it was easy to get lost in your thoughts and just run. The fact that nothing but a chain link fence separated you from the bad guys didn't seem to faze me for some reason.

As I jumped back into the general support missions, things slowed down for me. For the first time since our arrival, I felt like I had a little time to think. My self-awareness perked up in conjunction with that.

Part of that was the added distraction of deploying for the first time as a field grade officer. I was not only the OPSO for the combined squadron but also the Detachment Officer in Charge (OIC) for the half of us who had deployed from the west coast. With all the natural stress that had occurred due to mashing two halves of two squadrons together for a deployment, I knew I had a significant role to play there. It was the most challenging leadership opportunity I had ever faced. And the whole squadron needed me to nail it. I had a good reputation coming in, but executing the TRAP fully solidified my credibility with everyone. I knew that gave me the influence I needed to help ensure our unit's success, but I had to wield that influence smartly.

During my previous combat deployments, flying had been the stressful part. Now it was my escape. As an aviator, I was in my prime and peaking. I was as good in the aircraft as I would ever be. I knew that. I was cruising past 2,200 flight hours and had just come off a tour teaching the best of the best at MAWTS-1. I was back in the show, putting it all to work where it mattered. I had never felt more prepared or more comfortable in the aircraft. I was ready for any mission. No matter how difficult. I was exactly where I was supposed to be and enjoying it.

At that point in the deployment, I had firmly established a great relationship with Jake and his team in Maintenance Control. Not only for how we were functioning between operations and maintenance, but in the other ways that I was willing to help as a pilot. Every squadron has aircraft with assorted types of gremlins.

Some pilots are very particular about some of those things and will down any aircraft in the chocks that isn't damn near perfect. I was the total opposite. If I could get all three engines started and the head spinning, I would most likely take the aircraft. I knew how to work around minor issues and wasn't going to bitch about it. I would always make it work. As a result, Jake and his team often assigned me those aircraft to fly.

He would say, "Sir, this one has a tricky #3 starter. The AFCS is squirrelly in this one. Comm two sucks. The FLIR isn't working."

None of that shit mattered to me. So long as the aircraft wasn't hard down for a safety of flight issue, I would fly it. I always viewed that as the unwritten contract between pilots and maintenance control. You need me to fly this particular aircraft, because it best supports the maintenance plan to support everything we are doing. It was on me to fly whatever aircraft they needed me to fly. I enjoyed that, and it further strengthened the bond of our operations and maintenance relationship.

The general support missions got me dialed back into the Area of Operations (AO) as a whole. FOB Dwyer, FOB Payne, Marjeh, Kajaki, and Lash Kar Gah. The Marine Corps was scattered at FOBs across the AO, and it was primarily up to us to ensure they always had all the supplies they needed. I hated going into Marjeh during the day. We weren't far removed from the huge fight that had taken place there, and there were always too many people around.

Lash Kar Gah was my favorite approach to landing. To get into the LZ at Lash, we flew down what we called the *Star Wars* trench, a gap in the housing we could fly at low altitude then make a quick stop before dropping over a wall into the compound that made up the FOB. On short final, little kids would often sit on the wall near the LZ, throwing rocks and launching assorted projectiles at us with slingshots. Something about those kids was equal parts admirable and amusing.

As we settled in, it quickly became apparent that the feeling our unit could execute on a high level wasn't only internal. In the wake of the Chinook TRAP, higher headquarters immediately saw us in a different light, as did everyone else in-theater. As the only Special Operations Aviation unit in the game, the Night Stalkers received more requests for support than they could fill.

Having proven we could execute on a high level, the overflow quickly started making its way to 2nd MAW (Fwd) for us to execute. During turnover, I was impressed that HMH-361 had executed over 70 named operations. We were now being handed so many named operations, we executed one almost every night. Thankfully we had eleven pilots who were at least Night Systems Instructors (NSIs). Seven of us were also WTIs. Those pilots were the flight leads for almost every named operation. Between the two shifts, we typically had two or three pilots in that group out flying and another two or three planning the named operation for the next night. That depth and operational organization allowed us to keep up.

A couple of weeks later, I was out on a general support mission, but I was also giving the Helicopter Aircraft Commander (HAC) in the other aircraft a Section Lead evaluation. The flight ended up being one of those reminders that the bad guys, terrain, and the weather also get a vote.

It started simply enough with a quick run down to Musa Qaleh and Now Zad just before sunset. I tended to always scan the Direct Air Support Center (DASC) frequency in the background to make sure I heard if anything unusual popped off. As a result, I heard the warning that there was a storm rolling into Bastion and all aircraft relatively close should try to return to base. I immediately came up on our interflight frequency and let the other aircraft know. We needed to get going. Quickly.

I was holding out by Edinburgh while he was unloading at Musa Qaleh, but I told him I was pushing to Now Zad to unload my cargo in order to expedite my return to Bastion. He caught up with me on deck a few minutes later. By the time we got airborne, to push home, we were on our NVGs. I knew the storm was already over the airfield at Bastion because I couldn't see the lights. We could always see the lights at Bastion from at least 30 miles away when it was clear outside.

Since the other aircraft was getting an evaluation as the flight lead, I wanted to give him a chance to figure it out. Then he did exactly what I didn't want him to do. He turned 180 degrees and headed in the opposite direction! I came up on the radio and asked where he was going. He said the weather was coming in, so we needed to get back on deck somewhere. There was no guarantee we could outrun the storm back to one of the FOBs we'd just come from. I told him to turn around, call approach, and we would then split up and execute individual instrument approaches back into the airfield. I could tell he didn't want to do it, but he made the call to approach.

We got in touch with approach, dialed in the discreet squawks we were assigned, and started taking separation from one another with instructions from approach. When we first punched into the storm, it was a wild ride for a couple of minutes, but that always happened in the desert. We ended up executing our approaches without incident and safely returned to Bastion. After we shut down, I could tell my copilot was a little rattled. I didn't think what we had done was a big deal. It didn't even register with me as stressful. We were all instrument rated naval aviators. There was zero reason not to recover with an instrument approach. That's the job.

By late April, I was starting to feel the deployment. We were crossing the halfway point and fully immersed in the grind. It takes a special type of endurance to keep a squadron running 24 hours a day for 180 days straight. There is no weekend; there is no day off. It is an endless series of Mondays that seemingly have no end. The only real variation day to day was whether or not I was personally on the flight schedule. As slight as that variation was, I welcomed it. It was the only thing that didn't make every day the same.

I was hitting that point in the deployment where the guilt about not being home started to set in. Kids are resilient, but not being home is still not being home. It is time you can never get back. All those seemingly meaningless interactions at home on any given day matter in the grand scheme of things. There was a cost to not being there. I always just hoped that all of the time apart wouldn't come back to haunt us.

The weather had also officially changed from being cold to full-blown desert heat. Some of our crews were feeling it. It was one thing to be out in the aircraft for 8-10 hours when it was cold or cool outside. It was something else entirely when it was really hot. You had to be in good physical shape to handle it.

On those long flights, I always went through the entire 100oz of water in my Camelbak. It was necessary to at least try to stay hydrated. I was used to functioning that way from my deployments to Iraq, but it was starting to wear on some of the crews. But we had plenty of snacks and little treats like knockoff energy drinks. Our crew chiefs would typically pack a few of those on flights. Any time I started to feel it a little bit late in a flight, I would ask them to pass one of those up to me in the cockpit. Purple "Rip Its" were my favorite. Overall, our living conditions were pretty great considering our location. And some things were unique to Bastion that we all enjoyed.

. . .

One of our favorite "Bastion things" was the British Air Traffic Controllers. They were predominantly female, and their accents made them sound like angels on the radio. Something about their voices soothed. One of our guys asked the Brits about the female Air Traffic Controllers, and the Brit told him it was by design because the pilots find their voices calming. For all I know, it was totally random that they were mostly female, but they were very calming. That was especially true when returning to the field at the end of a mission. As soon as you switched to the tower frequency and called inbound and heard that voice, you knew you had lived to fight another day.

I was also starting to work on the redeployment plan. We would get home late in the summer, which is the tail end of Permanent Change of Station (PCS) season when everyone up for orders executes them and moves to their new duty station. I would take over as the XO of our squadron when we returned to Miramar. I needed to work on the overall personnel plan with the current XO to make sure we knew who was outbound, who was inbound, and what billets all of the officers would occupy. Working on the plan was important, but it made me think about returning to Miramar. I needed to balance that with staying dialed in on the current mission.

The named operations and general support missions were still rolling, but some standard headache type tasking also started to materialize. We had to create a special shift for a few days to serve as the backup for what they called a "Very, Very, Important Person (VVIP) movement" of Afghan President Hamid Karzai. Apparently, once you are a president, you rate the extra "Very." The Afghan National Air Force was the primary, and they apparently pulled it off because we never launched after jumping through hoops to rearrange our schedule for a couple of days.

We did end up launching for something comically ridiculous,

though. Someone decided it would be a good idea to bring a "steak team" out to the AO to grill steaks for Marines at the various FOBs. That's one of those things that sounds kind of nice until you start thinking about the logistical nightmare surrounding it. For a couple of days, our general support missions consisted of hauling this group from Texas and their grills all over the AO. There was constant chaos and confusion surrounding those movements. It seemed so ridiculous, you just had to laugh.

At the end of the month, TITS McKeon was out flying with one of our other guys one night, and they managed to ding their tail pylon on a HESCO barrier going into FOB Oulette. They got lucky that nothing really bad happened, but we still had to go through the whole mishap procedure. It was quickly determined that TITS had made a mistake that was a potential causal factor. He was likely going to be done flying for the deployment while waiting on an official determination. The possibility that it could lead to real consequences for him immediately came up. We had to get Wing to let us have a little Operational Pause the next day so that we could talk about safety and flying smart.

Coming out of the Operational Pause, we immediately had a crew lose a map. Those maps were highly classified because they contained all of our FOB locations. The combination of those two things had the CO running at max stress. I had seen COs exhibit inconsistent decisions about what would and would not be made into a big deal over the course of my career. Sometimes it felt like there was no real rhyme or reason to any of it. But in the case of our CO on that deployment, he was consistent. He would do everything 100% by the book, no matter what.

It was a little different for me, but at least I knew what to expect. I still needed to try and solve for TITS McKeon, and the Wing gave me a golden opportunity. They tapped us to provide an officer to go to Al Udeid Air Base outside of Doha, Qatar, to temporarily fill a billet. I immediately offered up TITS. Getting him out of sight and out of mind for a while would be the best thing for him. By the time I told the CO about it, he was already on an airplane and gone. I justified it with the fact that he wasn't allowed to fly, anyway. No sense sending someone else that could be out there flying.

A couple of days later, the Taliban sent a letter to the commander of U.S. forces, saying that they would be complete with their poppy harvest and starting their spring offensive on May 1, 2011. The summary of the letter basically told us to get ready because on May 1, the Taliban was going to kill all of us. The letter was distributed to all the commands in-country so that we would all be on our toes heading into May. It was such a ballsy thing for them to do, I respected it.

On April 29th, we executed a low light level insert of 86 Marines into a poppy field on the west side of the Helmand River just across from FOB Nolay. We were a mixed division with Dolf's CH-53D squadron next door, and he was in the flight. I enjoyed it when we got to execute missions with them. For the deployment, their callsign was "Closeout," which is a surfing term for a type of wave. It was fitting for a K-Bay squadron. They had a great squadron, and with Dolf running Ops, they were always pros to work with. A KC-130 dropped LUU-19 battlefield illumination for us on insert, and it worked perfectly.

Once on deck, the smell of the poppy field struck me. It smelled like dead fish. One of our crew chiefs stuck his hand out the crew door, grabbed one of the poppy seed pods, and brought it up onto the jump seat. Whoever was working that field had already made cuts on the seedpod, and the milky opium was oozing out of it. I told him to toss that back out the window ASAP. The last thing I needed was anyone thinking we had Marines with Opium! On our way back into Bastion, we switched to the tower frequency, and Dolf called inbound for all of us, "flight of four shitters inbound from the south." The contrast between his deep intimidating voice and the always angelic female British controllers sounded stark. It made me smile.

By that point, not only was Dolf next door, but the OPSO in the skid squadron on the flight line had also been a MAWTS-1 Instructor with us. It made for a great working relationship between the squadrons. And when everything is easier, all of the squadrons execute at a high level.

On May 1, 2011, the Taliban kept their word. There were a lot of them out and about, and almost all of our aircraft that flew that day took fire. Nobody got hit, but we understood the game had changed a little bit. On May 2nd, we executed another mission that was a mixed division with our squadron and the CH-53D squadron next door. Aflak led the flight with me, Dolf, and his CO rounding out the division. It was another mission handed off to us by the Night Stalkers. It was a low light level division insert on the outskirts of Nolay. At the last minute, we learned that we had lost our airborne Battlefield Illumination (BI) support to help facilitate our landing. Aflak jumped through some hoops and coordinated BI from an artillery battery to substitute. Overall, it was a high degree of difficulty insert. Before we walked, Aflak and I had joked about what the Night Stalkers might be executing that night. If they handed this one off to us, what high-speed mission were they doing? When we got back to Bastion, we found out.

As soon as we walked back into the squadron spaces, they were buzzing. The TV in the ready room was on, and they were reporting that a Seal team had killed Usama Bin Laden on a raid across the Pakistani border. We knew immediately what the Night Stalkers had been doing! We were jealous we didn't get the opportunity to participate in that somehow. But it was a huge win for the country and a morale boost for our squadron. Wins like that reinforce the understanding that your work in a war zone is accomplishing something.

On May 6th, my Dad emailed to tell me he planned to marry his new girlfriend. I was happy for him, but it was a random reminder that there was a whole world back home where people were living their lives. It also reminded me how disconnected I was from that world. There was a gap there that had slowly grown over the course of several deployments. In moments when things got quiet, I sometimes wondered if I would ever be able to close that gap and get back to something resembling "normal." I wasn't even sure what normal was anymore.

On May 16th, we received a request for a feasibility of support to recover another downed Chinook helicopter. This time, the aircraft was Canadian. Having already done this once, I was happy to plan it, but I thought someone else should get the opportunity to execute the lift. That someone was our Aviation Maintenance Officer (AMO), one of the HMH-461 guys. He was a highly competent and experienced aviator, so I was certain he could do it. This one was much closer to home, so we launched early the next morning to execute.

I went into the objective area first to ensure the aircraft was rigged properly and ready to lift. I landed near the downed aircraft and left my copilot in the seat while my crew chief and I got out to coordinate with the Canadians. The guy in charge greeted me with a McKenzie Brothers, "How's it going, eh?" I chuckled a bit.

After looking everything over, the only glaring issue I found was that they had not de-fueled the aircraft, so the weight was going to be too much for us to execute the lift. We had to get as much fuel out of there as possible. After giving me a few confused looks, one of the Canadians pulled out an ax and started wailing on the fuel sponson. An unconventional approach, but in his defense, it worked.

The next thing I knew, fuel was pouring out everywhere. After seeing that, I thought it might help reduce the brownout a little bit for the lift. Once the fuel drained, I returned to my aircraft and took off to get out of the way. From there, the execution went off without a hitch.

At the end of May, one of my guys banged the tail skid of his aircraft while landing on a named operation. It was a close call that damaged the tail skid actuator, but it ended up being a non-event. Regardless, it resulted in me being back in the CO's office for another one-way conversation. We had grown to understand each other, but he still didn't care for the fact that I tended to be significantly less emotional than he was about pretty much anything. He articulated that by saying, "You can't always be the coach or the big brother!" It was one more conversation that I stored away for my personal leadership file. I was who I was, and my style worked for me. I wasn't ever going to be the excitable guy who ran around chewing people's asses. It just wasn't me.

I had brought a handful of young copilots with me that were on their first deployment. Two were turning into total rock stars. One wasn't a surprise at all. He was the kind of guy you knew would be a WTI the day he checked in. He just had "it" in every way. The other was a surprise. She was extremely shy and quiet. When she first checked in, I was concerned she might not have the necessary demeanor for any of this. But once we got in-country, she slowly came into her own. I flew with her quite a bit and loved watching her confidence grow.

By that point in the deployment, I had started putting them on the schedule as copilots for some of the named operations. The moment was never too big for either of them. They could keep up. It was rewarding to see that development happening. I was fully transitioning from being the guy who wanted to fly the mission to being the guy who wanted to ensure that everyone else developed sufficiently to fly the mission.

A couple of days later, we had a Helicopter Aircraft Commander (HAC) round table discussion that I missed because I was out flying. During the discussion, the CO said, "Tail skid." One of my guys chuckled. That resulted in me getting called in for a follow-up one-way conversation. It had gotten better, but there was still a separation between the two halves of the squadron, and it was typically my guys who highlighted that.

The whole situation was a real challenge for me. I knew keeping my guys in check was critical to keeping the whole thing together, but the truth was that the perception of the CO and the combined squadron wasn't exclusive to my guys. He had made that for himself. There wasn't anything that I or anyone else could do to change that perception for him. His to own, but mine to manage for another few weeks.

In early June, we planned our first mission with the Australian Special Operations Forces (SOF). They, too, had a Task Force in-country that was looking for Assault Support aviation. It was a division insert, and Aflak was going to lead it. On the night the Australian Task Force guys were in our spaces doing the initial planning, I was in and out of the ready room while also working on some things in my little office. I had a phone in there that could call back to the states, but I was always conscious of not abusing that privilege. It wasn't easy for the Marines to call home, so I felt I should be selective about doing so myself.

That night I had a few minutes, so I called Kerry to say hello. She was telling me about the kids and talking about everyday things like how they were doing in school, play dates, and dental appointments. In the middle of that, Aflak walked into my office with a question. I asked Kerry to hold on for a second.

Aflak said the Australian Task Force guys wanted to know how many dead bodies we could carry. I answered that there weren't any rules about that, so the number would just depend on whatever capacity we had at that point for the additional weight. Based on the mission profile, we should be able to take several if necessary.

Aflak said thanks and walked out to deliver the news. The contrast between my conversation with Kerry and what I was doing there could not have been more profound at that moment. On one end, it was taking kids to dental visits in San Diego. On the other end, it was how many dead bodies we could carry. I felt totally disconnected from the real world.

That first mission with the Australian Task Force ended up being a wild one. Aflak led a flight of four to conduct a division insert into the Kajaki Sofa Bazaar. An ambush awaited them on short final, and the sky lit up with tracer fire and RPG shots. Somehow, they all waved off and managed to get the fuck out of there without taking any real damage. But it was an eye-opener about how wild working with the Aussie Special Forces might become. In the days that followed, our guys started to refer to that flight as "The Talamo" and reached back to the states to have shoulder patches made that said, "Remember the Talamo." It is one of many patches underneath the glass on the desk at my home office to this day.

A couple of weeks later, we were back on with the Australian Task Force for another mission. This time it would be to a little village in a high-altitude mountain valley north of Kajaki. According to intel, the Taliban was stashing injured fighters up there to recover, and there were supposed to be a lot of them. The Australian Task Force wanted to be inserted to surround the village at night, fight all day, then be extracted the next night. Aflak would lead the mission, but I was going with him this time and helping him plan it.

The objective area looked like shit. There was no good way to get into that valley, and once we were down in it, there would be nowhere to go. We knew the Taliban would have spotters scattered up and down the valley to alert them to any inbound aircraft. They would swing into action for a fight as soon as they heard us. The high altitude village and steep valley was surrounded by small, tiered fields. We planned to take four aircraft up there and land in four different landing zones around the village, each one with its own little tiered field. The imagery we had sucked, but one of the 461 majors had a buddy in the U2 squadron in Korea. He requested a favor - some updated imagery. Amazingly, we got it back in the span of 48 hours, which was huge in finalizing the plan.

I also worked out with Sniper and his boss, the Wing OPSO,

the notion of positioning purple air (joint aircraft) up high over the objective area to provide Imagery, Surveillance, and Reconnaissance (ISR) for a few days before the mission. The idea was basically to have the ISR aircraft collect information from their communication and sound false alarms for their spotters. When we went to execute, we wanted them to be slightly complacent. It worked. In the early hours of June 24th, we showed up at the squadron ready to execute, only to learn that the entire mission was canceled. The purple air ISR support we needed in execution had fallen out, making the mission a no-go. We ended up executing some general support tasking instead.

The next night I was out with one of our young HACs, giving him a Section Leader check. We were dropping some externals at FOB Crusher on one of the last runs, and I was on the controls. Seated in the left seat and on final approach, I saw two Military Aged Males (MAMs) pop out of a compound with AK-47s. They started to shoot at us. We had skid escorts with us, and I immediately called out, "Two MAMs at 10 o'clock low."

The skids rolled right over the top of us and neutralized the threat while we were on short final. I set our load down and took off without incident. When we returned to Bastion after the flight, my copilot was worked up. After we shut down and got out of the seat, he started yelling at me. "Sir, what the fuck is wrong with you?"

I wasn't sure what he was getting at. Everything had gone pretty smoothly as far as I was concerned. He said, "I almost pissed my pants back there, and I looked over at you, and you looked completely unfazed. You are like a fucking robot!"

At that moment, I realized he was struggling because his reaction to the situation had been so vastly different than mine. The truth was, I knew I was the weird one. His response was normal. I had to acknowledge to myself that I had become completely desensitized to the fear of death. Not only that, but I also still enjoyed the excitement of those situations. It wasn't normal, and I knew it. I did my best to calm him and shrugged it off as "experience." I knew that was bullshit, but I wasn't going to psychoanalyze myself to a young captain. That was going to be mine to figure out when my days of being a combat aviator came to a close.

In mid-June, we finally got Wi-Fi in the cans where we lived. I was typically only in there and awake for about an hour a day before going to sleep. I spent most of that time journaling, but finally getting Wi-Fi allowed me to augment that by emailing and surfing the internet. It was a small creature comfort but a morale booster nonetheless.

On June 30th, we had one month to go. We were cruising well past 100 named operations executed, so we had already shattered the record. It had been a wild ride, but finishing was never easy. Our tasking was also accelerating, so there would be no coasting to the finish. It was going to be game day every day for another month. TITS McKeon also came back from Qatar that day, and the CO decided not to pursue any significant consequences for him. Instead, he only received some routine administrative discipline. It was a win. He had made a mistake, but I was happy to see that it wasn't going to result in anything significant for him. It was also good to see the CO take a measured approach. It felt like a peace offering of sorts for our entire detachment, and our guys genuinely appreciated it.

Right on cue, Sniper informed us that our insert with the Australian Task Force was back on for the 4th of July. I was a little bit concerned about that one. The village where the insert was going was called Meyhan, and as previously planned, we would land in four different fields surrounding the village.

Aflak would take the lead, and I was his dash two. The way the sticks were arranged, I wound up with the Australian Task Force Commander in my aircraft. As we pushed up toward the objective area, we climbed up into the mountains just shy of our maximum altitude at 10,000 feet Mean Sea Level (MSL). Our route had us waiting as long as possible before diving down into the valley that comprised the objective area.

We had the appropriate purple air above us in the form of an EC-130 Compass Call and an MC-12 Liberty. With that combination, we had a perfect comms relay and real-time Imagery, Surveillance, and Reconnaissance (ISR). As we drew closer, the ISR aircraft relayed there was cell phone chatter about our potential arrival. It sounded like our approach would be contested.

Aflak came up on the radio and asked, "Whiskey, what do you think?"

There was a brief pause, and I could feel the anticipation awaiting my response. I replied, "Let's keep pressing and see what happens."

The Australian Task Force Commander went wild on the ICS in our aircraft. "That's what I'm fucking talking about, mate, huge balls; let's go in there and kill all of these motherfuckers!"

Those guys were fearless, and I loved it.

A few minutes later, we started our descent into the valley. It was an extremely dark low light level night. Although we knew the terrain was high on both sides of us, we couldn't see it. It was like descending into a bottomless black abyss. When we hit our final approach, the KC-130 overhead dropped some covert Battlefield Illumination (BI) flares for us. Through our NVGs, they immediately lit up the entire valley. It was like turning on a light bulb. The purple air also marked our LZs with infrared (IR) strobes for ITG.

Nothing was more comforting than seeing that "finger from god" pointing at your landing spot. Nobody fired a shot during our insert, which was almost disconcerting. We had expected it to be contested, so I felt vulnerable as soon as we were on deck. Were they just waiting for us to land to light us up? As I thought that, I looked around and realized a donkey stood about five feet outside of my rotor arc. Frozen solid, it just stared at us. I couldn't believe it hadn't taken off running. I also couldn't believe how lucky we had gotten that our rotor blades hadn't hit it. An animal that size would have caused enough damage to completely take us down in the LZ. Truly a random stroke of luck.

As soon as the Australian Task Force guys were off-loaded, we pulled power and took off. We were off the hook until the extract the following evening. Before we launched for the extract the next night, we got word that the Australian Task Force would be bringing one of their own casualties out with them on extract. It put a somber feeling on us in the brief, but it also served as another reminder of what the stakes were every time we took off.

We had the same lineup of purple air for the extract, and the whole event was a rinse and repeat of the previous night. They could hear us coming, and there was cell phone chatter, but in the end, it was another uneventful extract. The only difference was that on the extract, there was a cow in the landing zone instead of a donkey.

We watched in silence as the Australian Task Force guys carried a body bag to our aircraft. When we dropped them back off at their FOB, we all sat there turning for a few minutes while they did a brief ceremony for their fallen comrade on the flight line. A heavy night. Despite mission success, everyone remained somber during the debrief.

On the night of July 7th, we had a quick All Officers Meeting (AOM) in the ready room to say goodbye to our Advanced Party from HMH-465. A small portion of our detachment was heading home to Miramar. Aflak was the senior guy leaving. Executing these last three weeks without him was going to suck, but it was time for him to head home. He received a Navy Commendation Medal for everything he'd done on the deployment.

In his remarks, he said, "Special thanks to Major Lee, the guy behind the curtain who runs this place. He knows how to get the absolute best out of everybody."

He had earned the right to make that comment. Amazingly, I never heard a thing about it from the CO.

A couple of days later, the Advanced Party crews from

HMH-464 and HMH-462 were in our spaces, and we started doing turnover. My counterpart as the incoming OPSO was also an old friend. She had been right behind me coming out of flight school and had spent her entire career on the east coast. Before returning to the fleet as a major, she had completed a tour at Marine Helicopter Squadron One (HMX-1), where she became the first female aviator selected as a "Marine One." Marine Ones were the select few allowed to sign for the aircraft when flying the President of the United States. She was great to turn over with, which made the last few weeks a lot more enjoyable. Their squadron also had a female CO, a first for our community.

The following week, Dolf came over to fly with me. Since he was in a CH-53D squadron, he needed to punch a current fly day in a CH-53E. Technically, I was giving him a NATOPS check so that he had a current check ride, but we were able to work that into a regular general support mission. It was really cool to get to fly with him again. Back home, it was also Tristen's 9th birthday. I was able to call her before we took off and catch her on the phone. I felt like an asshole for being gone so much, but it was nice to chat with her. I took a flag in my helmet bag that day, just like I had done for Dalton around his birthday earlier in the deployment. I would have them both mounted in cases for them when I got back home.

I spent the next week flying left seat, right seat missions with our replacements. It was a positive distraction to keep my mind off the fact that we were counting down the days. In our last week, I was on the flight schedule for four out of seven nights. It was the best way to accelerate time. One morning we were still out shortly after sunrise. We were on deck, off-loading at one of the FOBs. About 50 yards out in front of us, some local villagers were busy at work in a small field of vegetables. I saw a little boy emerge out of the field, dragging what looked like a sheet with a pile of vegetables on it. He appeared to be around the same age as my son, Dalton. He couldn't have been any older than four. The difference between his life and our son's struck me. Dalton was back home in San Diego, in a nice house, probably eating Goldfish and drinking juice. This kid was helping his family harvest vegetables to survive. I felt a simultaneous rush of guilt and thanks. It reminded me I was ready to go home.

Our last flight was in the early hours of August 1, 2011. I put the CO and myself as the aircraft commanders in the section. If someone was going to be on the hook for not fucking it up at the finish line, it should be us. A general support flight that launched shortly after midnight, it was busy. The plan had us going from Bastion to FOB Edinburgh, to Now Zad, and back to Bastion. Then to Kajaki, Nolay, and back to Bastion to pick up the RC Southwest CG. The last stop was delivering the CG to Lashkar Gah. As was customary, we gave the RC Southwest CG an ICS cranial so he could chat with us on the flight to Lash. He was very complimentary about us as a squadron and thanked us for all that we had done while in-theater. He talked about how many lives we had saved by taking the fight to the enemy in Kajaki and the mountains to the North. Taking the fight to them in their safe havens had shaped the future clearing of the remaining Taliban strongholds.

I flew with one of the captains from HMH-462, and it was his first time flying down the *Star Wars* trench into Lash. I handled the approach and landing myself to show him how it was done. That last quick stop to a landing felt good. I couldn't believe we were wrapping it up. When we got back to Bastion and shut down, it hit me. I had completed my fourth combat deployment. I had logged almost 1,000 hours of combat flight time. I didn't know if I would ever fly in combat again. At that moment, I didn't care. The only thing that mattered to me was that I was still undefeated in combat. Through four combat deployments, we hadn't lost a single Marine. It was a remarkable statistic, and I was beyond thankful for it.

What we had accomplished as a squadron was historically significant. As difficult as it had been, we had set a new bar for named operations, executing 144 of them. We had doubled what

HMH-361 had done on the cycle before us. It was a mind-boggling number for a CH-53E squadron, as well as the greatest sense of accomplishment I had ever felt. Not just for me personally, but for the whole squadron. It was a team event, and despite several significant challenges to overcome, we had done it. We could all be proud for the rest of our lives that we had been a part of it.

The CO was happy. He was smiling and laughing when we got off the aircraft and back into maintenance control. The pressure was finally off, and he could breathe again. He was like a completely different person. I think that deployment had aged him about ten years. It was easy for us to critique how he had handled things since we weren't doing his job. It certainly hadn't been easy at times, and my guys had added the majority of the stressful events to his plate. I knew the weight of the responsibility he had been carrying was heavy. In the end, we reached the desired outcome for the squadron under challenging circumstances. I learned a lot working for him.

I had filed all my thoughts and observations away so I could navigate that role if and when I got the opportunity. When I got back to my office after debriefing and doing my post-flight paperwork, I sent the email below back home. The subject line... "Heading Home."

For all practical purposes, my fourth combat deployment has drawn to a close. We are mission complete. The thought of being back in San Diego in less than a week still feels a bit surreal.

Thank you again for all the emails, cards, care packages, and support. Please know that it is all very much appreciated.

Overall, this deployment has been more challenging than my previous combat tours both inside and outside the wire. There are many reasons for that, and at some point, I am sure I will bore all of you with the details over a few beers.

In short, bringing 140 Marines out here from the west coast and fully integrating with another half of a squadron from the east coast brought out some expected internal friction. Despite the initial friction, the Marines in the squadron did what they always do - they pulled together to make it happen. Returning home to separate coasts will be bittersweet.

The last few months have also been unprecedented from an operational standpoint for the Marine Aircraft Wing. The stars lined up, and we had the right people in key places. The end result has not been good for the enemy. They are definitely ready for us to get the hell out of town.

While we primarily supported the Marines on the ground out here, we also got the opportunity to support a multitude of operations with our sister services and coalition partners. The fight out here is truly joint and working with some of those units was extremely interesting. Ask me about the Aussie commandos sometime. Impressive.

Like my previous combat deployments, this one has been a great education. Simultaneously exposing yourself to the best and worst that humanity has to offer tends to give me a unique perspective on things. I am grateful for that.

I am proud of our Marines for a litany of reasons. In part because they just busted their asses 24 hours a day for the last 180 days to ensure that we accomplished the mission. In part because I, once again, saw some of them do some of the gutsiest shit that you could ever imagine. But more than anything else, I am just proud to be one of them. My favorite thing about the Marine Corps has always been the Marines themselves. No other organization on the planet has such a high concentration of individuals who exude the finer qualities of the human spirit. Fittingly, combat deployments always seem to bring out the best in all of them.

See you soon.

Isaac

21

BONUS DEPLOYMENT

THE TRIP HOME from Afghanistan was long. Our first stop was back at Manas Air Force Base, Kyrgyzstan. Fittingly, our follow-on flight home kept getting delayed, so we spent three nights there just sitting on our bags, waiting for a ride. Once our flight finally showed up, we got on board, and everyone promptly fell asleep. A few hours later we made a quick fuel stop in Anchorage, Alaska, then pressed on home to Miramar. We landed at Miramar at 0800 on August 6, 2011. We had been gone just shy of eight months.

I could see the families waiting for us in front of the Passenger Terminal on the flight line. That was always awesome to see. As the senior Marine on board, I let all the other Marines get off the aircraft first. I was the last Marine to walk off the aircraft and slowly walked across the flight line to find Kerry and the kids. Seeing our Marines in front of me finding their families was awesome. I finally found Kerry and the kids in the crowd. That first family hug was great. Dalton didn't want to let go, so he clung to me for quite a while as I said hello to several other families. It was great to be home.

The next morning I was up early, drinking coffee in the kitchen. I was looking out the window across the San Pasqual

Valley at the same view I had just before leaving for the deployment. Only this time, I wasn't wondering what was waiting for me in the Sangin River Valley in Afghanistan. I knew what was there, and I missed it. A few days prior, I had been fighting and flying in Afghanistan. The change was too abrupt. I sat there drinking coffee, looking at the peaceful San Pasqual Valley, and missing the war. I had to find a way to try and turn that off so I could be at least somewhat present for Kerry and the kids. We all needed that.

After the post-deployment 96, I returned to the squadron. I moved up into the XO position under Dobie. The plan was that I would stay there and remain the XO after he executed a Change of Command with the next inbound CO the following spring. Getting back to work was the best thing for me. It wasn't combat, but I was at least flying and helping to train the squadron.

Moving into the XO position was also a great education for me. Until then, I had only worked in the two biggest departments in every squadron. Maintenance and S-3 Operations. Those were arguably the most important, and I knew those departments well. But being the XO made me learn a lot more about the other departments. S-1 Administration, S-2 Intelligence, S-4 Logistics, S-5 Civil Affairs, S-6 Information Systems, Safety, and Medical - each department played an important role, and I enjoyed working with all of them.

Being back in the squadron as a major and a department head still felt a little strange. It would take some getting used to. As I acclimated to the XO position, I also realized I would likely be competitive for selection to command a squadron. In the blink of an eye, I went from being a captain unsure about remaining in the Marine Corps to a major who might be competitive to command a squadron. Talk about a mind-blowing thought. But that heightened awareness also proved helpful. I could closely watch Dobie and the other COs in Hangar 4. I could study the manner in which they conducted themselves. For the first time, I started to think about how I might do it if I received the opportunity to become a squadron CO.

Since I had deployed so quickly after checking in, I still had two years on station before I would receive orders and move again. I hoped to persuade the monitor to let me stay in San Diego. I would be up for orders in the Summer of 2013, but the Command Board was also that August. If I had an opportunity to be selected for command of a west coast squadron, I didn't want to take orders and move the family if I might be informed soon after that I had orders to return to Miramar.

I had that on my mind, but it was still two years away. Our squadron was out of the Afghanistan rotation after our deployment, so the only thing looming on the horizon was providing a couple of 31st MEU detachments. The 31st MEU was still operating out of Okinawa, Japan. It was also different than the SoCal MEUs in that there was no workup period prior to the deployment. West coast Marines always joked about how the 31st wasn't a real MEU for that reason. But it was still a deployment, and we had detachments to get trained up. I tried to settle in and just enjoy being back at Miramar.

Things at home were relatively peaceful. We loved our neighborhood up in the San Pasqual Valley, and the kids were both enjoying school. The four-year break that was MAWTS-1 and Command and Staff College had helped Kerry and me settle back in a little bit. The deployment had been challenging, but it felt good to have it behind us. I wasn't expecting to deploy again as a major, so we had a couple of years in front of us that felt like they could be fairly normal. Things felt calmer and more manageable than they had in a long time.

On February 22, 2012, I was out flying in the Yuma Range Complex with one of our captains. We were setting everything up for a couple of other aircraft from our squadron to come out and execute NSI check flights with MAWTS-1. I was on deck at LZ Bull, where we always did our external lift training, when I heard what sounded like an explosion. I had seen a brief flash of light out of the corner of my eye, but that was it. Nothing after that.

We scanned the range frequency, and no one came up on that frequency to say anything. I assumed that what I'd heard had been some type of ordnance coming off another aircraft in a nearby range. We finished setting up the zone and then pushed out to do some other training once our flight of two showed up to execute the NSI Checks. Like any night training flight, we headed back to Miramar just prior to the field closing at 2300. We shot an instrument approach down through the marine layer to land. I knocked out the paperwork, debriefed, and headed home around 0100. The next morning, Kerry woke me up early. She was really upset, so I knew right away that something bad had happened.

She proceeded to tell me that one of my fellow MAWTS-1 instructors had been killed the night before. He was an AH-1W Cobra pilot and a peer of mine. His wife was also a Marine who had worked in MAWTS-1 operations with me. Kerry and I were good friends with her. His squadron had also been doing NSI checks and had just taken off from a Forward Arming and Refueling Point (FARP) when his Cobra collided with the Huey they were flying with. There were no survivors. I just knew that was the explosion in the nearby range the night prior.

I had completely lost my grief response, although I felt a ton of empathy for his wife. I felt terrible for her and their son. It also bothered me that something like that had happened to him. Like me, he was a senior major serving as the XO in his squadron and a highly regarded and experienced aviator. Things like that weren't supposed to happen to guys like him. He probably looked down for two seconds, and it got him. If it happened to him, it could still happen to me. That thought really fucked with me.

Spending time with the friends still with us always helped after such a loss. Apollo was serving as one of the department heads in HMH-462 at the time, so we still saw each other often.

He was set to get married that March, and he asked me to officiate the wedding. After filing the appropriate paperwork, I married him and his fiancée on March 31st. I put the entire script in one of our Naval Aviation "blue brains" checklists and used that as my guide for the ceremony. It was a great day and a perfect reminder to try and enjoy the ride.

In April, we executed Dobie's Change of Command ceremony. I stayed in the XO billet under the new CO, who'd also been in HMH-465 with us for a bit when I was a young captain. Both he and Dobie had been on the 15th MEU, where Spooner made a name for himself as the squadron WTI. I didn't know the new CO nearly as well as I knew Dobie, but there was enough familiarity that the transition was totally fine.

In mid-May, the new CO and the major slated to be the Officer in Charge (OIC) for our 31st MEU detachment about to deploy went up to MAG-16 to give the MAG CO the customary pre-deployment brief. About an hour later, I got a call from the MAG XO. He told me that the brief did not go well and that the MAG CO had fired our Detachment OIC during the brief! All four CH-53E squadrons on the flight line had twenty-four hours to nominate a major to serve as the replacement. I knew right away that I was the only other major in our squadron with the requisite qualifications to take that detachment on short notice, so I told the MAG XO that, by default, I would have to be our nominee. I also reminded him I'd already deployed as a major and several other majors in the MAG needed a deployment to update their Overseas Control Date. I could tell he didn't give any fucks about that, but it was worth throwing it out there.

I went home that evening and told Kerry what was going on. She asked me if I thought I would be picked. I told her that I didn't think so. It just didn't make a ton of sense. I knew those other majors needed to execute a deployment. She reminded me that we had just booked a summer vacation to visit a few of the National Parks in Northern California. I knew my vacation plans weren't going to have anything to do with this decision. The decision was with the MAG CO, and he would ultimately do what he thought was best.

The next morning, I got a phone call from the MAG XO. He told me that the MAG CO wanted me to come to his office. I knew exactly what that meant. I was going on deployment. When I got over to the MAG and reported to the CO, he told me to have a seat. He proceeded to tell me that I was going to be the Detachment OIC for the deployment. He told me that he had the utmost trust and confidence in me, and he believed that would be the best thing for our Marines. As much as I didn't want to take off on another deployment, I totally agreed with his perspective. I knew it would be the best thing for our Marines, too. I told him that I would take care of the detachment and that we would execute at a high level. He didn't need to spend any time worrying about it. He replied that he appreciated that and told me he would keep a close eye on the rest of the squadron back home. We shook hands, and I was dismissed.

I went back to the squadron and reached out to the CH-46E squadron in Okinawa, which was going to serve as the 31st MEU Aviation Combat Element (ACE). That squadron was the HMM-262 "Flying Tigers." They were sixteen hours ahead of us, so I just sent an email to their CO and XO to let them know that I was now coming to lead our detachment. I knew they were expecting a more junior major, so they were going to have to figure out what to do with me in terms of a billet in the squadron.

I then ran home to tell Kerry what was going on. I walked into the house around lunchtime, and she knew before I even said anything. "Let me guess; they decided to send you, didn't they?" I told her she was correct. She took the news much better than I anticipated. She was so used to the Marine Corps making me disappear, she had succumbed to that reality.

I had exactly three weeks to get my shit together to deploy. I also had to communicate quite a bit with HMM-262 to sort out some details. They had planned to make our Detachment OIC the S-1 Administration Officer. I was more suited to one of the more senior billets, but we were also only going to be there for six months. It made the most sense for them to just put me in S-1 and have me focus on helping train the entire squadron for higher-level flight qualifications. The CO assured me that he would annotate the situation in my Fitness Report to prevent it from looking like a demotion. I was good with all of that.

On the night of June 5, 2012, I had our friend Dalton pick me up at the house to take me to the squadron. It felt like we had just done this, and saying goodbye to Kerry and the kids again was brutal. The older they got, the more difficult it became. The guilt of just always being gone was eating at me.

A few hours later, I was on a bus to March Air Force Base and then on a flight to Okinawa. I hadn't been to Okinawa since making that short pit stop in late 2003 to take the Okinawa aircraft back to Iraq for OIF II. But when I got there, everything was still frozen in time. MCAS Futenma was a tiny little postage stamp of a base. Nothing had changed. The only issue I knew needed fixing was that the Echo Chamber had been shut down. About a year prior, an officer had fallen out the window of the Scar Bar, so the base CO had shut down both the Scar Bar and the Echo Chamber. One of my goals for the deployment was to get those reopened.

I struggled privately with the idea of being on a non-combat deployment. Especially a 31st MEU Deployment. It just felt like a waste of time to me. But I knew I needed to find a way to make the most of the situation for the Marines on my detachment. Many were first-time deployers, and some were getting a "break" from the combat deployments. They deserved the best experience possible. I decided to take advantage of the opportunity and focus on my leadership. It was unusual to get the opportunity to be a Detachment OIC twice as a major, and I needed to be smart enough to make the most of that. I wanted to work on creating a great culture with our detachment. Everything I did was me dialing in on exactly how I would run an entire squadron if I were to be slated to command one in the next couple of years.

The schedule for the MEU was basically that we would train on Okinawa for a few weeks, then get on the ship to spend a few months cruising around the Pacific to participate in some training exercises. We would return to Okinawa for about a month before going home. Breaking it up like that would make the deployment a lot more tolerable. HMM-262 was hospitable, and I knew a couple of their majors and we got along well. The CO was a great guy, and I really liked him right away. That made the overall situation feel a lot better for me.

For those first few weeks, I was heavily involved in all the flight planning and execution that the combined squadron was doing to prepare. When I arrived, I was the only pilot in the squadron with the Air Mission Commander (AMC) designation, making me the default AMC for every flight that required one. The AMC is ultimately responsible for the planning and execution of the entire mission for the ACE. In execution, I preferred to fill that role while riding as a passenger in the back of a UH-1Y Huey. I could sit right next to the commander of the Ground Combat Element (GCE) and ensure that everything went off without a hitch. While filling that role, I simultaneously trained another pilot to earn the qualification. That kept me busy, and it was a positive distraction.

When not planning and executing flights, I arranged activities for our detachment. I wanted our detachment to get tight before we got on the ship. We spent a lot of time having cookouts and drinking beers together at the bowling alley on base. It worked. I was always telling the Marines on our detachment that we needed to execute like professionals and stay off the radar. Translation: nobody gets in trouble for any shenanigans in their downtime. They bought into it.

On August 20th, we flew about half of the squadron onto the USS *Bonhomme Richard* (LHD-6). There was a typhoon bearing down on Okinawa, so we wanted to get about half of the aircraft and all of the pilots who still needed to finish their Carrier Qualifications on the ship. The ship would sail away from the typhoon so that our pilots could complete the last of their training. I sent our captain WTI with our last couple of pilots who needed to do that. He could finish training them. I stayed in Okinawa with about half of our Marines to finish getting the last couple of aircraft in shape while we rode out the storm.

On August 31st, the rest of us flew onto the ship, and we got underway. I had spent a little bit of time on the USS *Bonhomme Richard* (LHD-6) when I deployed to Iraq for the first time. We had a couple of aircraft on the "Bonnie Dick" for the transit, and I was one of the guys who went over to test them up and get them ready to fly off. I had also been at that ship's christening when I was a student in flight school, so I had some history with it. It felt familiar.

I was in a room with the skid Detachment OIC, the AV-8B Harrier Detachment OIC, and a Japanese Liaison Officer. It didn't take long to be reminded that I did not care for life on the boat. At all. I would take a "dirt det" to Iraq or Afghanistan over living on the boat any day. But I couldn't bitch too much. Living in a stateroom as an officer was a hundred times better than what the Marines were dealing with down in the bowels of the ship. They were packed in there like sardines with zero privacy. It was brutal down there.

One week into it, we were in the vicinity of Guam executing our Certification Exercise (CERTEX) as a MEU. I thought the whole thing was a clown show. The MEU staff pushed everything like we were about to invade North Korea, but it all felt disorganized and chaotic. I was getting a first-hand look at why Marines called the 31st MEU the "thirty worst." This was the tradeoff for not having a six-month workup period. Since I wasn't in a major department head billet, I just sat back and watched the show. It was annoying but not as annoying as it would have been if I had been the OPSO or the XO.

I remained in the lead on all the actual flying operations,

which I enjoyed. At least in doing that, I felt productive. For one of the CERTEX missions, we flew an airfield seizure on Tinian. We landed on the same runway that the Enola Gay took off from with the atomic bomb. The bomb pits were still there. I had over-flown Tinian en route to Guam on my first deployment eleven years prior but hadn't landed on the runway. A little eerie but cool to see.

On the morning of September 15th, we received terrible news. We learned of an attack on the flight line at Camp Bastion, Afghanistan, the same flight line I had been on for our deployment a year earlier. The CO of the AV-8B Harrier squadron had been killed. He'd also been a MAWTS-1 instructor with me. I felt awful. The news immediately reminded me of the war still underway, while I was stuck on a useless MEU in the middle of the Pacific. The situation was maddening, but I needed to manage my thoughts and emotions. I couldn't let our Marines know it bothered me. They needed me to be right there in the game with them. Focusing on that helped me to quickly compartmentalize my frustration and anger.

A few days later, I received permission from the CO to fly back to Tinian to reenlist one of our best Marines. We both jumped out on the runway and did it right there. He was pumped, which reminded me that I needed to stay focused on the Marines. I was there for them. By the time we finished CERTEX, I had given four AMC evaluations and was ready to take a little break.

We received a few days of liberty in Guam, which was timely. Our Marines ended up right back at "The Viking," just like we had back in 2001. One night a couple of the captains on my det came to tell me our Marines were getting wild in there, so I made a late-night run to the "The Viking" to save them from themselves. Violent Kay wasn't there any longer, but they had some other girl doing the same show, whipping drunk guys who were holding onto a ship's wheel. It was ridiculous, but the Marines all thought it was the funniest thing they had ever seen. Some things never change. On September 29th, we successfully got everyone back on the ship and set sail for the Philippines to participate in an exercise called Philippines Amphibious Landing Exercise (PHIBLEX).

While underway, I started to receive emails from a few senior officers about my next assignment. My desire was still to find a billet in San Diego to avoid having to move the family again while waiting to see if I got slated for command. Those senior officers didn't care about that, though. They were all pushing me to take orders to Headquarters Marine Corps Aviation at the Pentagon. Headquarters Marine Corps Aviation was more commonly referred to as "Aviation Hallway" and consisted of the Deputy Commandant for Aviation (DCA) and his principal staff.

Orders to the Hallway were similar to orders to MAWTS-1 in that they were invitation only. The DCA and his staff hand-picked the officers slated to go there. More often than not, those officers would subsequently slate for command. I still wanted nothing to do with it, but I could tell it was trending that way. I assumed I would soon be told I'd been selected. I decided not even to mention it to Kerry until it was official.

Back at Miramar, our squadron wasn't doing well. I was getting emails from the CO and the officer who had taken over for me as the XO. They were feeling the heat from higher head-quarters. I was only going to have six months left on station when I got home, so the thought of returning to the squadron held little appeal. Right on cue, I got an email from the MAG CO, telling me that he was hearing nothing but good things about us on the deployment. He also told me that when I got home, I would have a choice between going back to the squadron or coming up to be part of his staff for six months while waiting to execute orders. I quickly accepted the offer to join his staff.

I hated the idea of not going back to the squadron, but I knew with only six months remaining on station, there would be little I could do to help get things back on track. I was really frustrated that the situation had come to that. I'd brought half the squadron home from a successful deployment to Afghanistan the previous year. Some of the struggles associated with being out of the combat deployment rotation immediately reappeared. There were many lessons learned there that I was taking on board as I continued to think through how I might execute if selected for command.

On October 5th, we flew off the ship and into Basa Air Base, Philippines, to set up shop for PHIBLEX. Basa was a shithole. We pitched cots in what looked like a condemned building. With no fences or gates around the base, we could walk down the street and out into a little neighborhood. On the corner, we found a little cluster of street food places serving traditional Philippine food. The pancit and lumpia at those places were awesome. They also had things like Balut. A few Marines on our det tried it, including me. I didn't care for it.

In general, the living conditions sucked, but it was a bit of an adventure and better than being on the ship. Hot and humid as the Pacific could be, I stopped wearing a T-shirt underneath my flight suit. There was no point. I would immediately sweat through it and then feel like I was walking around wearing a wet towel all damn day. Flight suits were made of a different material and quickly dried out. So wearing it without a T-shirt was much better. Most of our Marines followed my lead and also stopped wearing T-shirts. They always referred to not wearing a T-shirt as "belt fed," which I found amusing.

Throughout the deployment, I constantly reminded our Marines that our goal was to do our jobs well and stay off the radar. That turned into "Belt Fed and off the radar" about two days into PHIBLEX. Our Marines were constantly saying that to everyone. Nobody else understood what it meant, which was comical. That phrase would ultimately end up on our deployment plaque. We also had to take malaria pills while we were there, and those always made me feel a little queasy. Between the malaria pills and constantly sweating my ass off, I wasn't loving PHIBLEX.

One cool thing was that an active volcano called Mount Pinatubo was only a short flight from Basa. It hadn't erupted since 1991 and had formed a little lake in the cap with a shore around it that was big enough to land a CH-53E. Naturally, we flew in, landed, and got out to take a few photos.

On October 12th, we only had five days of PHIBLEX to go when one of our CH-46s crashed while trying to land with 11 passengers on board. While doing a pinnacle landing to a little LZ atop a mountain, they somehow managed to slam the belly of the aircraft into the side of the mountain as they approached the LZ. Amazingly, the entire crew and all the passengers egressed safely, but the aircraft was a total loss. That resulted in us canceling our entire schedule for a day. An Aviation Mishap Board (AMB) immediately convened to start an investigation.

The next morning the CO let me know that he needed me to lead the Field Flight Performance Board (FFPB) that would ultimately determine the fate of the two pilots involved. It made sense for him to have me do it. I was an experienced senior aviator, and I didn't really have much of a ground job in the squadron. Since I was basically done leading the big missions and training new AMCs, I had time. He also trusted me to appropriately determine the fate of the two aviators, both part of his organic CH-46E squadron which made up our MEU ACE.

The next morning the CO came back to me with an additional request. The Philippine government had told the Marine Corps that we absolutely needed to remove every bit of the CH-46E off the side of that mountain. The CO hoped I could externally lift the various sections with one of our CH-53Es to get it out of there. I told him I would need a good Helicopter Support Team (HST) and would also need to go look at the site in person. A few hours later, I was in the back of a UH-1Y Huey with the HST leader, being flown up to the crash site to take a look.

When we walked onto the crash site, I was amazed that

everyone had survived. The aircraft was destroyed and burned. I felt certain we could get most of what was left of the aircraft off the mountain by using nets to wrap around the assorted sections. We could then hook up and externally lift those net loads. The one thing I wasn't confident about was the aft transmission, which now rested about twenty feet below the edge of the LZ. It wasn't quite a cliff, but that slope was approximately seventy-five degrees. It was really steep. Way too steep for any HST Marines to walk down in order to rig that aft transmission for an external lift.

The HST leader thought he could get down there with mountain climbing gear and rig it. The slings would barely make it back up to the LZ, meaning I would need to hover extremely low to get it hooked up, but I felt comfortable with that approach. We slapped the table on our plan, jumped back into the Huey, and headed back to the squadron to brief the boss.

When I told the CO I thought we could do it, I could tell he was relieved. He had a lot of shit on his plate, and he welcomed anything that checked something off the list. I understood his attitude and was happy to be able to help. Getting that wreckage off the mountain was high profile enough that the MEU CO also wanted me to brief him on it before we were cleared to execute. He came down the next day, and I talked him through the plan. I could tell he was concerned, but he trusted me to pull it off. Everyone up on high wanted a warm fuzzy that we could clean this one up.

After finally getting approval to execute, HST rigged everything exactly the way the team leader and I had discussed. We were set to execute on October 18th. We were also supposed to fly back to the ship that afternoon, so I didn't have any room for error. I had to get everything that was left of that aircraft off the side of that mountain. We briefed at 0500 and took off at first light.

I picked the forward transmission first and worked my way back to the aft transmission that was resting down on the side of the mountain. I intended to do it last. After each pick, I flew down to the bottom of the valley to drop the loads next to a couple of heavy trucks on standby to load it up and haul it away. Then I would land and wait on deck while they pulled the slings off the load I had just dropped off. They returned the slings, and I would fly back up to the LZ and do a low pass so my crew chiefs could drop the slings. I would then hold out to the west while HST used the slings to rig the next load. Once they were ready, I would come back in and make the next pick. It was five picks total, and I was ready to be done when we got to the aft transmission. I executed a really low hover, and HST managed to hook it up. When we lifted it off the side of the mountain and pushed out, HST came up on the radio and said, "Hell, yeah." We had pulled it off.

After dropping that last load, we took off and headed back out to the ship just off the coast. It was one of those rare instances during which I felt thankful to be on a Navy ship. The AC was working, and there was hot water in the showers. We had also been living off of MREs and T-Rats, so the food in the wardroom seemed like a five-star restaurant. I was tired but happy that PHIBLEX was over.

We pulled into Subic Bay for a few days of liberty the next morning. We slept on the ship, but everyone was free to get off in the evenings and enjoy all of the wonders that Subic has to offer. They had fenced off the area we were allowed to be in, but there was plenty to do there for the Marines. There were restaurants, bars, tons of vendors, and of course, brothels. The girls were aggressive and would yell all kinds of crazy shit at us as we walked down the street. It was wild. In the evenings, I took the officers from my detachment out for a leisurely dinner with plenty of San Miguel.

After dinner, we would make our way down to the end of the street, where a big open-air pavilion had a live band covering American rock music every night. They sold Mojo there, which I thought of as the Philippine version of Soju. Mojo is another unregulated alcohol that is quite strong. They mixed it with Kool-Aid and sold it in pitchers. By the time we got down there, our Marines were staggering around shit-faced drunk with pitchers of Mojo and talking about the adventures they had at a few other establishments on the street earlier in the evening. At the end of the night, we would round them up and herd the cats back to the ship.

The second night in Subic, I ran into the MAG-36 CO at a bar shooting pool. He came over to thank me for getting that CH-46E off the side of that mountain. He asked if there was anything he could do for me in return. I told him he could give me the keys to the Echo Chamber. He immediately agreed. He told me to come see him as soon as we got back to Okinawa, and he would give me the keys to open it back up. As a bonus, he threw in the Scar Bar. I had essentially traded what was left of a crashed CH-46 for the keys to a bar. I was just about mission complete for the deployment. By the time we left Subic, I couldn't wait to get the fuck out of the Philippines. But the Marines did a good job. They stayed "Belt Fed and off the radar."

Our next stop was Kota Kinabalu, Malaysia. I booked a hotel room to share with the skid Det OIC. He and I got along well and enjoyed hanging out with each other. But the day before we got off the ship, I was in the gym working out when I started to feel bad. I hardly ever got sick, but I knew something was wrong. I went to see the flight surgeon. He told me I had a kidney stone, likely due to the cumulative result of how much water I had lost while we were in the Philippines. It was my going away gift from the Philippines. I'd never had a kidney stone before, but I was alarmed when he told me it was a downer. If I couldn't get rid of it quickly, it would remove me from flight status. I asked him for any suggestions he might want to offer. He suggested I hydrate like crazy and pass it before we got back on the boat to leave Malaysia. I knew exactly what to do.

I told the skid Det OIC I was about to set a personal record for drinking beer. Flushing my system would be my only shot at passing that kidney stone. We stayed in a hotel on the water, and they had a free happy hour every evening. The first night we started there, and I went to work. The squadron had also set up a "Westpac O Club," which was just a hotel room stocked with booze and beer. We hit that second, then hit some of the bars. By the time the night was over, I had consumed far too much Heineken and Tiger beer, but it worked. The next morning the kidney stone was gone. Somewhere in there, I had passed the stone and didn't even notice. I chalked that up as a win. Kota Kinabalu was a good time. We even had a squadron Kangaroo Court at a bar on our last night.

Our last stop was in Hong Kong. I had never been before, so I was excited to see it. I got a hotel room with a couple of our captains. It had two tiny beds in it and a little pull-out bed. Once that was set up, you could barely even walk through the damn room. But it didn't matter; we spent almost no time there other than to sleep. On the first day, we went to Sam's Tailor in Kowloon. My buddy Dalton had told me that his Dad had turned him onto it a few years prior. Sam made suits for high-ranking American officials, including a few Presidents. Naturally, we wanted a few of those suits for ourselves. After that, we enjoyed a nice dinner at a restaurant in a high rise. It remains the best Chinese food I've eaten to this day.

We spent our days in Hong Kong roaming the open-air markets and soaking up the culture of the city. We rapidly became experts on their public subway system. It was the cleanest, most organized, and most packed public transportation system I have ever seen. We got a sidewalk table at a bar downtown on Halloween night and ordered bottle service. People there were way into Halloween. We drank Johnny Walker Black and just took in the scene. It was a cool way to wrap up our little mini-float on the 31st MEU.

The next day we jumped back on the ship and headed to

Okinawa. For all practical purposes, the deployment was over. I had a little time to think on the way back to Okinawa, which wasn't always good for me. I thought about everything that had transpired and considered my reactions. I was slowly realizing that I thrived on risk. Combat had become my drug of choice, and I had been chasing that dragon for a long time. But at the heart of it was risk in any form. That's what I was really chasing. In the absence of real life and death risk, I subconsciously created it. It was the underlying thing that led me to drink way too much and to raise hell when I got the opportunity to do it. I spent 99% of my life totally under control. I was disciplined, regimented, hard-working, and steady. It felt good to roll the dice and let the chips fall where they may some of the time. I was in the early stages of starting to understand that.

I also started to consider my time in the Marine Corps, and I realized there were always a couple of guys like me in the squadron. It wasn't specific to pilots; sometimes, it was a crew chief or a maintainer. But there were always a handful of high performers around who pushed limits during downtime. I started connecting the dots. The Marine you most needed on the darkest night is also the Marine most likely to get hammered and dive into a bar fight over the weekend. I was one of them. That realization felt like a breakthrough in self-reflection and personal understanding.

We had a month to kill in Okinawa, executing training flights and administrative closeout. I also knocked out the FFPB for the pilots who crashed the CH-46E in the Philippines. We were in the Echo Chamber when we weren't at the squadron. The MAG CO made good on his promise and allowed me to reopen it. The skid det also got to reopen the Scar Bar. It was glorious. We had another detachment from our squadron coming to replace us, but the CH-46E squadron we had been attached to would remain the MEU ACE. They were about to do it all over again with new detachments of skids and CH-53Es. That wasn't my problem, though. We'd completed our portion.

On Thanksgiving Day, most of my officers and the officers from the skid det went to eat Thanksgiving Dinner at the Camp Butler Officers Club. We all wore our Hong Kong made suits, but the captains were so hungover from the previous night most wore flip-flops with their suits. It was a miracle none of the senior Marines there flipped out about it.

A couple of days before we headed home, I found out I had been selected for the rank of lieutenant colonel. It would be at least a year until I pinned it on, but it was nice to know in advance. It also meant I would be screened for command the following summer. I then officially received orders to Aviation Hallway in the Pentagon. A normal reaction would have been to be very happy about both of those things, but I felt ambivalent. Neither was a surprise. I knew I would have to go home and inform Kerry that we were moving back to Northern Virginia in a few months. I knew she wasn't going to love the idea of moving cross country with the possibility of having to do it again one year later. The Marine Corps always gets theirs.

On December 6th, we made the return trip to Miramar. It was the usual flight to Alaska, then March Air Force Base, where we took buses back down to Miramar. We got back to Miramar around 2100 on December 6th. It was great to see Kerry and the kids. Kerry had a photographer there to photograph the home-coming. One of the photos ended up being one of my all-time favorite photos of us. It's a photo of our family hug, but it is focused on Tristen who was holding a little American flag in her hand. She always seemed to handle deployments well, but you can see the emotion on her face in that photo. Her facial expression perfectly captured how we all felt. The bonus deployment was over, and we were all relieved to have it behind us. Now I needed to get the family prepared to move back to Northern Virginia.

22

THE HALLWAY

WHEN WE RETURNED FROM OKINAWA, I took the customary 96 to catch up with the family, then I went back to work and began the checkout process from HMH-465. I had some admin to clean up and still had to give the MAG CO and the 3rd MAW CG post-deployment briefs. In terms of heavy maintenance, flight hours executed, and training completed, it had been one of the most productive CH-53E 31st MEU detachments in the last decade. The Marines had done an outstanding job, and staying off the radar had been a great bonus on top of that. I was proud of them.

It was bittersweet to check out of HMH-465 for the second time. I had returned to the squadron I grew up in and completed two more deployments as a Detachment OIC. I hated leaving, knowing that I still had a few months left on station, but I also knew that going up to the MAG for that time was the best thing for me and the squadron. I checked into MAG-16, where I took over as the MAG S-1 officer from the lieutenant colonel about to take command of HMH-462. Being on the MAG staff was a nice break for a few months while I prepared to move back to Northern Virginia.

We considered not moving Kerry and the kids at all. The

command slate was going to come out in August, and I had a decent chance of being selected. But if we elected to leave Kerry and the kids in San Diego, it would have meant we were all apart for another year. It was also possible I wouldn't be selected on my first look. Then we would really have a nice little mess to work through. None of those choices were good, but we decided that keeping all of us together would be better than being apart again. Even if that meant we would move across the country for one year.

We rented a house in Vienna, Virginia, about a mile from the Vienna Metro station. I would commute to the Pentagon every day on the Metro, so living close to one of the stations was a win. I had to be there in May of 2013 to check in, but the kids would not finish school until the middle of June. Fifer was living there and also working in Aviation Hallway, so I arranged to stay with him for that first month. At the beginning of May, I took off by myself and drove across the country to get checked in. I still didn't like the idea of spending time at Headquarters Marine Corps Aviation, but I didn't have a choice. I needed to make the most of it, spend time with the family, and think about what I wanted to do long term.

I was assigned to Aviation Plans and Policies (APP) 2, which was the budget arm of the Hallway. I was personally in charge of the Marine Corps Flying Hour Program. In the simplest of terms, that was the budget for all the money the Marine Corps needed to fly every aircraft in the Marine Corps for an entire year. An obscene amount of detail went into the justification for all that, and that is what I was responsible for. It was a $2.5 billion dollar annual budget. I didn't know a damn thing about how that process worked when I arrived, but I got up to speed quickly with the help of a couple of other guys in the shop who'd already been there for a year or two. After immersing myself in it for a month, I knew enough to be dangerous.

It was also a bit of a reunion for me. Several of the other officers there had also been MAWTS-1 instructors. We had all returned to the fleet, completed department head tours and were now on staff at the Hallway. All on the same track, we waited to see if we would be slated for command later that summer.

I flew back to San Diego in early June to meet the movers and load up Kerry and the kids. Fifer and I had managed not to get in trouble for that first month, so I considered that a win. It had been great catching up with him. We kept our house in San Diego and rented it out to another Marine Corps family. As soon as the movers were out of there, we loaded up my truck, and I drove across the country for the second time in two months. We settled in quickly and decided not to unpack anything we didn't really need. We took all the boxes that fell into that category and stacked them up in the basement.

As I settled into my new job, I decided to try and make the most of the Pentagon experience while I was there. The Pentagon was like a living museum. We had a list in the shop of all the things to see around the building. On most days, I would take a short break and go for a walk to find one of the things on the list. In doing that, I quickly got familiar with the building. Almost every room was its own secure space, and we all had badges that only gave us access to the spaces that we needed to access. I would walk down the hallway sometimes and not see another person for a bit because every door was closed and locked. For a building with over 20,000 people working in it, I always thought that felt really strange.

I also liked being able to go for runs at lunch. I would head down to the gym in the basement to change over, then take off out the back of the building. It was close to the Arlington Memorial Bridge, so I would run across that bridge, which would spit me out next to the Lincoln Memorial. I would run down the mall until I got bored and worked my way back. Depending on my motivation level and how much time I had, I would turn around somewhere between the Washington Monument and the United States Capitol building. Those runs were always a nice way to break up the day.

I was diving back into my job and quickly gaining a better understanding of how the money worked. Everything at the Pentagon was about money. Before I had executed orders there, another officer had told me, "That place will make you sick. Every decision is based on money, not what the warfighters actually need." He was correct. It was an amazing education, but at times I wished I wasn't learning how it really worked. Despite that, I became well-versed in budget preparation and budget defense. We were constantly preparing the Deputy Commandant of Aviation (DCA) to defend requirements before the Senate and House Armed Services Committees. It was fascinating, sometimes disturbing, and a lot of work.

In August, the command slate came out, and I learned I had been slated for Command of HMH-462 back at Miramar. To facilitate that, we would return to San Diego in the summer of 2014, and I would execute a Change of Command in the fall. We would officially only be in Northern Virginia for a year. As annoying as it was that we had moved across the country for a single year, I couldn't complain. We wanted to return to San Diego, and I knew I was fortunate to have been slated for Command of a fleet squadron.

Once we knew that we were going back to San Diego, we decided to treat our year back in Northern Virginia like tourists. We bought metro passes for the family, and almost every weekend, we took a "field trip" somewhere. We hit all the monuments, museums, and historical places around the area. Tristen was in 6th grade, and Dalton was in kindergarten, so they were at a good age for the historical exposure. We also spent a lot of time with Kerry's family. We made the most of our Northern Virginia year.

It wasn't perfect at home, but we were working at it. Kerry carried a lot of resentment, and moving back to Virginia for one year didn't help. Moving the kids across the country in back-to-back summers meant they would only spend one year at a new school in Virginia. It was a difficult lifestyle, and she was over it. It was a fair perspective.

It gave me a lot to think about as I contemplated my future. I would get back to Miramar the following summer in 2014. I would promote to lieutenant colonel a couple of months later and then take command of the squadron that fall. By the time all of that was over, I would be a lieutenant colonel with two years of time in grade and nineteen years of service. I would be one year away from being eligible to retire. If I decided to retire at that point, the Marine Corps would have to leave me in San Diego for that final year of active duty. I was fairly certain that was what I would do, but I wanted to leave my options open.

I had the better part of a year remaining in Northern Virginia, and I decided to focus on two primary things. The first was to do all the preparation I wanted to do to get ready for command. The second was to get a head start on preparing to retire and transition out of the Marine Corps. I knew I wouldn't have time for any transition preparation when I was in command, so I wanted to take advantage of the time to get in front of it.

I knew that HMH-462 was slated to deploy to Afghanistan that year. They would be getting home from that deployment shortly before I returned to Miramar the following summer. One of the good things about only being at the Hallway for one year is that I would not have to do a full refresher syllabus as a pilot. I would only need a few warmup flights to regain currency. That was the second time I had avoided having to do a refresher syllabus, and it saved me a lot of time. It would also prevent me from becoming an additional training requirement for my own squadron when I got there. I started working on my full command plan. After everything I had seen and learned over the years, it was a great exercise to plan out how I wanted to approach leading a squadron.

My primary observation over the years is that there were four HMH squadrons in Hangar 4, and at any given time, one was awesome, two were mediocre, and one was terrible. The playing field was perfectly level. Every squadron had the same number of Marines, the same aircraft, the same parts supply system, and was living in the same, or at least similar, deployment cycles. The only real variable was squadron leadership. The Marine Corps changed squadron COs every eighteen to twenty-four months around the deployment cycle for a reason. When a squadron went from awesome to mediocre or from mediocre to awesome, it typically happened during the tour of a specific CO. I had observed that it was hard for a CO to make a squadron great but easy to screw one up. I knew my plan needed to keep things as simple as possible for the Marines. Keeping the main thing, the main thing, was a must.

I worked up a full twenty-page document that outlined exactly how I wanted to approach everything. I started thinking through every aspect of the squadron. Command philosophy, squadron culture, family readiness, and of course, maintenance and operations. I knew that the HMH squadrons at Miramar were struggling with aircraft readiness, so I spent a lot of time thinking about that. I had some ideas, but I knew I would need a couple of strong majors to help me execute. I immediately started working on that.

Major Kelly "Big Red" Allen was already in HMH-462, but he would need to extend for a year on station to stay and deploy with me. I immediately called him to ask if he would be willing. He was, and I was able to get the monitor to make his extension official. With that taken care of, I still wanted to get one more really strong major, but I would have to wait until we got a little closer to taking command to start working on that one.

As I contemplated my future, I also closely watched the colonels in the Hallway. They worked twelve-hour days and were stressed out as hell all the time. The DCA and the other general officers were wearing those guys out. Until then, most of the colonels I had come across had "cool" jobs like being MAG COs or the MAWTS-1 CO. But those were the exceptions. Most colonels were grinding on general officer staffs like the colonels I worked for in the Hallway. I quickly concluded I wasn't particularly interested in doing that. It was one more thing pushing me towards retiring as a lieutenant colonel in three years.

While I was at the Pentagon, a CO in Hawaii was relieved of his command. He was a great guy, and we all knew him. The story slowly trickled in, but it was essentially due to some shenanigans that had happened at a Squadron Kangaroo Court. Nothing about what we heard sounded particularly bad to us. It was just Marine Corps aviators being Marine Corps aviators. It sounded to me like the type of thing that might result in someone getting their ass chewed and probably a great callsign. But someone got offended, and the CO ended up being relieved. None of us could believe it.

The Marine Corps was changing, and I knew it was changing in a way that would be difficult for me. I had grown up practicing the "work hard, play hard" philosophy in the squadron. Play hard was slowly being eliminated. Now, COs were being relieved for it. My callsign was "Whiskey." Despite everything I had done well to that point, I assumed that, somewhere down the line, the Marine Corps wouldn't want a guy with the callsign "Whiskey" in any role that was too prominent.

I also understood that, in Marine Corps Aviation, CH-53 pilots did not fare well at the rank of colonel. At that point, there had not been a CO at MAG-16 who was a CH-53E pilot since I was a lieutenant. MAWTS-1 had never had a CH-53E pilot as the CO. If I stuck around, those would be the two O-6 Commands that I was most interested in. Understanding that neither was likely, I felt more and more certain that squadron command would be my last hurrah.

The good part about that is that it allowed me to view my preparation for command through a slightly different lens. My peers would need to consider what higher-level commanders would think if they implemented new or different ideas. I wasn't thinking about that at all. It gave me a little more freedom of creativity in planning how we would approach things like squadron culture and aircraft readiness. I could focus on what would be the best thing for the squadron without considering what anyone above me might think about it. It allowed me to be innovative and take some additional risks.

I couldn't tell anyone that I was leaning towards retirement after command. The expectation for all squadron and battalion commanders was that if their command tour went well, they would continue in the Marine Corps. To that point, I had checked all the right boxes, and I was on track. Guys like me weren't supposed to even think about getting out. Being aware of that, I kept it to myself.

I started doing some more homework. I reached out to a few officers I knew who had retired as lieutenant colonels post-command. The things they told me verified my thought process. I remained aware that most people tend to give what I still referred to as "look how great I turned out advice," meaning they would tell you that you should do what they did. Marine colonels would tell me that I should stick around and be a colonel. Even if they were obviously fucking miserable doing it themselves. But the guys who had punched out at twenty years honestly seemed happy with their decisions. That was not lost on me.

I always understood that, for every Marine, it ends one of two ways. Either you leave the Marine Corps on your terms, or the Marine Corps will eventually tell you that your service is no longer needed. I liked the idea of leaving on my own terms. With that in mind, I took a little time to do things like work on my LinkedIn profile on the weekends. I had always been someone that was overly prepared. I wanted to head back to San Diego prepared for command and with a head start on whatever I ultimately decided to do next.

I checked out of the Hallway in early May 2014. The family that had rented our house back in San Diego for the last year was super understanding and moved into another rental house around the corner. As usual, the kids had a few weeks of school left, so I drove back to San Diego alone. This time I planned to remodel the kitchen. I spent my first few weeks back in California sleeping on an air mattress and knocking that out.

I checked back into MAG-16 in late May and took a position on the MAG-16 staff in charge of the Personnel Support Detachment (PSD). That made me the primary officer working all inbound and outbound orders for the MAG, which was perfect. I still needed to get one more strong major.

I was able to work it to get Major Carlos "Choco" Chavez slated for HMH-462. I had first run across Choco when turning over with HMH-466 in Iraq in 2005. He impressed me again when I did his NSI evaluation as an Instructor at MAWTS-1. He had since gone to HMX-1 and completed a tour flying the President of the United States before heading to school for a year. Like me, Big Red was a former MAWTS-1 Instructor, so Choco having a slightly different background was good.

Big Red's callsign was appropriate. He was a big red headed guy from the Pacific Northwest. He was extremely competent but also had a great sense of humor and an easy demeanor. Choco was from Chicago and had served on the Chicago PD as a police officer prior to joining the Marine Corps. He was highly intelligent and had a tendency to get fired up much faster than Big Red and I did. They were both great leaders who I expected would go on to become COs themselves. The combination of backgrounds and personalities gave us a nice balance. Having them on the team was going to make everything I wanted to try and accomplish for the squadron much more feasible.

Kerry and the kids drove across the country with my mother-in-law in June. We settled back into our house, and the kids could resume at the neighborhood school they had left one year prior. We had been referring to San Diego as our "Marine Corps home" for several years. We all wanted to make it our permanent home at some point, and now that I had managed to get orders to come back to San Diego one more time, we would have the opportunity to do that.

On August 1, 2014, I was promoted to lieutenant colonel. I was making my final preparations to take command in October. It was the last time I would ever be a part of a fleet squadron. And I was going to be the CO. It felt like an appropriate way to wrap up my career, and I was ready to get started.

23

RETURN OF THE SCREW

I TOOK command of the HMH-462 "Heavy Haulers" on Friday, November 7, 2014. The ceremony was on the flight line at Miramar in front of Hangar 4. It was the perfect setting to start my last and, arguably, most important assignment as a Marine Corps officer.

HMH-462 had a long and storied history as a squadron. The squadron had deployed to Vietnam in 1968. That had turned into nearly ten years of consecutive overseas service. A large portion of that time had been spent based out of Okinawa, Japan.

In 1975 the squadron, still based out of Okinawa, participated in the evacuation of Phnom Penh during OPERATION EAGLE PULL. Seventeen days later, the squadron also participated in the evacuation of Saigon during OPERATION FREQUENT WIND. Somewhere in those years overseas fighting the Vietnam War, the Marines of HMH-462 started to refer to themselves as the "Screw Crew." The connotation is that they got screwed in being overseas that long. The name stuck.

A "Screw" logo was born out of that, and Marines of the Screw Crew wore it like a badge of honor. I have no data to back it up, but that screw has to be the most common tattoo in the entire CH-53 community. Squadron Command is not only about taking care of the Marines; it also comes with the responsibility of stewardship. Living up to the legacy of the unit. I was very aware of the HMH-462 history, and I intended to honor it.

When I was a major, HMH-462 hit a rough patch, and the 3rd MAW CG had outlawed all use of the "Screw Crew" and the accompanying screw logo. My predecessor as the CO had been low-key campaigning to bring the screw back. For our Change of Command ceremony, he had the Marines paint the screw logo on the tail of one of the aircraft that was part of the static display. It was a ballsy move, but he had a little more latitude after a successful command tour, so he pulled it off. Immediately after the ceremony, the MAG-16 CO told me I needed to make it disappear quickly.

Despite the screw logo on the static display, the ceremony went off without a hitch. I assumed command. We had a lot of family and friends in town for the ceremony, and we had a great weekend celebrating with all of them. My parents were able to be there for the weekend, which was nice. They were both doing well, which made for a comfortable family event. Amid the festivities, I was very aware that I was celebrating something I hadn't done yet. In the grand scheme of things, the only thing that mattered was if I would be able to make the most of the opportunity for the Marines of the Screw Crew. I knew I would have to earn that.

I had been fortunate to observe several COs throughout my career. I believed that to be successful, I needed to keep things as simple as possible for the squadron. I didn't ever want there to be any questions about our priorities. Every CO in the Marine Corps is required to publish a "Command Philosophy." Over the years, I had seen and read more Command Philosophies than I could count. My observation was that they often said a lot of great things, but they were completely ineffective. There was too much information contained in them for the Marines to remember and use as a guiding light.

I was able to get mine down to one word. "Fundamentals."

The fundamentals were defined as follows:

1. Fix Aircraft
2. Fly Aircraft
3. Take care of ourselves, our families, and each other

That was it. If those three things were always our focus, I liked our chances of being successful. The CH-53E had been the newest aircraft in the fleet when I had checked into HMH-465 fourteen years earlier. When I took command of HMH-462, it was the oldest aircraft in the fleet, and it was showing its age. Aircraft readiness was a significant issue across the entire Marine Corps fleet, and parts were prioritized for deployed units. When I took command, the CH-53E squadrons of MAG-16 were all struggling with aircraft readiness. I knew we needed to remedy that quickly.

The squadron had recently returned from Afghanistan. For the next rotation, we were scheduled to deploy to Okinawa for the Unit Deployment Program (UDP) and to support the 31st MEU. Having done combat deployments and Okinawa UDP deployments, I knew Okinawa was the tougher deployment to prepare for. It sounded like a vacation, especially to the Marines who hadn't been there before.

Bouncing around the Pacific doing exercises could be a lot of fun. But I had also seen it eat units alive. It was easy for Marines to get in trouble. It was easy for morale to go into the tank because you are away from home and don't feel there is a real purpose for being there. It was a lot harder than it looked.

I was fortunate to have Big Red and Choco with me as majors. Our other majors were also solid, but I saw those two as future COs. Initially, Big Red was the Aviation Maintenance Officer (AMO) and Choco led our safety department. The plan was for Big Red to move into the Executive Officer (XO) billet and have Choco replace him in leading our Maintenance Department for deployment. I also got lucky and was paired with

Sergeant Major Dustin Kazmar, who served as my senior enlisted advisor.

Kazmar was a physical stud who had been a drill instructor and had spent time as a real operator deploying as a member of a Marine Forces Special Operations Command (MARSOC) unit. When it came to the Marines, Sergeant Major Kazmar just had "it," and the Marines loved him for it. I couldn't have asked for a better group of primaries. The squadron also had some A players at every other level. Overall, we had a good group of officers, Staff NCOs, NCOs, and junior Marines. A great foundation. We developed some new concepts for managing maintenance and put them into practice. They worked. The squadron bought in, and our aircraft readiness quickly came around.

With six months to get the squadron ready to deploy, we took off running. I dusted off my old playbook, and we took training detachments to Naval Air Facility (NAF) El Centro to increase our efficiency. The proximity to the Yuma range complex always maximized our training time. We pushed hard through the holidays. In January, we went to Marine Corps Air Ground Combat Center (MCAGCC), Twentynine Palms to participate in an Integrated Training Exercise (ITX). It would be a five-week exercise. The California desert is cold at that time of year and a perfect setting with enough shared adversity for the squadron to get tight. On the fifth evening of the exercise, I was in the hangar on the flight line waiting to hot seat into one of our aircraft to take a couple of our young copilots out for some night training.

There were a lot of Marines in the hangar and on the flight line, as all of the units participating in the exercise were executing hot seats and trying to launch aircraft for night training. There was a UH-1Y Huey inbound to land on the runway. Something looked off as I watched it, but I couldn't tell exactly what it was. Then, suddenly, the Huey just fell out of the sky and burst into flames when it hit the desert floor. I knew immediately there were no survivors.

All the Marines in the hangar and on the flight line stood

there in stunned silence as the crash crew rolled out towards the crash site off the runway. It was awful. It would later be determined that their main rotor gearbox had failed.

Our majors came and found me, asking if I still intended to fly. I told them that I was still going. I had already asked the rest of my crew if they were still good to go, and they assured me that they were. I felt I needed to set the example and be the first to get out there and fly. I would address the ready room when I got back. The mood for our crew was somber as we executed our training. When we returned from our flight, I got the officers together in the ready room to talk about what had happened. It was the first time most of them had been close to a mishap that included loss of life, and they were taking it hard. We got them through it and went on to have a productive exercise.

In February, we were only three months away from deploying when something happened that we couldn't have prepared for. The fleet was hit with an Airframes Bulletin, which suspended all CH-53E operations until a detailed inspection of the entire aircraft cabin was performed. The inspection focused on fuel lines, hydraulic lines, and electrical wiring. We knew it would take forever to complete those inspections on every aircraft.

The bulletin was based on a mishap involving a Navy MH-53 that had caught fire in flight, so there was a legitimate reason for it. But attacking it would be difficult and cumbersome. Our squadron immediately went to work on a couple of our own aircraft and quickly got them back into the fight. That, at least, gave us a couple of aircraft to fly while we made our way through the inspections on the remainder of our aircraft. Meanwhile, our sister squadron in Okinawa - which we were slated to replace - was struggling. We heard they'd disassembled all the fuel lines, but they weren't putting any aircraft back together. I was immediately concerned. When we deployed, we always traded aircraft with the other squadron on both ends. That meant they would get all the aircraft we had inspected and repaired, and we would get theirs.

If our Marines were making good progress on our aircraft at Miramar and then had to leave and fall in on a completely down fleet of aircraft in Okinawa, it would feel like a gut punch. I immediately started campaigning to our MAG-16 CO and the 3rd MAW CG to be allowed to at least take two of the aircraft we had built back up with us to Okinawa. That would give us something to fly while going to work on the aircraft in Okinawa. I was persistent enough that they finally relented and allowed me to take two of our aircraft with us.

Fifer was still working at Aviation Hallway, and they were tracking the inspection progress across the fleet. He was keeping me updated on what we would face when we reached Okinawa. I briefed him on our plan, and he was confident we would get the Okinawa aircraft back up quickly after falling in on them.

I left the house for my seventh deployment on the night of May 12, 2015. Saying goodbye to Kerry and the kids again hadn't gotten any easier. Dalton cried himself to sleep while I was lying there with him. I felt extreme guilt. Tristen was more stoic when I said goodbye to her. I worried she was already too adept at compartmentalizing her emotions.

Kerry and I said our goodbyes, and I walked out the door without looking back. I drove myself and picked up a couple of our majors on my way to the squadron. One of them only lived a few blocks away. He was my first stop, so there was no time to wallow in it. Kerry was going to pick up my truck at the squadron the next day. The majors and I stopped and grabbed food at the McDonald's on Miramar. It was appropriate for our last meal on American soil. We were on buses to March Air Force Base a few hours later to catch our flight to Okinawa.

Upon arrival in Okinawa, we officially fell in on the worst material readiness in the fleet. Big Red had been in charge of our Advanced Party and had already started getting us organized to get those aircraft appropriately inspected and put back together.

My challenge to the Marines was that we were going to take our aircraft readiness from worst to first during the deployment. They immediately rose to the challenge. I briefed a get-well plan to the MAG-36 CO and 1st MAW CG. They thought my timeline might be too aggressive. We beat it. Our 31st MEU detachment also got their aircraft back up quickly. We all worked together to ensure that happened.

We pushed the Marines hard, but we were also organizing a lot of group activities to smartly spend our downtime together as a unit. We had bowling parties, cookouts, and Kazmar put together CrossFit type competitions. The majors, Kazmar, and I got together and made dinner every Sunday. All of that time was well spent. The squadron was getting tight.

Prior to leaving on deployment, I had officially received permission to bring "the screw" back. But I planned to wait and do that after a successful deployment. I first wanted to lean into the squadron history of the Vietnam era. We reproduced the squadron patch from that era and wore it on Fridays. I often mentioned our squadron legacy in Okinawa and the Pacific to the Marines. Choco came up with the idea to have shoulder patches made with the screw on them that annotated higher-level maintenance qualifications. Those qualification patches were the only way our Marines could wear the screw logo. It was an added layer of motivation for our Marines to earn those qualifications. It worked.

The Echo Chamber had been closed again prior to our arrival. This time the base CO had ordered that everything be taken off the walls and put into storage. It was just an empty room. I had our captains conduct a recon mission to find those items in storage. MCAS Futenma was a tiny base, so there were only so many places to look. They found the stored items within a few days, and I went to work on the MAG-36 CO to get our "heritage room" reopened again.

Living in the barracks in Okinawa left me with a lot of downtime, which wasn't good. I never liked having too much time to sit around and think. I was chatting with our Flight Surgeon one day about how frustrated I was that the Marine Corps seemed to be getting progressively stringent on disciplinary issues of all kinds. Especially those involving alcohol. It seemed like once a week, I heard about some Marine in trouble for an Alcohol-Related Incident (ARI). When I was a captain, I had never even heard that term, which is fortunate since I had been involved in plenty of things that would have been considered ARIs by modern standards. I was frustrated because it was typically our best Marines getting caught up in these incidents.

Our squadron flight surgeon helped me to connect the dots. I was venting to him in my office one day when he explained that, in many cases, our best Marines are also the most prone to getting in trouble. They have an attraction to risk and will often subconsciously seek it out. That can make them great in the aircraft and in combat. But it also makes them prone to drinking too much, getting into bar fights, and a host of other shenanigans. In many cases, those Marines had personal lives that were a disaster zone as a result.

Pappy Boyington was a great historical example. I felt like he was talking about me personally. I completely identified with that mentality. He also validated the perspective I had come to believe a few years prior. It made sense. It wasn't just me. I knew a bunch of Marines like that.

On July 9th, we had to hangar all our aircraft due to an inbound typhoon. It was shitty timing because we were one week away from flying four aircraft to Clark Air Base in the Philippines for an exercise. After being delayed for a few days, we finally launched for the Philippines on July 15th. We were following a flight of KC-130s from VMGR-152 "Sumo" so that they could aerially refuel us over the Pacific. Shortly after 9-11, I had flown across the Pacific bound for Guam with Browner and Fifer. Now, I was the CO of a squadron leading a detachment on a similar flight. I had come full circle. On our second aerial refuel event, one of our captains struggled to get into the basket to fuel his aircraft. I fell back to the observation position above his aircraft and gave him talkies over the radio, just like I would have if I were sitting next to him. The whole time, I thought through what we would need to do if he couldn't get fuel and had to ditch his aircraft in the Pacific.

I could feel the tension in his voice over the radio. We finally got him into the basket to get some fuel, but he didn't get enough. Our quick math said that we were going to have to divert to an airport in the northern Philippines as soon as we hit land. I still felt relieved. That was a hell of a lot better than ditching in the open ocean.

About forty-five minutes later, we landed at Laoag International Airport on the northern tip of the Philippines. It was a tiny little commercial airport, and they were surprised to see us. They initially rolled some armed guards out, but when we got out of the aircraft waving a government credit card and giving the universal signal for "need gas," they relaxed, and we got our fuel. The delay cost us, though. There was weather rolling into Clark Air Base, and I was concerned that we wouldn't be able to get there. Once we got our gas, we took off and gave it a shot. We didn't get very far before the thunderstorms were too much to navigate. We had to turn back to Laoag International Airport.

The airport manager was great about it and told us that we could crash on the floor in the terminal once they finished operations for the night. We were all tired and sweaty as hell, but at least there was some shelter. We all crashed on the tile floor in the tiny little airport.

The next morning we received word that the storms were not going to lift for a few days. We were stuck. I called back to Okinawa and talked to Choco. Since he had been at HMX-1, traveling around the world supporting the President of the United States, I knew he had connections there that could find us a safe place to stay. Within a few hours, we had a reservation at a resort down the road, and a driver showed up in a Jingle Bus to give us a ride. We went four to a room, but the Marines didn't care. Fort Ilocandia Resort had everything they could have wanted, including a casino. The Marines enjoyed themselves for a few days, waiting for the weather to break.

One afternoon, I was sitting at the resort and trading texts with Kerry and Tristen. They were celebrating Tristen's 13th birthday. It was a nice exchange, but the guilt really hit me that I was missing one more family event. I was already leaning hard toward retiring at 20 years, but I became certain as I sat trading texts with them. It was going to be my last deployment. I would officially submit for retirement as soon as we got back home.

When the weather broke, we pushed to Clark Air Base and settled in for the exercise. Over the exercise, we did a lot of flying, and I got to revisit some of the places I had flown as part of the 31st MEU in 2012. That included landing inside the Mount Pinatubo volcano. It was fun to show some of our Marines flying in the Philippines. They had a blast. Meanwhile, we still had elements of the squadron operating in Okinawa, the Philippines, and our 31st MEU Det was finishing up in Australia. I felt great about where we were as a unit. On July 24, 2015, I sent the below email to the entire squadron.

Screw Crew, in the last week, we have supported FRAGs in the Philippines, FRAGS in Okinawa, ferried a previously Long Term Down aircraft to Korea for IMP induction, and our 31st MEU Det got back on the boat after carrying the load for the MEU ACE at Talisman Saber. We also just executed long range HAAR 832nm over water complete with a weather divert. The CH-53E hasn't had that level of presence in the Pacific in over a decade.

We did that on 10 aircraft that hadn't flown in 3 months prior to our arrival + 2 aircraft we broke down and brought with us.

On my first day, I shared this Vince Lombardi quote with you.

"We are going to relentlessly chase perfection. Knowing full well that we will never catch it. Because nothing is perfect. But in the process we will catch excellence. I'm not remotely interested in being just good."

That is where we are as a squadron. Catching excellence. Every Marine is doing their part.

We are not without flaws. We will make mistakes and learn from them, but we will never stop being who we are. We are aggressive, and relentless. We push ourselves and each other to get better. We will always play to win.

We will stay focused. We will not get complacent. We will continue to work hard but smart. We will continue to focus on the fundamentals as we fix and tactically employ the CH-53E. We will always have a long-range plan. We will continue to play hard but always take care of ourselves and each other while doing so. There is no other way.

I am proud to be one of you. I love every one of you like family.

Leaders, wherever you find yourselves, please take a minute to share this message with our Marines. SgtMaj and I will be sure to do that here in the PI.

s/f

LtCol Isaac G. Lee "Whiskey"
HMH-462 Commanding Officer

We flew back to Okinawa on August 14th. It was nice to get the whole unit back together after having some adventures. As soon as I was back on the island, I got the keys back to the Echo Chamber. Our Captains quickly went to work building a new bar and putting everything back on the walls. There was a wall covered with Velcro that had previously had groups of name patches belonging to the CH-53 squadrons deployed there. As the resident old guy, I took it upon myself to sort those patches and get them back up by unit. Several groups of those patches pre-dated me, but I remembered enough names and stories to piece it all back together. It felt good to successfully re-open The Echo Chamber for a second time. I wanted our young officers to experience the camaraderie possible in that room.

The shenanigans started right away. I had a blast hanging out in there with the other officers in the squadron. There was a lot of fighting over the music, and the captains' selections were significantly different than they had been when I was a captain. Instead of Metallica and Motley Crue, it was The Weekend, Taylor Swift, and Katy Perry. Despite the different tastes in music, we still had a blast. Someone hooked up a PlayStation 3 and had updated rosters for the old college football game. I had always been pretty decent at that game, so I jumped on and beat one of the captains the first weekend it was hooked up. After that, it became an event when I was playing. All of the captains wanted to beat me. I made it through the remainder of the deployment without losing to any of them. I also started adjusting my schedule on the weekends to accommodate watching college football in the early hours of Sunday morning. A few of our captains joined me. I really enjoyed that.

It felt much like the first portion of my first deployment before 9-11. The squadron was working hard but also having fun. We were constantly out and about, running around the island. Dinners at Sam's Anchor Inn, Yoshi's Sushi, and Coco Ichibanya Curry House were common. We lined up buses to take everyone to the Churaumi Aquarium and then on to the Okinawa Battle Sites Tour. We wanted the Marines to experience the island.

On Saturday, November 7, we enjoyed a very informal cele-bration of the Marine Corps Birthday. Instead of doing a traditional Birthday Ball, the Marines had voted to have a giant cookout. That ended up being my all-time favorite Marine Corps Ball. It lasted all day, and the entire squadron had a blast.

It had been a strong deployment, but I was ready to go home. It was time. When we ordered our squadron deployment plaque, I had the captains put a giant Screw in the middle of it and added "Return of the Screw" as the tagline. It was an homage to our squadron history in returning to the Pacific, and we were literally bringing the screw back. It was fitting in multiple ways.

November 19th was our last day in Okinawa. I got online and officially Removed myself by Request for consideration for Top Level School (TLS). In doing so, I was essentially ending my career. I did so without a single conversation with any colonel. On November 20th, we boarded our flight at Kadena Air Force Base to return to Miramar. I was officially done deploying.

It was the usual routine coming home. We arrived at Miramar on the afternoon of November 20th. Kerry had arranged for us to go to Disneyland to spend Thanksgiving there as a family. When we walked into the park, Dalton started to cry. When we asked him what was wrong, he said that he was happy. He had been looking forward to that little trip for months. It was the finish line for him. And when we got there, he really felt it. I knew for certain that my decision to retire was the right one.

When I returned to work, I immediately visited our new MAG-16 CO. He had taken over while we were on deployment, and I had never met him in person. My introduction to him was me saying hello and letting him know that I had removed myself from consideration for TLS, because I planned to retire the following summer. He was shocked. By the time I got back to my office, I received a phone call from the 3rd MAW Chief of Staff telling me that the 3rd MAW CG wanted to see me. That didn't take long.

I headed over to the 3rd MAW building and reported to the CG. He asked me to talk him through why I was planning to retire. I did, and he was understanding about it. He was clear that he wanted me to continue in the Marine Corps, and he laid out all the reasons why the Marine Corps needed me. But he also understood that, for me, it was just about trying to put my family and myself first for a change in hopes that we would all be able to stay together and get to a good place. There were no guarantees either way, but I knew what I needed to do. In the end, he told me he would support my decision. The tradeoff is that when I finished up command, I would come up to the Wing and be his Deputy Operations Officer. I was happy about that. I had always enjoyed working in operations, and doing so on his staff would be a good way to spend my last year in the Marine Corps.

I still had six months remaining in command, and we still had a lot of work to do. But I wanted to reward the squadron for everything they had done to that point. On December 4th, we had a Dining Out to make up for the fact we hadn't had a formal Marine Corps Birthday Ball while on deployment. Everyone wore their dress blues and brought their significant others. A good friend from back home, who had gone on to play in the NFL, came out to be the guest speaker. It was the perfect tie-in to "Fundamentals."

After the speeches, I announced that, due to our outstanding deployment, we were again legal to proudly wear and display all things "Screw Crew." I had black flight suit patches made up that displayed the screw logo on them and said, "Screw Crew" in place of "Heavy Haulers." The majors immediately started walking around, throwing fistfuls of the patches on the tables. The Marines went berserk. It was an awesome night.

We were working in some little breaks through December, but we were going full speed again by January. My former MAWTS-1 squadron mate, Eric "TULSA" Purcell, was at the MAG, waiting to take command of one of the other squadrons when he was informed that he would instead be going to Hawaii to replace a squadron CO who had been relieved. He was checking into the squadron on January 14, 2015. That night two CH-53Es from the squadron, with twelve total aircrew aboard, collided with each other off the coast of Hawaii. There were no survivors. It was a tragic event for both the squadron and the entire CH-53E community. It reminded everyone that, even though the long war was winding down, we still worked in a very dangerous business. About a year later, I would be one of a few senior CH-53E pilots selected to brief a few of the families on the investigation results. A parting gift from the Marine Corps.

My last six months of command went well. In March and April, we executed a large training detachment to NAF El Centro, while also providing tactical support to the spring WTI class. I spent a lot of time in El Centro myself. It was great to have one last big push with the squadron. Shortly before my Change of Command, we were recognized as the HMH squadron of the year for the Wing. We had a lot to feel good about.

On Wednesday, May 4, 2016, I flew a CH-53E for the last time. When I taxied back into the flight line in front of Hangar 4, the entire squadron was out there waiting for me. They dumped water on me, and I spoke to the Marines as a group for the last time. It felt good. I was handing the squadron off to the next CO in good shape.

Two days later, on Friday, May 6, 2016, I executed my Change of Command Ceremony. I had spent almost ten years of my career in the CH-53 squadrons of MAG-16. I had deployed seven times and done just about everything that there was to do as a CH-53E pilot. I'd had a good run. It was time for me to do something else.

24

SEEKING CLOSURE

ONCE A MARINE, always a Marine is a real thing. Becoming a Marine is, in itself, a transformative experience. To serve for twenty years through multiple combat deployments leaves one with a significant burden of experiences and life lessons to sort out. That said, I regret nothing. I would do it all over again without thinking twice about it.

Simultaneous exposure to the best and the worst humanity has to offer leaves you with one hell of a perspective on all things. I genuinely appreciate basic things like running water and climate-controlled environments. I truly value people and relationships. I am very aware of the fragility of life.

For every individual, the combat experience is unique. The one common thread about the combat experience is the part that I believe is most frightening for all who have experienced it. It is also the thing I appreciate the most about my personal combat experience. Combat tells the truth about you as a person. When the bullets start flying, and your friends start dying, you quickly find out who you are.

Warfighting is the purest test of will and the human spirit. You simply cannot bullshit your way through it. Once that truth is revealed, you will spend the rest of your days on this planet living with whatever you learned about yourself.

On one extreme, some find themselves paralyzed with fear and unable to perform. At the other end of the spectrum, some like me discover that they grow into enjoying the combat experience for a mix of complex reasons. In both cases, it can lead to a depth of self-loathing that can eat you alive from the inside for years to come.

Thankfully, most who experience combat fall somewhere in between. They don't like it, but they have the training and intestinal fortitude to endure and survive it. When you toss in a bit of survivor's guilt and a dash of post-traumatic stress disorder (PTSD), it can be a lethal cocktail. The post-combat road is littered with veteran casualties. Substance abuse problems and failed marriages are common. The worst cases ultimately contribute to the twenty-two suicide per day statistic that haunts the veteran community to this day.

For many years I expected that death was near for me. It seemed like an inevitable end to the life I had chosen for myself. It was difficult for me to imagine it ending any other way. I had so many close calls, I figured that, at some point, my ability to stay a half-second faster than death would end. Something was destined to catch up to me.

I figured I would live hard, love hard, fly hard, fight hard, and inevitably die at the controls of a CH-53E. In some ways, that sounded better to me than being one more war veteran out there trying to stay sane while fading away in the suburbs. Then something happened I hadn't planned for. I lived.

Not all of us came home. I lost my first close friend in Iraq in 2004. That first one fucking hurt. It hurt a lot. After that one, saying goodbye to those who died became strangely normal. I could go through the motions of the memorial service. I could console my fellow Marines. I felt empathy for the loved ones left behind. But inside, I felt nothing.

My grief response disappeared. I was completely numb to it.

Death was just part of the deal. That level of compartmentalization comes with many strings attached.

I relinquished command of HMH-462 on May 6, 2016. I was
slated to spend the next year as the Deputy in 3rd MAW Operations until my retirement ceremony. Before relinquishing
command, I decided that my last flight would be as the
Commanding Officer of HMH-462. It was important to me that
my final flight happened as a contributing member of a fleet
squadron.

I wanted no part of being the soon to be retired Wing guy,
asking a squadron for one last lap in the pattern for old times'
sake. Not my style. I also knew I needed to spend my last year in
uniform preparing for the future I had not planned for. If I
intended to make a successful transition back into the real world,
I needed to take meaningful steps away from being "Whiskey"
the combat aviator and focus on preparing "Isaac" for a
successful integration into corporate America.

My first stop was the San Marcos, CA Vet Center. I walked in
the door for the first time one week after giving up command of
HMH-462. I had one year to get my shit together before I retired,
and the Vet Center would be an essential part of that process. My
friend, author, and former AH-1W Cobra pilot Dan "Shoe"
Sheehan turned me onto the San Marcos Vet Center in his first
book. After reading *After Action*, I reached out to Dan and
discussed it with him.

The San Marcos Vet Center was a safe place to begin counseling and to start unpacking everything I had experienced. I
also needed to find out if all the things I had come to believe
about myself were true. Was I just bullshitting myself? Was it all
just one giant excuse? Time to find out. I had chased the dragon
as far as I could without letting it destroy me. I had lived on the
fringe of my dark side. Now, it was time to let it all go. To do
that, I needed to better understand the person I had become.

To this day, I consider my decision to seek counseling one of
the best personal decisions I have ever made. I needed to wade

through a lot of shit in order to find my way to a version of myself I could be happy with. A version that could experience somewhat normal human emotions. A version who could be a present husband and father for many years to come.

Now, I have the opportunity to live a chapter of my life I never expected to have. I want to make the most of that.

I conducted my retirement ceremony on Friday, May 5, 2017. The 3rd MAW CG was my retiring officer, and we conducted the ceremony in Hangar 4 at Miramar. It was the most appropriate setting for me to conclude my career as a Marine Corps officer. Hangar 4 had been the finish line for all seven deployments. It had always felt like home to me. It was the only place I wanted to be when I said goodbye to the preceding twenty years of my life as a Marine Corps aviator.

I often think back on my experience in the Marine Corps. It will always be a significant part of who I am and how I define myself. I continue to work on finding closure for that chapter of my life, but I'm not sure I ever really will. Writing this book has been a major part of my quest to do that, despite the many emotional moments I experienced alone in my office while writing about the experience.

I listen to music while writing. Now and then, a song will pop up that takes me back to some specific part of the experience. On other occasions, a song will come up that I once imagined would play at my memorial service. Chris Cornell singing "Say Hello to Heaven" always makes me think of that. I am certain that sounds very dark to anyone who's never spent a significant portion of their lives expecting to die. A part of me will always struggle with the fact that I survived. Why did I survive when so many good people did not? Those of us who came home must answer that question for ourselves.

I reconcile that by trying to make the most of the chapter of my life that I didn't expect to have. Every day I try to make a positive impact on people. Primarily my family, friends, co-workers, and just about any veteran who reaches out to me for any reason. I make an honest effort to live in the present and stay focused on the future. If my story were fiction, it might have been better had it ended tragically. But this isn't fiction. As anticlimactic as that might be, being where I am today is infinitely better than a tragic alternative. Even if the alternative might have made for a better story.

My counseling process continues to this day. I won't ever be "normal," but the incremental progress continues. It took me a long time to fully accept that my PTSD is a big part of who I am. I learned early on in counseling that I had PTSD, but I didn't totally accept that reality until almost six years into my counseling journey. Until that point, I lived in the land of what some call "comparative suffering."

What I experienced seemed insignificant in comparison to what a lot of other Marines I knew had experienced. While still in uniform, it was easy for me to tell myself to shut the fuck up and keep being the guy my fellow Marines needed me to be. Once I was out of uniform, I gradually let myself off the hook and slowly accepted the impact my experiences had on me.

Sitting down and writing the first draft of this book contributed greatly to that self-acceptance. At the tail end of that process, I finally submitted my diagnosis to the Department of Veterans Affairs. It's official now. It's in my record. I have PTSD.

In addition to individual counseling, I also now participate in a weekly PTSD group at the San Marcos Vet Center. The group is primarily Vietnam Veterans. They are outstanding mentors to me.

Six years removed from the experience, I can tell you that life around our house is closer to something resembling "normal" than it ever has been. Life, on the other side, is not without its challenges, but it has been a positive change for our family. We exist in a never-ending state of working towards being as happy and healthy as possible. For the most part, it usually feels like we are trending in a positive direction. A couple of years after my retirement, we were eating dinner when something came up that I shrugged off.

Dalton said, "A few years ago, Dad would have been mad at me. You went to war therapy after the Marine Corps and chilled out."

He was right. Today, I run operations for a great company, work out a lot, play amateur handyman around the house, work with transitioning veterans, and try to be the best version of myself for my family and friends. When I have some spare time, I mostly spend it sitting in the backyard watching baseball or football on TV.

We still live in the San Diego area, just a few miles up I-15 from Miramar. I often drive by Miramar on I-15 and see the FA-18s, KC-130s, MV-22s, and CH-53s on final approach to Runway 24 Right. It's an approach I must have flown a thousand times. When I see those aircraft, I don't think anything of it most of the time. But every now and then, like the pictures on the wall in my home office, seeing them takes me back to a time and place when I was a professional warfighter. When I was out there at the controls of the mighty CH-53E, pushing any and all limits.

Hangar 4 is still there, as are the CH-53E squadrons of MAG-16. Periodically, I am invited back to attend a Change of Command or some other ceremony. When I get out of my truck, I always stop and just look at the hangar for a minute before I walk across the street to go through the gate. The hangar still looks and smells the same. I kind of love that it is frozen in time.

A part of me will always long to be out there somewhere with my fellow Marines. I miss booming around at the controls of a CH-53E on a low light level night while going "downtown" on a high-risk mission. I miss being with my fellow Marines, drinking way too much, talking shit, and ultimately hugging it out in some shithole of a bar in a foreign country.

A part of me will always want to be back there doing those things. We lived and fought fearlessly. Sometimes to our detriment. The one constant was the way we all felt about each other. We rarely said it, but the purest form of love was ever-present. I will always love them. Unconditionally.

The greatest gift that the Marine Corps gives is the honor of being in the presence of other Marines. For two decades, I walked among giants. I will forever cherish every one of those relationships. Especially those relationships I had with the great ones who never came home.

PLAYLIST

1. **Operation Matador:** Metallica "Seek and Destroy"
2. **Learning to Fly:** Pink Floyd "Learning to Fly"
3. **Warhorse:** Aerosmith "Make It"
4. **Far East Chronicles:** Def Leppard "Rock Rock (Til you drop)"
5. **9-11:** The music stopped…
6. **Put us in Coach:** AC/DC "For Those About to Rock"
7. **Growing Up:** Depeche Mode "Enjoy the Silence"
8. **The Magnificent Seven:** Metallica "For Whom The Bell Tolls"
9. **Welcome to the Show:** Guns N' Roses "Welcome to the Jungle"
10. **Jalibah:** AC/DC "Hells Bells"
11. **Home:** Sheryl Crow "Home"
12. **Going Back:** Metallica "Am I Evil?"
13. **Reality Check:** Temple of the Dog "Say Hello 2 Heaven"
14. **Round Three:** AC/DC "Highway to Hell"
15. **Addiction:** Metallica "Master of Puppets"
16. **Warfighter Without a War:** Pink Floyd "Wish You Were Here"

17. **MAWTS-1 "Heavy Metal":** U2 "With or Without You"
18. **Back in the Fight:** Aerosmith "Back in the Saddle"
19. **It's a TRAP!:** Metallica "The Four Horsemen"
20. **The Guts to Try:** Metallica "All Nightmare Long"
21. **Bonus Deployment:** Metallica "Wherever I May Roam"
22. **The Hallway:** Metallica "And Justice For All"
23. **Return of the Screw:** Audioslave "Cochise"
24. **Seeking Closure:** Eagles "Hotel California"

BIBLIOGRAPHY

1. Marine Corps Combat Development Command. CH-53 Pilot Training and Readiness Manual. NAVMC 3500.47A. Washington, D.C.: Headquarters United States Marine Corps, March 8, 2011.
2. MAWTS-1. *(U) Combat Aircraft Fundamentals CH-53*. Naval Tactics Techniques and Procedures NTTP 3-22.3-CH53. Nellis, AFB:561st Joint Tactics Squadron, November, 2008.

ACRONYMS

AAA - Anti Aircraft Artillery

AACG/DACG - Arrival Airfield Control Group/ Departure Airfield Control Group

AAMO - Assistant Aviation Maintenance Officer

ACE - Aviation Combat Element

AFCS - Automatic Flight Control System

AFL - Assault Flight Leader

AFN - Armed Forces Network

AGL - Above Ground Level

AJ - Anti Jamming

AMB - Aviation Mishap Board

AMC - Air Mission Commander

AMO - Aviation Maintenance Officer

AO - Area of Operations

AOM - All Officers Meeting

AOPSO - Assistant Operations Officer

API - Aviation Preflight Indoctrination

APP - Auxiliary Power Plant

APP - Aviation Plans and Policies

ARI - Alcohol Related Incident

ASD - Assault Support Department

ASE - Aircraft Survivability Equipment

ASR - Assault Support Request

ATF - Amphibious Task Force

ATO - Air Tasking Order

BBC - British Broadcasting Corporation

BCT - Brigade Combat Team

BI - Battlefield Illumination

BIM - Blade Inspection Method

BOQ - Bachelor Officer Quarters

BP - Battle Position

BPS - Ballistic Protection System

BRAC - Base Realignment and Closure

CACO - Casualty Assistance Calls Officer

CAS - Close Air Support

CASEVAC - Casualty Evacuation

CAX - Combined Arms Exercise

CERTEX - Certification Exercise

CFIT - Controlled Flight Into Terrain

CG - Commanding General

CHOP - Change of Operational Control

CIWS - Close in Weapons System

CO - Commanding Officer

CWO - Chief Warrant Officer

DA - Density Altitude

DART - Downed Aircraft Recovery Team

DASC - Direct Air Support Center

DCA - Deputy Commandant for Aviation

DET - Detachment

DFAC - Dining Facility

EFL - Escort Flight Leader

EGA - Eagle, Globe, and Anchor

EMV - Enhanced Mojave Viper

EPW - Enemy Prisoner of War

FAA - Federal Aviation Administration

FAM - Familiarization

FARP - Forward Arming and Refueling Point
FCF - Functional Check Flight
FCP - Functional Check Pilot
FFPB - Field Flight Performance Board
FITREP - Fitness Report
FLIR - Forward Looking Infrared
FOB - Forward Operating Base
FOD - Foreign Object Damage
FOPSO - Future Operations Officer
FORECON - Force Reconnaissance
FRS - Fleet Replacement Squadron
FWD - Forward
GAIT - Ground Air Integrated Training
GCE - Ground Combat Element
GPS - Global Positioning System
HAC - Helicopter Aircraft Commander
HMH - Marine Heavy Helicopter Squadron
HMLA - Marine Light Attack Helicopter Squadron
HMM - Marine Medium Helicopter Squadron
HMMWV - Highly Mobile Multi Wheeled Vehicle
HMX-1 - Marine Helicopter Squadron One
HST - Helicopter Support Team
HUD - Heads up Display
HVT - High Value Target
ICS - Interphone Communication System
IFAV - Interim Fast Attack Vehicle
IMC - Instrument Meteorological Conditions
IMDS - Integrated Mechanical Diagnostics System
IP - Initial Point
IR - Infrared
ISAF - International Security Assistance Force
ISR - Imagery, Surveillance, and Reconnaissance
ITG - Initial Terminal Guidance
ITX - Integrated Training Exercise
IWO - Integrity Watch Officer

JSDF - Japanese Self Defense Force

JTAC - Joint Terminal Attack Controller

KAL - Korean Airlines

LAR - Light Armored Reconnaissance

LCE - Logistics Combat Element

LFOC - Landing Force Operations Center

LZ - Landing Zone

MACCS - Marine Air Command and Control System

MAG - Marine Aircraft Group

MAGTF - Marine Air Ground Task Force

MALS - Marine Aviation Logistics Squadron

MAM - Military Aged Male

MANPADS - Man Portable Air Defense System

MARSOC - Marine Forces Special Operations Command

MATSG - Marine Aviation Training Support Group

MAW - Marine Aircraft Wing

MAWTS-1 - Marine Aviation Weapons and Tactics Squadron One

MCAGCC - Marine Corps Air Ground Combat Center

MCAS - Marine Corps Air Station

MCB - Marine Corps Base

MEF - Marine Expeditionary Force

MEU - Marine Expeditionary Unit

MMCO - Maintenance Material Control Officer

MOS - Military Occupational Specialty

MRAP - Mine Resistant Ambush Protected

MRE - Meal Ready to Eat

MSL - Mean Sea Level

NAF - Naval Air Facility

NAS - Naval Air Station

NATOPS - Naval and Air Training and Operating Procedures Standardization

NBC - Nuclear Biological Chemical

NCO - Non-Commissioned Officers

NEO - Noncombatant Evacuation Operation

NICU - Neonatal Intensive Care Unit

NIPR - Non-classified Internet Protocol Router
NSI - Night Systems Instructor
NVG - Night Vision Goggles
OAT - Outside Air Temperature
OCS - Officer Candidates School
ODO - Operations Duty Officer
OEF - Operation Enduring Freedom
OIC - Officer in Charge
OIF - Operation Iraqi Freedom
OODA - Observe, Orient, Decide, Act
OPSO - Operations Officer
ORM - Operational Risk Management
OSO - Officer Selection Officer
PA - Pressure Altitude
PCS - Permanent Change of Station
PFC - Private First Class
PFPS - Portable Flight Planning Software
PFT - Physical Fitness Test
PHIBLEX - Philippines Amphibious Landing Exercise
PJ - Pararescue
PME - Professional Military Education
POC - Point of Contact
PSD - Personnel Support Detachment
PTO - Pilot Training Officer
PTSD - Post-traumatic Stress Disorder
PZ - Pickup Zone
QAO - Quality Assurance Officer
QRF - Quick Reaction Force
RC - Regional Command
RCT - Regimental Combat Team
REIN - Reinforced
ROTC - Reserve Officers' Training Corps
ROZ - Restricted Operating Zone
RPG - Rocket Propelled Grenade
RSO&I - Reception, Staging, Onward Movement, and Integration

SAM - Surface to Air Missile
SINCGARS - Single Channel Ground and Airborne Radio System
SIPR - Secret Internet Protocol Router
SNCO - Staff Non-Commissioned Officer
SOAR - Special Operations Aviation Regiment
SOCOM - Special Operations Command
SOF - Special Operations Forces
SOP - Standard Operating Procedure
STA - Surveillance and Target Acquisition
T&R - Training and Readiness
TAA - Tactical Assembly Area
TACAIR - Tactical Air
TACC - Tactical Air Command Center
TBS - The Basic School
TCN - Third Country National
TERF - Terrain Flight
TERFI - Terrain Flight Instructor
TFA - Test Fire Area
TFOA - Things Falling Off Aircraft
TLS - Top Level School
TMS - Type Model Series
TQ - Al Taqqadum
TRAP - Tactical Recovery of Aircraft and Personnel
TTPs - Tactics Techniques and Procedures
UAV - Unmanned Aerial Vehicle
UDP - Unit Deployment Program
VCP - Vehicle Checkpoint
VIP - Very Important Person
VMGR - Marine Aerial Refueler Transport Squadron
VSI - Vertical Speed Indicator
VVIP - Very, Very Important Person
WTI - Weapons and Tactics Instructor
XO - Executive Officer

Milton Keynes UK
Ingram Content Group UK Ltd.
UKHW012340010424
440454UK00011B/170/J

9 798885 280808